Praise for *Your Inner CEO*:

"One of the greatest challenges that leaders confront is to motivate their people and organizations to reach beyond themselves to achieve their true potential. Allan Cox, in his inimitable way, writes that leaders may be undervaluing a key ingredient in reaching that goal—reaching *inside* to achieve the leaders' full potential—professionally, personally, and spiritually—as a prerequisite for leading subordinates and peers to greater accomplishments. The message of *Your Inner CEO* for me is clear, understandable, and compelling: 'Leaders, reach inside and create *your* real potential, *then* lead your organization and its people to similar success.'"

—Dr. Dana Mead, Chairman of the Corporation, Massachusetts Institute of Technology and Retired Chairman and CEO, Tenneco, Inc.

"Imagine having a wise counselor with your best interests at heart. Now imagine your counselor taking you on a personal journey, albeit a difficult one.  With dozens of insight exercises and real-world examples, Cox enables you to face your fears, dig deep and discover your true strengths, create your positive future and live into it."

—Wayne Baker, Ph.D., Professor of Management and Organizations, University of Michigan Ross School of Business; author of *Achieving Success Through Social Capital*

"Allan Cox helps nurture people and corporations the way perceptive executives treat a great brand."

—Wally Olins, Co-Founder & Chairman of London-based Saffron Brand Consultants; author of *On Brand*

"In this incisive book, Allan Cox guides the reader to powerful self-discovery—both personal and organizational—in ways she never could have imagined."

—Julie Meier Wright, President & CEO, San Diego Regional Economic Development Corporation

*"Your Inner CEO* takes you beyond theory to common sense wisdom. Cox's insights are exactly what is needed for the development and release of today's global executive."

—Jan Bubenik, Managing Director, Bubenik Partners, Prague, Czech Republic


"Allan Cox grounds his primer on leadership and performance in the revolutionary work of Alfred Adler. *Your Inner CEO* is a clear and pragmatic guide to finding one's individuality and courage as a leader."

—Raymond E. Crossman, Ph.D., President, Adler School of Professional Psychology, Chicago, USA and Vancouver, Canada


"Allan Cox knows and shows what it takes to become a superior CEO."

—William A. Roper, Jr., President and CEO, Verisgn, Inc.

# ALLAN COX

# YOUR INNER
# C E O

## UNLEASH THE
## EXECUTIVE
## WITHIN

CAREER
PRESS

Franklin Lakes, NJ

YOUR INNER CEO
EDITED BY GINA TALUCCI
TYPESET BY EILEEN DOW MUNSON
Cover design by The Design Works Group
Printed in the U.S.A. by Book-mart Press

To order this title, please call toll-free 1-800-CAREER-1 (NJ and Canada: 201-848-0310) to order using VISA or MasterCard, or for further information on books from Career Press.

CAREER
PRESS

The Career Press, Inc., 3 Tice Road, PO Box 687,
Franklin Lakes, NJ 07417
**www.careerpress.com**

**Library of Congress Cataloging-in-Publication Data**

Cox, Allan J.
    Your inner CEO : unleash the executive within / by Allan Cox
        p. cm.
    Includes bibliographical references and index.
    ISBN-13: 978-1-56414-955-8
    ISBN-10: 1-56414-955-2
        1. Executive ability. 2. Management—Psychological aspects.
        3. Self-perception. 4. Corporate culture. 5. Mentoring in business. I. Title.

HD38.2.C693 2007
658.4'09--dc22

                                                                    2007016599

# Dedication

## $\mathcal{F}or\ \mathcal{C}her$

※❀※

# Acknowledgments

Thank you to my friends who bore with me during this project, who faithfully read several incarnations of the manuscript, and who offered suggestions and support, especially Gene Croisant, Al Gini, Doug Gray, Joe Hannon, Phil Jacklin (the younger), Wayne Lerner, Richard Senior, Alan Sorkin, and Bob Unglaub. In the middle of the project, Arieh Shalhav lent his hand in his own, incomparable way.

I also owe a real debt of thanks to Marci Kaminsky, Warren Batts, and Elmer Johnson for their insights on board of director issues, which helped me write Chapter 5. Marci, senior vice president of communications at USG, as her title suggests, is a superb communicator and student of human behavior. Warren, the retired CEO of Premark, now adjunct professor at The University of Chicago Graduate School of Business, was honored as the director of the year for 2006 by the National Association of Corporate Directors. Elmer, old friend, tower of an attorney, astute board observer, social theorist, former executive vice president of General Motors, and CEO of the Aspen Institute, serves as my ever-present sage.

Thank you to all my clients who have taught me so much over the years. They include Avery Dennison, Bacardi, Child Welfare League of America, Coca-Cola Foods, Columbus McKinnon, Consolidated Communications, Cummins Engine, Foremost Foods, Jones Lang LaSalle, KFC, Kodak, Kraft, Board of Owners of the Minnesota Vikings, Motorola, Navistar, Northwest Airlines, PepsiCo International, Rehabilitation Institute of Chicago, and Travelers. Special thanks also to Don Kelly and the late Bob Palenchar of Esmark. Thank you to Hal Pendexter, the retired senior vice president and chief administrative officer of USG, who has a special place in my heart. Hal introduced me to Bill Foote, USG's big picture leader, who more than any other CEO I've met or studied, fully understands and has lived by Robert Frost's admonition, "The best way out is always through." USG provides a sterling model for corporate mission.

I deeply appreciate the work of Jim Lienhart, whose graphic design brilliance I've enjoyed for decades, and who has won "corporate identity" awards on my behalf, designed our Website, and turned my scribbles into the charts and diagrams that appear in these pages.

To all the people at Career Press, I offer my gratitude for the seamless and effortless (on my part) editing, production, and marketing that brought *Your Inner CEO* to market.

Michael Snell, my agent and writing mentor, "pushed a pencil" through every line of the manuscript and gave me a postgraduate course in book development. For all that effort, I'd like to paraphrase Lao-tse: "Good editors are best when writers barely know they exist, not so good when writers always obey and acclaim them. Worst when writers despise them. Of good editors, when their work is done, and their aims fulfilled, the writer will say, "I did this myself.""

*But listen, the day one decides to take the reins of one's own life into one's own hands, to captain one's own ship, that's the day the dance around the edges starts to slow down, bringing that person to a place where gnawing questions will no longer lie still.*

—Sidney Poitier

# Contents

Introduction .............................................. 11

Chapter 1: Goals .......................................... 15

Chapter 2: Changes ....................................... 37

Chapter 3: Facades ........................................ 59

Chapter 4: Boundaries .................................... 81

Chapter 5: Boards ........................................ 107

Chapter 6: Visions ....................................... 135

Chapter 7: Futures....................................... 155

Chapter 8: Models ....................................... 177

Chapter 9: Mentors ...................................... 201

Appendix: Your Inner CEO Bookshelf .................... 225

Bibliography ............................................. 229

Index .................................................... 233

About the Author ........................................ 239

# Introduction

*You can't build a reputation on what you're going to do.*

—Henry Ford

Every time you start a new job, you go back to square one. About 25 percent don't survive the first year, and of those who do, another 25 percent don't achieve their full potential. Those odds produce a lot of fear and anxiety, whether you're a rookie sales person or a newly minted CEO.

However, there is a way to manage your career so that fear is removed, strengths are summoned, and achievement is ensured: grounding.

> *Ground (n.)* **1.** Something that serves as a foundation
> or means of attachment for something else. **2.** The
> foundation for an argument, a belief or an action.
> *(v.)* **1.** To provide a basis for action. **2.** To build on
> fundamentals.

In *Your Inner CEO*, we'll use the concept of grounding to help you become more aware of your unique talent, to harness that talent to your unique Destiny, and to achieve extraordinary results. Some people strive to wield power, but that's the wrong course. Raw power does not guarantee extraordinary results. Those who rely on it not only fail, they create and suffer debilitating fear and anxiety. Successful CEOs, I have discovered, share power with others, strengthen everyone with whom they come in contact, and treat all stakeholders in their enterprise with kindness, generosity and humility. They know that success stems not from their own efforts, but from a clear understanding of who they are and what Destiny they pursue.

Unfortunately, most executives and their organizations propel themselves toward the wrong goals—goals inconsistent with their true talent, or goals to which they pay lip service, but in which they don't actually believe. Think about it: If you and your company (even if it's only a "company of one") say one thing and do another (the rule rather than the exception), how can you possibly pursue your personal or organizational Destiny? You can't; and if you can't, you will never achieve either extraordinary results or peace of mind.

The solution to this common problem: face your fears, summon your strengths, and get grounded. Of course, that's easier said than done. Where do you start? My extensive experience coaching leaders has convinced me that CEOs and their organizations obey a compelling central goal *of which they are unaware.* Kept buried, such goals can either enhance or erode personal and organizational achievement. I didn't pull this idea out of thin air. I first heard it in graduate school when I took a course called Theories of Personality. It was a theory proposed by the brilliant psychiatrist, Alfred Adler, who asserted that all people pursue hidden goals. Throughout the years, I have successfully applied his ideas to countless executives and organizations.

*Your Inner CEO* offers insights into the application of Adler's seminal work and presents chapter exercises that will help you uncover your hidden goals, face your fears, summon your strengths, and propel yourself to a wonderful future. You'll learn about your own "Style-of-Life," determining whether it acts as a guardian presence or a looming threat. Once you do so, you can nurture the guardian or extinguish the threat. You'll ask and answer penetrating questions about your deepest beliefs and desires and connect your goals to those beliefs and desires. You'll excavate the true Style-of-Life that matches your inner CEO.

You'll also benefit from verifying and closing the gap between your organization's rhetoric and its action, its good intentions and actual performance. You'll find that "let it happen" works better than "make it happen." You'll learn to articulate your company's actual destination, and how to adjust it to make the company great. Fears will fall by the wayside; strengths will take hold and flourish. By looking at boundaries (those ubiquitous dividers you seldom see) in a new way, you'll master the art of redefining your life on a daily basis, consistently connecting to a spiritual dimension that adds richness to all aspects of your work and life.

Once you tap all your largely hidden or untapped talents, you will become a model and mentor for your associates and anyone with whom you come in contact. Finally, you and your organization will reap the benefits of *Your Inner CEO.*

Here's a glimpse of the journey ahead. I've used real people, real organizations, and real names to illustrate each chapter's lessons, but I've relied on fictitious names in other examples where the subject is sensitive and requires discretion. Other examples are hypothetical or composites of two or more situations, designed to make the point as sharply and briefly as possible.

The journey begins in Chapter 1, with the excavation of your Style-of-Life, and concludes in Chapter 9, where you learn that every teacher learns and every learner teaches. In between, you'll encounter seven chapters that I hope will multiply and sharpen your skills as a world-class leader.

Chapter 2 gives you the tools to answer penetrating questions about your deepest beliefs and desires, and to connect your newly discovered goals to those beliefs and desires. You'll traverse the boundary that separates fear and self-doubt from courage and conviction. In this chapter, you'll plan and track changes you want to make in your true "SELF."

Chapter 3 explains the significance of excavating your organization's Style-of-Life, just as you did your own. You'll learn how to discern the gap between your organization's rhetoric and action; its good intentions and actual performance; its façade and essence. As you measure the overlap between its ideal and real personality, you'll determine the need for crafting your own organic mission around a "guardian presence" Style-of-Life. You'll sense the benefits of mastering the art of meditation.

Chapter 4 helps you recognize the crucial fact that you are always moving *away, toward* or *against* something. To ascertain your level of mastery in any area of performance that concerns you, you'll measure yourself against what I call the BAM Grid. You'll make boundaries concrete, as well as pinpoint the events when you can create authentic contact with significant people in your work and life. You'll learn to distinguish between the apparent and real purpose of a boundary, thereby acquiring the means to define accurately any situation you face.

Chapter 5 reveals eight specific steps that can prepare you to become a CEO who serves as the energy source between your board (be it a formal or informal one) and top team. You'll gain awareness of the new board accountability that has emerged in corporate governance, and, along with it, the need for you as a CEO to serve as a catalyst. You'll learn how to prepare, plan, and execute good board meetings, secure your board's best judgments, and you'll take away valuable insights from the CEO Boundaries Quiz, such as the fact that first-rate leaders accomplish more with less control.

Chapter 6 demonstrates that true vision arrives in two phases: vision here-and-now, and vision there-and-then. It argues that the force acting on your organization does not push you from behind, but pulls you forward like a magnet. You'll learn that who you are now as an organization provides the single best indicator of who you're going to be. You'll learn how to define your correct direction and destination. You'll see, perhaps for the first time, your organization's keel-of-boat values that lie beneath the waterline, where, often unseen, they control your direction nonetheless.

Chapter 7 shows how each structure (form) in your company *always* undergoes change to serve an unshakable purpose (function). This chapter also stresses that the future, more than the past, causes the present. This revelation gives you an entirely new perspective for understanding why your company acts the way it does, and how you might influence desirable changes in those actions. Finally, you'll learn how to articulate your company's Style-of-Life, vision, and mission in a fresh, compelling way.

Chapter 8 suggests that you are like all other people, like some other people, and like *no other person.* That latter singularity will help you grow into a stand-alone model. The Centering Statements you'll write will help you manage *all* the boundaries of your life, not just those at work.

So, that's the satellite view of our journey. Join me now, with your feet firmly on the ground, as we take the first few steps toward unleashing your inner CEO, and creating a more prosperous and rewarding future.

Allan Cox
*www.allancox.com*

# Goals

*Two o'clock in the morning courage: I mean unprepared courage.*

—Napoleon Bonaparte

Ted Engdall, a freshly minted MBA from the University of Chicago's Graduate School of Business, moved rapidly up the management ladder, first at a major building materials manufacturer, then at a large real estate development firm. After a successful stint there, Ted, age 40, landed a job as senior vice president of facilities operations for a leading Arizona bank, Valley National, with a wide-spread and growing network of 250 branches. There, he oversaw all new construction, maintenance, janitorial services, food service, and much more, starting with the downtown Phoenix headquarters tower (where he occupied a corner office on the top floor), and spreading out to expanding branches throughout the state.

You would expect Ted to feel quite happy with his life at this stage, but you'd be wrong. When I met him 30 years ago, though pleased with his progress and grateful for his job, he felt curiously restless and disengaged. Serving as his executive coach, I helped him peer into his deepest self. Who, really, was Ted Engdall? How did he define his life? What goals truly motivated him? Should he look more deeply inside himself to discover hidden goals, the pursuit of which could cause his current unease?

I advised him to take his time and answer these questions in 10 words or less, using non-business language. After several weeks of pondering, of peering deep inside himself and scanning back to his earliest childhood experiences, he eventually crafted his answers:

| | |
|---|---|
| **I am:** | a preparer. |
| **Life is:** | clutching support. |
| **My central goal:** | to ride on a hero's coattails. |

These definitions may seem rather innocuous to you, but in Ted's mind they detonated a bomb. The new contact he had made with himself prompted him to make some dramatic changes in his outlook, replacing excess caution with more risk-taking action. This led him in other directions: to stop depending so much on others and start standing on his own two feet; to eradicate envy of others' accomplishments with pride in his own initiative; and to offer support to others rather than seek it.

Right off the block, he understood what anyone would realize if he or she is to live a life based on authentic Destiny: To learn who he truly is and act on it, he has to unlearn who he isn't, but thinks he is.

Ultimately, Ted recrafted his answers to the Big Three Questions:

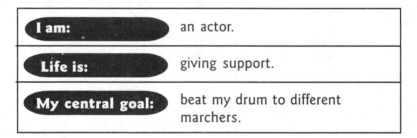

| | |
|---|---|
| **I am:** | an actor. |
| **Life is:** | giving support. |
| **My central goal:** | beat my drum to different marchers. |

Within six months he quit his job, wrote a business plan, and raised $1 million in venture capital to launch his own janitorial services firm, The Sunrise Group. Conquering occasional self-doubt and the inevitable obstacles that got in his way, this "reborn" entrepreneur acquired an impressive array of customers: large office buildings, sprawling shopping malls, and professional sports arenas. In a few short years, he presided over his own mini-empire.

Seven years ago, Ted Engdall sold his company to a much larger conglomerate, Sanitors, Inc., and became president of their western division. The merger was a successful one and Sanitors, with Ted's help, has been on a tear. Then, on May 22, 2007, Sanitors announced it had been acquired by ISS Group of Copenhagen.

The ISS Group is one of the world's leading Facility Services Group, with annual revenues of approximately $10 billion, and more than 410,000 employees in 50 countries across Europe, Asia, North America, Latin America, and Australia. Ted remains a key player in this new combine, and was quickly off to his first meeting of this global enterprise in Instanbul. Though he's approaching retirement age, he doesn't know the meaning of the word. Money means little to him now. Sure, he's made millions, but no amount of money can bring him his greatest achievement: feeling completely comfortable in his own skin. Twenty-five years later, he "came home" to that smart, winsome, autonomous kid who somehow lost his way early in his career.

Though Ted is approaching retirement age, he doesn't know the meaning of the word, and money means little to him now. Sure, he's made millions, but no amount of money can bring him his greatest achievement: feeling completely comfortable in his own skin. Twenty-five years later, he came home to that smart, winsome kid from Chicago's St. Ignatius High.

You may think that Ted's metamorphosis seems too easy or too hard: "How can a person grasp something so elusive, so deeply buried in her makeup? In the pages ahead you will learn how to resolve that paradox.

In Ted's case, I didn't send him off without some guidance. First, I met him face to face and spent time getting acquainted. And when I did assign his homework, I handed him a self-survey similar to the one in the next chapter. However, I want to focus on one key point: Nobody but Ted could have arrived at the answer. During several contemplative weeks, he courageously experimented with definitions of just who he is. Trial and error brought him to the right answers; you can do the same.

The three answers should weave an integrated theme: They should hang together. When you look at Ted's answers of "preparer," "clutching support," and "riding another's coattails," you can see they create a picture, not a healthful one, but a complete one just the same. When you examine his replacement answers of, "actor," "giving support," and "beat my drum to different marchers," you see another picture emerge—one that's brimming with vitality, and the real Ted eager to take on the world.

At first, you too may feel as though you can take on the world, and that exhilaration is just fine. This is because you've gained a new self-knowledge along with a freedom that rings true. Alternatively, you'll soon level off to a more determined resolve. You'll engage not only with the task of building your career, but also of building love and community—local and global.

Some figure out their goal first, and then go back to their "I am" and "Life is" readings. Others do the opposite, figuring out what their actions reveal, and what kind of a life they lead before gaining insight into their goal.

## 27 Sample Descriptions

| | | |
|---|---|---|
| ‣ Architect | ‣ Fixer | ‣ Plodder |
| ‣ Arguer | ‣ Helper | ‣ Questioner |
| ‣ Catalyst | ‣ Hurdler | ‣ Ripper |
| ‣ Complimentor | ‣ Joiner | ‣ Seeker |
| ‣ Critic | ‣ Limiter | ‣ Untangler |
| ‣ Developer | ‣ Lover | ‣ Voyager |
| ‣ Energizer | ‣ Martyr | ‣ Waster |
| ‣ Enveloper | ‣ Nay-sayer | ‣ Wisher |
| ‣ Evader | ‣ Pleaser | ‣ Yearner |

The list could be a lot longer. I suggest these "I am" examples just to prod your imagination. To describe the life you lead, state it in terms of action, of doing something—what you typically do that expresses who you are, and where you're headed. For example, an "architect" (not someone who literally makes her living as an architect) might say, "Life is: designing solutions to problems"—any kind of problem. A helper might write "Life is: giving comfort." A pilgrim might observe "Life is: following an open road." A voyager might note "Life is: embarking on something new." A waster might say, habitually, "This situation doesn't have much to offer."

If your central goal is a positive one that serves you well, think of it as a guardian presence. Cherish it, nourish it, let it pull you toward a bright future. If, however, it is a negative one, you should replace it (because it does more harm than good), and face up to it as a looming threat. I use the term "looming threat" because it may not damage you today, but if you let it thrive unabated, it can eventually choke off your life force. Question it, change it, but don't let it pull you to a dark place. And don't forget: This is a goal that shapes and explains all your life, not just your career.

If you need a replacement goal, make the new one as large and overarching as possible—one big enough and positive enough to govern the rest of your life as you believe it authentically needs to be. You want it to diminish your fear and stimulate your courage. After all, it takes courage to become the person you're really meant to be. Make the goal fit with this person you now believe truly exists—the one you've kept bound up all these years.

Consider these examples of limiting and enhancing goals:

| Negative/Limited/ Looming Threat | Positive/Expansive/ Guardian Presence |
| --- | --- |
| Become wealthy | Add value wherever I go |
| Get the top job | Nurture reunion between others |
| Seek perfection | Be available |
| To have power | Mentor others |
| Claim victories | Feed my gifts |
| Be eloquent | Speak like a journeyman |
| Live long | Live wise |
| Control the future | Adapt to the future |

Remember: You will want to ask the Big Three Questions periodically, because you will change, conditions will change, the world will change, and your goal may evolve over time, becoming clearer, sharper, and more powerful.

## Have You Lost Your Way?

When I agree to serve as a CEO's counselor, I come to fan a flame, whether the CEO has won a reputation for abrasiveness, meanness, and volatility, or for brilliance, charm, and warmth. These traits are little more than smoke, masking the flame flickering in a person's soul.

In the more than three decades that I've consulted with CEOs and boards, I've completed more than 200 top-level executive searches; facilitated dozens of top management team-building off-site meetings

for companies large and small; led many lengthy mission development projects that helped organizations reclaim their spirit and frame
new purpose; helped resolve dangerous conflicts between top executives; advised boards on their expanded role in the development of
their CEOs; completed a handful of corporate culture studies that
laid the groundwork for corporate transformation; and extended career counsel to hundreds of top executives.

This rich experience has taught me a lot, but more than anything
else, I've learned that I can best serve my clients by peeling away the
complexity of a situation and address the simple core issue that demands the most attention. It's a bit like Pareto's law, where 20 percent accounts for 80 percent, though in my work, 1 percent usually
accounts for 99 percent.

At the very beginning of any assignment, I issue this statement:
"I've found, almost without exception, that by the time executives get
married, take on a mortgage, raise kids, cope with the crabgrass, climb
the corporate ladder, do their best to manage career pressures, and
build their net worth and get into their forties, they've lost touch with
what they believe in and care about most deeply."

I can see these words register in the eyes of my audience, whether
it's a Ted Engdall or the Board of Directors of AT&T. It touches a
nerve—often a tender one.

Most people, regardless of their position in life, can't or won't
touch that nerve themselves. They need someone (or a book like
this) to do it for them. Eric Hoffer, the longshoreman-philosopher,
writing late at night after his arduous days on the San Francisco docks,
put it best: "That which is unique and worthwhile in us makes itself
felt only in flashes. If we do not know how to capture and savor those
flashes, we are without growth and without exhilaration."

Have you lost touch with what's worthwhile in you? Have you
lost your way on the road to success and fulfillment? If so, you are
probably suffering from the *disconnect* between who you are and who
you think you are, as Ted Engdall discovered after deep soul-searching. His hidden goal was a personal looming threat, one he needed to
face and overcome before he could possibly find true fulfillment. Ask
yourself the tough questions, and the answers may startle you. It's
nothing to feel ashamed of; rather, it's something to welcome and
embrace. It's a boundary for you to cross.

You'll notice my frequent use of the word *boundary* throughout this book. (In fact, I think it's so important, I'll devote a whole chapter to it later). No other word better describes the choices we face, big and small, each and every day. Picture a circle with a line down the middle. The left side is black—a "looming threat"; the right side is white—a "guardian presence."

On the dark side of the boundary you encounter a personal looming threat that ignites fear and self-doubt. On the right side, you discover courage and conviction. Here you feel together, focused, unfettered, integrated, centered, authentic, and powerful. Here you can generate a high-octane performance.

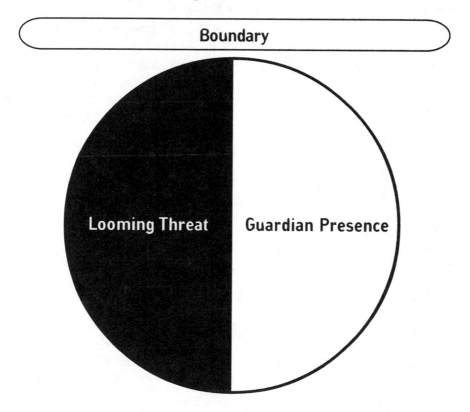

I often use one word to capture this phenomenon: grounding. As we discussed in the beginning of the chapter, grounding removes fear, summons strengths, and ensures achievement.

Grounding will help you cross the boundary to reach your Destiny. Never shy away from it, but eagerly plunge toward it. Welcome and work your way through what Joseph Campbell calls the dark night of the soul. Similar to most of us, you may meet, perhaps for the first time since your youth, your true self.

Not long ago, I looked across the desk at Jay Geldmacher and asked him a simple question: "What keeps you awake at night?" Jay is a group vice president and responsible for an exemplary multi-billion dollar group of electronic divisions for Emerson Electric; nothing ever seems to scare him. He grinned. "Reality. Nobody's got it all figured out. To truly come out in the right place in this job, or any like it, you have to walk through the valley of death."

Reality. It's scary. It's full of boundaries, threats, and opportunities, and no one, not even the most admired and successful CEO, can duck reality, ignore boundaries, or avoid the "walk through the valley of death." It does take courage to take the stroll, to look closely at the dark side, at your personal looming threat, because, similar to most of us, you've probably erected almost impenetrable protective walls to shield you from all your unfounded, debilitating fears, catastrophic fantasies, false comforts, and any other uncomfortable factors in your life. Those walls will ultimately disintegrate, so why not dismantle them yourself?

## 2 a.m. Courage

I like Napoleon's observation about courage. Anyone, he thought, could act bravely in the clear light of day with a threat still miles away. But what about deep in the night when a threat blasts you awake?

Two o'clock in the morning, "the darkest hour." You lie there wide awake, naked and vulnerable, exposed to all the dark and troublesome fears that disrupt your sleep. You can toss and turn and try to clamp down on them, or you can muster the courage to look them squarely in the eye.

Two a.m. offers us a window into our soul. If we can see through it clearly to the core of those 2 a.m. fears, we may discover our hidden goals, the ones that inexorably draw us forward, whether they lie on the dark side or the bright side of the boundary.

Pretend it is 2 a.m. and do the following things:

- Define a boundary.
- Describe its dark side (looming threat).
- Detail its bright side (guardian presence).
- Set a specific time to cross to the bright side.

I posed this exercise to Anita Carlson, the 38-year-old head of a large paperback subsidiary of a major New York trade book publisher. Roger Altman, the CEO of the parent company, viewed her as the brightest star on his management team and had decided to groom her as his successor.

Anita's intelligence and interpersonal skills had taken her to the top, but, having majored in biology at a small college in the south, she lacked any formal business education. She should, Altman believed, fill that gap easily.

When he proposed that for her, she got really excited. Altman was, after all, one of the most respected leaders in the industry. She loved working with him, but she didn't know he thought so highly of her. "I want you to consider something," Altman urged her. "Choose one of the best business schools—Harvard, Stanford, Chicago, Wharton, your pick. Enroll in one of their advanced executive programs. The company will pay all your expenses. These programs usually run from eight to 10 weeks. We'll take care of your work here while you're away."

As much as the offer flattered and delighted her, she left her boss's office in a state of pure terror.

Where did that fear come from? Hadn't she just been offered the chance of a lifetime? Was it separation from her family—her husband, who had always supported her career, and their three young children, whom she adored? Yes, of course, that concerned her. But what really scared her was diving into a pool of skilled swimmers, in terms of business training, in which she could barely dogpaddle. Not only might she not measure up, but perhaps her present position was just a stroke of dumb luck.

This is when I entered the picture, invited by my old friend Roger Altman to spend a couple of hours over lunch with his protégé. After exploring her fears and dreams, I asked her to perform the boundary exercise. Here's what she wrote:

- Define the boundary: "I'm being put to the test."

- Describe its dark side—the looming threat: "I'll seem inadequate by comparison."

- Detail the bright side—the guardian presence: "I've always welcomed new tasks."

- "I can pass any test if I put my mind to it."

- Set a time to cross to the bright side: "Monday morning. I'll accept Roger's offer."

Did her fear suddenly disappear? No. It was just a little healthy apprehension, some pre-performance jitters that affect us all when we face a big test. But Anita had chosen courage. Long story short, she picked Stanford, where she won enormous respect from her fellow classmates. Back at work several months later, she saw a big payoff in terms of applying business acumen to decisions she often made with instinct alone. The absence from her family made her appreciate them even more, and to top it all off, a year later the board approved her appointment as president of the company, a position that acknowledged her as Roger Altman's heir apparent.

Similar to Anita, you can perform this exercise to pinpoint and analyze any boundary you encounter, from routine choices such as which sales manager to hire, to life-changing decisions, such as whether or not to quit your job and accept a new position, or face up to a marriage gone stale. Make it a habit, and you will more consistently cross your boundaries from the dark side to the bright side. That will make it much easier to confront the "big boundary—the one that may separate the "Who am I?" from "Who can I be?" or the one that may separate the right ultimate goal from the wrong ultimate goal.

## When You Say No to Your Wake-Up Call

When Anita Carlson heard her 2 a.m. wake-up call, she bolted out of bed and ran toward the bright side. But what happens when you ignore that wake-up call? George Brumner's story offers a cautionary tale. Walter Bingham, the chairman and CEO of a mid-sized Cleveland-based company that made and sold high-quality women's casual clothes nationwide, introduced me to George. Some years ago, the chairman had met 25-year-old George through a friend, and had hired him as a salesman. George shot up through the sales organization like a missile, and at age 28 became the southwestern regional senior VP of sales.

Thanks to George, his region had gone from dead last in sales to first place in just 18 months. George's star couldn't have shone more brightly. But there was a hitch.

The company had recently reorganized sales, and placed another regional VP (older than George by seven years, whose region had not performed as well) as executive vice president of the whole sales organization. That's when the chairman called to ask if I'd spend some time with his young star. The recent shuffle had upset George, who criticized it to anyone who would listen. Would his disappointment prompt him to leave? As the chairman confided, "We don't want to lose him, because we think he might take my place in a few years."

When I met with George over lunch, his warm personality impressed me. I could see why the chairman liked him so much. He exuded charm and energy, and displayed a quick mind and sharp sense of humor. I could see the CEO in him; not right now, though. He had one foot out the door, with the other on a roller skate. He was meeting with me out of courtesy to the chairman, he confided, and would resign as soon as he could arrange a meeting with his boss.

An impatient player with many options, George had exceled in a gossip-ridden industry where rising stars make their presence known quite quickly. A month later, he called me to say he'd taken a job in Boston as a president of an established, smaller competitor run by an aging owner who wanted George "to light a fire under the place." Light a fire he did, and throughout the next five years, he managed to triple sales and quadruple net profit. Imagine my surprise, then, when he quit that job in a huff. As he put it, "The old man was having too much fun now that we're a thriving business and wouldn't make me CEO or give me the equity he promised."

George vowed from that day on, he would only work for a publicly held company.

Shortly afterward, he landed a new job, and in less than a month he moved up to president at a small, promising division of one of the largest women's clothing companies in the country. He had quickly achieved a position that gave him a clear shot at the top job.

Five years later, George had grown his division tenfold in sales and sevenfold in profit, an astonishing feat accomplished through imaginative marketing, strong cost controls, and acquisitions. That was when, just by chance, I happened to meet with the CEO of George's new company for lunch. He didn't know of my relationship with George. When I asked him to rate his management team, he spoke favorably about them all, though he described the head of his fastest growing division as a superstar. "This guy is a true entrepreneur," he said, "a real piece of work. You normally don't see guys like this in companies like ours."

About 60 days later, George reached me in my office and asked for an appointment to, as he put it, "figure out the rest of my career." Of course I agreed, although I insisted he do a little homework before we got together. You know the assignment: Who are you? What life do you lead? What goal moves you forward? Three weeks later, George came to the office and proudly showed me his answers:

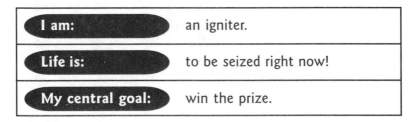

| I am: | an igniter. |
|---|---|
| Life is: | to be seized right now! |
| My central goal: | win the prize. |

Throughout the next hour, I learned from George that although he had racked up spectacular results for his division and won the open admiration of the Chairman (the CEO I had met for lunch), he was beginning to feel he just didn't fit in. His competition for the president's job, one of his peers who seemed to have stolen the inside track, seemed to be a shoo-in. Why her? Why not George?

Time for the boundaries exercise, I thought. I left him alone for a while in an adjoining office, urging him to identify his major boundary, frame up its dark and bright side, and the actions he could take to cross it, much like Anita Carlson did. This is what he wrote:

- Boundary: Promotion from division president to corporate president.

- Dark Side (looming threat): Impatience will drive me away from the company.

- Bright Side (guardian presence): A good result comes with time.

- Actions: Slow down, be patient, drop the old habit of quitting in a huff.

I thought he'd searched his soul and come up with a valuable insight. What, specifically, could he do to cross his boundary? Replace his break-neck timetable with a more patient and reasonable 1 to 3 year plan? Emphasize his passion for the piano? George (a jazz virtuoso) played beautifully; he even had his own trio, and earned good money playing in clubs on weekends. I suggested he rely on that source of pleasure to nurture his patience at work. We agreed to stay in touch, and, periodically, because of our fondness for each other, we did.

He stayed on at his company, told me he still wanted the top job, but from our communications I could tell that he had done little to curb his frenetic approach to work and life. Five years later, I learned from an officer of his company that he'd been fired for a host of reasons: drinking, judgment lapses on the job, and an overall deteriorating performance. He moved back to St. Louis, his hometown, financially independent but unemployable. He drank more. His natural charm never died, but the man inside shriveled and succumbed to liver disease 10 years later. The moral? Never say no to your wake-up call.

## Distinguish Between Ordinary Obstacles and Your Looming Threat

Let me pause to make an important distinction. Can you see the different between George's looming threat, which eventually destroyed him, and the ordinary obstacles that can also keep your inner CEO awake at night?

Not long ago, I had breakfast with Peter Georgescu, the recently-retired CEO of Young & Rubicam, one of the top five global advertising agencies, where in a 10-year run he had recorded a list of accomplishments as long as a limousine. Nonetheless, he recounted the challenges he had faced in his job. "When I first became CEO I felt I was on Mars. I had a good relationship with my CEO when I was COO and had been with the company my whole career. "We talked all the time, and he shared with me options he was considering, but I never had a clue as to the enlarged perspective that's required when you step into that corner office. It's lonely. You lose your friends in the company. The business comes first. The job is harder and more complex than ever. Even former CEOs who have been retired for some years don't have a full appreciation of how demanding the job is now."

He could have rattled off similar challenges for hours, of course, but he didn't need to. All you need to do is scan recent headlines:

- Skyrocketing fuel costs jeopardizing airlines and trucking companies.

- An Army General in Iraq losing respect when the press castigates U.S. troops' suspected brutality to local civilians.

- A small decline in quarterly earnings (down a penny from what the analysts predicted) decimating a company's stock.

- A nonprofit organization encountering trouble raising funds in the wake of a destructive act of nature because "I gave to the Red Cross after Katrina."

- A pharmaceutical company declaring bankruptcy when 7,000 lawsuits follow a negative FDA ruling that its product is unsafe.

- A school district superintendent dealing with a sex scandal involving one of its principals.

- A beef business declining because a Canadian supplier was quarantined when one animal in a herd came down with mad cow disease.

- A travel business languishing in the wake of September 11th.

- A Bishop of a local diocese coping with a priest's youth molestation charge.

These and countless other problems, roadblocks, and calamities may well keep CEOs awake at night, especially when feeling compelled to watch everything they say and do during a crisis. Any miscue (real or imagined) can bring negative consequences instantaneously. Any number of "threats" can spoil a CEO's good night sleep, but their destructiveness can't match the damage done by a personal looming threat, which can kill the inner CEO just as surely as a bullet to the heart.

About six years ago I sat in an audience of 1,200 at a dinner sponsored by The Economic Club of Chicago. Carly Fiorina, the featured speaker that evening, had taken the helm as CEO of Hewlett-Packard a year or two earlier.

I have listened to many speeches by CEOs, but never one as eloquent and compelling as this one delivered by a supremely talented woman. She had this black-tie audience enthralled, and when she finished, a hush fell over the room before we "came to" and erupted into thunderous applause.

On February 9, 2005, the Hewlett-Packard board of directors fired Ms. Fiorina. I don't know the inside story of the drama, but I can assure you her dismissal reflected more than flat earnings. A good part stemmed from her style, one that simply didn't work. You can detect clues to that style in an online Wikipedia entry:

> Fiorina's tenure at HP was nothing short of a prolonged controversy. Her unpopularity at HP was amplified by her many decisions, which some thought to be provoking. When she first started at HP, she removed the portraits of HP founders, William Hewlett and David Packard, from HP lobbies, and replaced them with her own. HP had long maintained an essentially no-layoff policy during the many years of following "The HP Way," immortalized in the book of the same name by David Packard. She, however, saw this as decidedly "old-school," and accelerated layoffs to increase profits.
>
> Then, while HP was undergoing massive layoffs, she approved the lease of two new Gulfstream jets, had HP

pay to move her yacht from the East to the West coast, and took endless trips to socialize with Hollywood movie stars and politicians, trips that could be justified as fortifying the benefits of one's political career, not those of shareholders and of HP. Her actions prompted the *San Jose Mercury News*, one of the prominent newspapers in the U.S. covering Silicon Valley, to speculate that she would run to become California governor, or a U.S. Senator, under the Republican ticket, after her career at HP was over. Fiorina never denied such rumors. According to family members of husband Frank Fiorina, as of 2005 she still hopes to land a high-level government appointment in a Republican administration, but her abrasiveness may preclude this possibility for at least several more years.

In any event, capability, brilliance, and experience could not avert a major career shortfall. An overlooked or unheeded boundary can bring down anyone—CEO or janitor—no matter how deep that person's reservoir of ability. That mistake, believe me, is a lot easier to make than coping poorly with a trucker's strike or a weak bottom line.

By the same token, crossing the boundary to the bright side can bring great rewards, especially in terms of a career-shaping appreciation of the hidden issues that stymie success for both individuals and their organizations as they encounter ordinary obstacles. Remember Ted and Anita, who crossed successfully, and George, who failed to embrace what he learned. While Ted broke a troubling and career-threatening pattern, and Anita put her finger on what might impair her progress, George did neither.

Can you probe your inner CEO and find your own pattern? Can you rid yourself of your personal looming threat and reclaim the unique strengths you may have neglected? That's the best way to discover and unleash your inner CEO.

## Excavating Your Style-of-Life

To identify a looming threat, look carefully for tip-off signs in your life. They may be as subtle as a tendency to avoid potentially painful decisions, such as firing a subordinate, or as obvious as losing your temper whenever you see someone making a mistake. Before you search for your own tip-offs, let's take a moment to review a centerpiece of psychologist Alfred Adler's theory of personality.

Adler introduced the phrase "Style-of-Life," meaning an organized set of convictions about life, which the individual, at best, is only dimly aware.

Given the elusive nature of our convictions, most of us lack total insight into our Style-of-Life. How do you correct this blind-spot? Simply by engaging in quiet introspection and trusting your natural intuition in a disciplined way.

Pause. Close your eyes. Focus on one of your strong convictions. State it in as few words as possible. For instance, suppose you avoid painful decisions. Your statement of that limitation might go something like this: "I don't like to hurt people." What does that really mean? "I want people to like me" or, "I don't want to feel badly myself?"

We each have (1) an orderly outlook on life, and (2) a consistent governance system for maintaining it, but by-and-large we remain unaware of both. The exercises in this chapter—asking the Big Three Questions and Analyzing Boundaries—give you practical tools for dredging up that habitual outlook, and that partially understood system from the depths of your psyche, and thus get a better handle on your Style-of-Life.

Adler's protégé, Rudolph Dreikurs, shed even more light on the Style-of-Life when he clarified that it consists of three elements. Whatever your convictions, subtle or obvious, they include:

▶ **Self-Image:** An indelible picture you've created of yourself, but seldom see as clearly as you should.

▶ **Worldview:** Deeply held beliefs about the structure and makeup of life that you may only dimly comprehend.

▶ **The Central Goal:** The magnet of your life that draws every particle of your existence into its service. This, too, remains largely unseen. It may, like your self-image and worldview, come from either the dark side or the bright side. It may sustain you or destroy you. While all these concepts entwine like the strands of a rope, the central goal precedes the other two. In a sense, the future gives birth to the present (more on this in later chapters).

Okay; back to your own Style-of-Life. Can you describe how you understand yourself (self-image), how you "scan" your horizon (worldview), and how you "navigate" the sea of life in accordance with a central goal (encompassing, hidden, magnetic)?

Tough questions; no easy answers. Yet, these three factors shape our lives. Obviously, we should strive hard to clarify them, excavate them from the depth of our souls, and consider how they influence our lives, for better or worse.

Your own introspections should help you answer the central questions I pose to all my clients: Who am I? What life do I lead? What pulls me forward?

Now we can try the exercise again:

Self-Image: _____

(Who am I?)

Worldview: _____

(What life do I lead?)

Central Goal: _____

(What pulls me forward?)

As we've seen, a Central Goal is often hidden, even though it pulls us forward like a powerful magnet. It functions similar to what physicists call "the strange attractor," the mysterious factor that binds invisible particles and fashions our universe. You don't see it, but as with filings to a magnet, every element of your existence, your every thought and act, is drawn irresistibly into its service. Dark or bright, a looming threat or a guardian presence, it exerts the same power. The threat can ruin your life; the guardian can save it.

Given the hidden nature of our central goals, you'll need to perform the Style-of-Life excavation process over and over again, so that you keep evolving and refining it. Reflections today may cause you to revise or replace one of yesterday's answers, and tomorrow's critical introspection may alter today's answers. It's like developing any capacity (such as what resides between your ears). Use it or lose it.

The more you work it, the stronger it gets. And it takes a powerful mind to excavate that slippery Style-of-Life that so strongly governs your life and work.

A couple of words of advice. Try to limit your definitions to short 2 to 3 word phrases. And, "To thine own self be true"—struggle for honest answers. Don't fall prey to the tendency to put a positive spin on your Style-of-Life. Otherwise, you'll never discover your looming threat or conceive a plan for crossing the boundary to a guardian presence.

Consider this transformation. Lindsay Cordell is a young woman who struggled with her answers until she defined them this way:

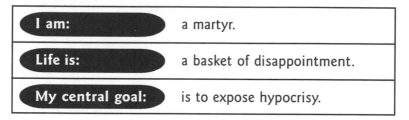

| **I am:** | a martyr. |
| **Life is:** | a basket of disappointment. |
| **My central goal:** | is to expose hypocrisy. |

Lindsay didn't like her Style-of-Life, but she did find the courage to state it honestly and set about making changes. Trained as a lawyer, she worked as an FBI agent, tracking and apprehending people who confirmed her self-image and worldview. After some soul-searching, she quit, made changes, and moved toward her guardian presence. She became a criminal law professor and world-class researcher, consulting with the federal prison system, directing studies on what might reduce recidivism (the incidence of repeat offenders). She replaced her former Style-of-Life with this one:

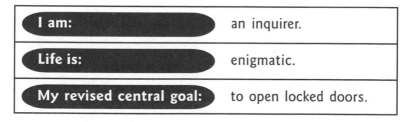

| **I am:** | an inquirer. |
| **Life is:** | enigmatic. |
| **My revised central goal:** | to open locked doors. |

She crossed the boundary from a dark world to a bright one, and she merely applied her skills to a more satisfying purpose. When she needed to elect a better life, she voted with her feet.

## Mouth Values vs. Feet Values

Similar to most people, you probably won't ferret out your Style-of-Life in a day or week. Play at it with patience. Let leisure rule. Stimulate new ideas and permit insights to bubble-up. Maintain a sense of humor, if you can. Don't try to force it. Sometimes great insights come when you least expect them, while you're doing something else, something pleasurable and distracting, such as playing tennis or strumming your guitar.

Another trick involves paying less attention to your mouth than to your feet!

Instead of listening to your words (the least reliable indicator of what you're going to do), watch your feet! Where did they take you yesterday? Where do they take you today?

In all these cases, ask yourself, "Toward whom or what?" "Away from whom or what?" "Against whom or what?"

Where will they take you tomorrow? To gain valid insights, trust visible movements. The visible can reveal the invisible. Accept your actions as an eloquent and trustworthy yardstick for measuring your commitments.

Body language can tell you more than mouth language, whether you're evaluating someone else or peering deep inside yourself. Talk the talk certainly, but pay more attention to how you walk the walk.

Astute market researchers know that focus group participants often state their intended buying preferences, then buy or don't buy based on preferences other than what they have stated. Obviously, factors other than articulated ones dictated their choices. This helps explain why true Style-of-Life can prove so elusive: self-image, worldview, and Central Goal play hide-and-seek with our minds.

To excavate your Style-of-Life, you'll first need to examine your behavior and your movement. Not until you've done this, can you come up with the right words to answer the Big Three Questions.

Does all this strike you as too touchy-feely, too abstract and philosophical, too ephemeral and ungraspable? Trust me. It's not. I'm as straightforward, level-headed, and down-to-earth as any of the CEOs I've consulted, and believe me, they and I always gain a lot by spending time reflecting on the intangibles in life.

As you grow more candid and unapologetic with yourself, you'll begin to notice a few signs that weave into a theme. Focus on those telltale signs, and search for more. Try naming the theme. Try more names until one rings true. Share it with your best friend, most valued associate, significant other, spouse, or sister. Do these caring mentors confirm your insight? Ask them for brutal honesty, the kind you've been applying to yourself.

### In this chapter you have learned how to:

→ Recognize lost dreams and desires.

→ Recognize your personal boundary that separates fear and self-doubt from courage and conviction.

→ Clarify whether your Style-of-Life acts as a "Guardian Presence" or "Looming Threat."

→ Answer your wake-up call.

→ Express your hidden self.

### Your Inner CEO Punch List

❏ Embark on a journey of discovery that will reveal your hidden goal.

❏ Ask the Big Three Questions over and over again until honest answers emerge.

❏ Learn how to identify and deal with boundaries.

❏ Don't listen to your words. Watch your feet.

❏ Repeat the "Who am I?" and boundaries exercises periodically. Life flows. Monitor the flow.

# Changes

*We can change our whole life and the attitude of
people around us simply by changing ourselves.*

—Rudolph Dreikurs

One night many years ago, dining alone in a Philadelphia hotel
restaurant, I made a startling discovery: I had been basing my whole
life on a false goal. While it hit me like lightning, its origin actually lay
in my distant past, when I had become fascinated with psychologist
Alfred Adler's work in graduate school. In particular, I admired his
idea of Style-of-Life, a concept we explored in Chapter 1. He defined
this centerpiece of his theory of personality as "an organized set of
convictions about life of which the individual, at best, is only dimly
aware."

In the restaurant, almost all alone, a dozen years into my consulting career, I surprised myself by asking, "What is *my* Style-of-Life?
What hidden conditions, for better or worse, govern my life?" The
answers surprised me:

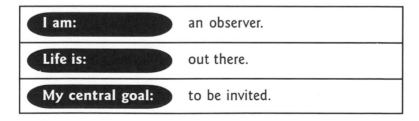

| I am: | an observer. |
| Life is: | out there. |
| My central goal: | to be invited. |

You'll notice that I stated my answers in plain non-psychological
or business language, and restricted my responses to 10 words or

less. I had looked into my innermost self, examined it honestly, and came away with answers that bothered me, but on the plus side, opened the door to positive changes. As an "observer," I sat on the sidelines, disengaged and distant from the action on the field of life. Life was "out there" where the action was, but I had confined myself to my own little compartment; and, rather than leaping into the fray, I just sat there waiting for an engraved invitation. To be sure, Style-of-Life can be healthful, serving you as a guardian presence, but it can also be destructive, always posing a looming threat, as mine did. Before dessert arrived, I began mapping out some productive changes I could make to transform my looming threat into a guardian presence.

When I returned home, I wasted no time sharing my self-discovery with my wife, who agreed that we would throw a large cocktail party, inviting a wide range of friends and acquaintances. We included almost everybody we had ever met, supposing that the approaching holidays would thin the crowd considerably. When the date rolled around, however, we found our large downtown Chicago apartment bulging with guests. On into the night we made merry with lively music, great food and drink, and a joyous crowd. The moral of the story: I participated fully, I put myself out there, and I did the inviting. I had changed my answers; I had changed myself.

With a newfound self and a deep sense of conviction, I soon designed and launched an experimental workshop for small groups of top executives, one that put them through the same sort of self-changing discovery process that had transformed me. These workshops grew quite popular, and many executives I coached said the experience prompted a much-needed mid-course correction.

## Grounding

At this point, let's assume that your answers to the Style-of-Life questions have convinced you to make some positive changes in your life. What, exactly, do you do with that insight?

You might do what Karl Ehrhart did. Not long ago, I coached a struggling new CEO named Karl Ehrhart, whose company, Lang Manufacturing, made and sold automotive wheel and brake systems, mostly to Detroit's Big Three. His former boss, Ed Herrsman, the chairman of the board and previous CEO of Lang, who'd hired Karl and had groomed him for promotion throughout the past decade, had urged him to work with me on the recommendation of Joyce Longford, head of Lang's human resources department. Joyce felt strongly that Karl could benefit from some objective coaching by someone who could help him sort out the priorities of his new job. When Karl resisted her suggestion, she went directly to Ed Herrsman, hoping he would change Karl's mind; He did.

Before I began the engagement, I did a little research. Lang, a typical rust belt heavy manufacturer, had enjoyed a long history of market leadership, but it had faltered throughout the last couple of years as its fortunes declined along with those of the American automobile companies it supplied. In order to restore profitability, Karl needed to reduce the company's dependence on Detroit, close and sell its marginal plants, revitalize management and the workforce, and seek new global markets.

The day I arrived in Harrisburg, Pennsylvania for the engagement, I could see that Karl wasn't thrilled to see me riding down the escalator to where he stood waiting in the baggage claim area. On this cold afternoon in mid-January, with people scurrying in all directions, I could easily spot Karl standing straight as a pillar of ice, arms folded firmly across his chest like bands of steel, his right hand crumpling a manila envelope as if it contained his death certificate. The look on his face could have flash-frozen Lake Erie.

After we chatted privately for an hour, however, he thawed out a bit. Clearly, he was exceptionally bright, imaginative, and tenacious, traits that were focused on the long-term viability of the business. Come hell or high water, he would make it happen with sheer overpowering determination. He would remain energized even if everyone around him gave up. After our warm-up session, I helped Karl look deep inside to his inner CEO and candidly answer The Grounding Quiz shown on page 39.

For the business to thrive as he wished, he ultimately concluded that he would need to face up to the central issue of his style, and engineer some difficult changes.

Karl got grounded when he acknowledged that he could never unleash the CEO he was hired to be, wanted to be, and possessed the tools to be, until he took his hand off everybody's throttle.

How could he make full use of his imagination and act as chief strategist (the number one job of all CEOs) if he got so mired in the

| The Grounding Quiz | |
|---|---|
| **Q & A** | **Karl's Considerations** |
| **Question #1** | "How many major decisions do you make alone—without seeking counsel?" |
| **Karl's answer** | "None." |
| **Question #2** | "Where do you seek help—is it from sources skewed toward avoiding difficult or uncomfortable decisions?" |
| **Karl's answer** | "Sometimes." |
| **Question #3 & 4** | "How do you assess/create an extraordinary management team and/or deal with a dysfunctional but talented individual, and how will you bring about Lang's transformation?" |
| **Karl's answer** | "I'd like you to help me facilitate these processes." |

day-to-day operations of the company? How could he articulate the future and the big picture to financial analysts and Wall Street if he never made time to reflect on those possibilities, and how he could help them become a reality? How could he demonstrate to the Board that he was ready to take this company to new heights if he had failed even to put someone in place who could run the business day to day? Could he balance trust in others with belief in himself?

Karl's answer to all these questions in his moment of truth stimulated him to make the changes necessary to accomplish his goals. As he did so, he felt exhilarated, as people invariably do when they unleash the executive within. Today, his board members take great pride in Karl's personal growth, and love telling their peers in other companies about how much fun they're having by being part of a classic turnaround.

Karl's examination of his inner CEO enabled him to achieve his goals: relying less on Detroit, closing marginal plants, revitalizing management and the workforce, and securing new global markets. He also brought in a capable COO. His actions worked to the extent that Lang's stock price multiplied 10-fold in two years. It's fallen off slightly as I write this, but that drift seems temporary and in tandem with the overall market. It still stands well ahead of the S&P 500 throughout the past three years.

Your own tailor-made Grounding Quiz might help you accomplish results in your job, whether, like Karl, you have recently won promotion to manager or CEO, or one day hope to do so. Karl Ehrhart and all the other personalities, vagaries, histories, cultures, structures, complexities, markets, products, trade-offs, talents, difficulties, successes, and failures you encounter in this book should help you, so that no matter what your unique situation, you can size it up and make the right choices to enhance life both on and off the job.

After working with CEOs from virtually all backgrounds, I've concluded that the most successful among them will admit that they weren't prepared for the job when they took it. It might come as a surprise to you that even the most celebrated leaders have had the very same doubts you may harbor about taking on a new challenge. Ironically, in fact, the greater the CEO, the greater the doubt. Winston Churchill felt fear, but he never accommodated it; he met it and conquered it head-on. He was grounded. Superior performers, those who lead their companies to greatness, somehow find a way to master doubt, and to master the job that turns out to be more complex and demanding than they ever imagined. They get grounded.

Sometimes this grounding kicks in immediately and easily when you take the job. In other situations, throughout time, after hard knocks and unanticipated forces converge to thwart your intended future, it takes time and effort to reach deep inside to your inner CEO.

CEOs who never reach inside almost always fail, without knowing why they failed. Those who succeed know who they are, comprehend what their unique strengths are, and know the same about their organizations. They appreciate and employ "best practices," but they also see the limits of what works for others, constantly searching for creative ways to address their own, and their organization's, special situation.

This brings us to a critical topic: the need to identify and channel your creative self.

## Your Creative Self

The insights that struck me about my own Style-of-Life in that Philadelphia hotel dining room led to changes far more momentous than that memorable party in Chicago. Yours might, too, if you do the work honestly and thoroughly.

Like many powerful ideas, confronting Style-of-Life is both simple and complex. You begin simply by disrobing yourself, your life and your central goal in plain English, limiting your responses to 10 words or less.

When you avoid business jargon, you expand your vocabulary to include words anyone can comprehend, especially friends, family, and colleagues with whom you might want to share your insights.

Here's where it starts to get a little complicated, though, because it's never easy to probe to the core of who you are, what sort of life you really lead, and what central goal (looming threat or guardian presence) guides you.

By the way, you might think you have pinpointed more than one looming threat, but that's doubtful. It's far more likely that seemingly second or third looming threats stem from the main message you're striving to give a *name* right now.

As you probe the corners of your life for signs of trouble in your actions and beliefs, bear in mind that what you find may not be bad, and, on the surface, seem to pose a threat. An apparent strength, such as confidence, can evolve into arrogance or narcissism. In such a case, a system becomes a danger and a liability.

For example, Steve Whiteside works as a product manager for Mosco Nutrition, a consumer packaged goods company that puts well-known brand-name food products on your kitchen table. He's an articulate and exceptionally gifted analytical thinker who regularly gets to the root of a problem faster than anyone else in the room. Because he does this so easily, he has come to rely on it to score points with his bosses. While they recognize his gifts, they also see the downside as well. Steve's peers, put off by his eagerness to strut his stuff, often bypass him, conducting critical discussions offline, without his knowledge. Of course, they derive a certain satisfaction when being "out of the loop" makes Steve look less than brilliant. They aren't dumb, either, and don't mind seeing him hung out to dry when, as one of them, Judy Pruitt, puts it, "he outruns his headlights."

Steve's "inner architect," or what Adler called the "Creative Self," can build a mansion, but it can also cause the walls to come tumbling on his own head. All of us are the creators of ourselves in ways that can enhance or limit our accomplishment. For better or worse, only we can be authors of our life stories.

Steve's Creative Self (architect) has produced a negative Style-of-Life (structure) that looks like this:

| I am: | a demonstrator. |
|---|---|
| Life is: | a vacuum. |
| My central goal: | to be first with the answer. |

By relying so heavily on his be-first-with-brilliance quality, Steve disowns or neglects other qualities that would make him a winner, such as his ability to listen carefully to others. Steve's bosses, peers, and subordinates all find him wearing, and his wife and kids wish he would just sit back and let them run their own lives. Clearly, he needs to make some changes.

My own Creative Self had somehow taken me out of the action, and I, too, needed to make some changes. I had let my architect separate and isolate me from the world and other people. This is what Joseph Campbell described as "refusing the call." The call he speaks of is, in my words, the call of *Destiny*. In my mid-30s I thought (but was mistaken), that I "got the memo" on Destiny. It's possible to craft a heady, masterful definition of Destiny, but for our purposes I'll simply call it living a life based on your uniqueness.

Fortunately, in my late-30s, in that Philadelphia hotel dining room, the ever-patient Unnamable (God, Allah, Tao, Buddha, The Universe, Fate, Reality—take your pick) commanded my attention. To what? To face a fear. To face it and cross a boundary from the darkness to the light.

Why had I become an observer of life waiting to be *invited* to the party? Fear. But fear of what? Failure? Rejection? Disappointment and disapproval? I could catch a glimpse of the fear that night, but it took years for me to grasp it fully. Until I fully grasped it, of course,

I could not properly *reframe* my Style-of-Life, and make the change that would put me on the path to being the person I was *meant* to be, living the sort of life I was *meant* to live.

In the end, I sliced through all the complexities to reach a simple name for my fear: *vulnerability*. We're all vulnerable to fortune, rejection, disappointment, and disapproval, but I had let my vulnerability paralyze me rather than motivate me. In a vain attempt to protect myself from danger or failure, I had let this fear suck all my behavior—all my thoughts and actions—into its service. A potential guardian presence had become a looming threat. How had I let this happen? To answer that question, I listed all the things that mattered most to me:

- Fine apparel
- Excellent food and drink
- Poise and self assurance
- Good taste
- Foreign travel
- Depth of personality
- Adaptability to all situations
- Warmth
- Non-submissiveness
- Perceptiveness
- Collaborative behavior
- Control
- Process (not product oriented)
- Physical fitness
- Fun
- Inclusiveness
- Reuniting those in estranged relationships
- Pretty wife
- Married life

What do you think? Not all bad things, right? Perhaps, but I came to see that vanity runs through the list like mortar holding together the bricks of my mansion. Unfortunately, I had come to value the mortar more than the bricks themselves.

This insight into how I *assembled, arranged, built, and created* my life to support a fear-inspired goal designed to keep me from my true Destiny inspired me to ask three more questions:

- Who am I *meant* to be?
- *What* do I fear?
- How has my fear held me back?

As I wrestled with these questions, certain items from my list of things that matter leaped out at me: Poise and self-assurance, dominance and non-submissiveness, control, and process (not product oriented). A pattern emerged. Each item masked my vulnerability. "Never let 'em see you sweat, stay in control, avoid risks, focus on constant activity, lest you be judged by the quality of that activity." Those were my matters. Could I change them in a way that would help me become who I am meant to be, to face my fear, and to stop letting that fear hold me back? The answers, I hoped, would come from an updated Style-of-Life:

| I am: | an angler (rather than jumping into the river, I stand on the shore). |
|---|---|
| Life is: | tricky (the river might sweep me away or drown me). |
| My central goal: | to be safe (stay on dry land to eliminate the risk of failure and disappointment). |

Now I could see the looming threat more closely. My safety zone had become a danger zone. My sense of vulnerability had stimulated me to create a life of invulnerability, but there's only one way to attain complete vulnerability, and that's to ensconce yourself in a mausoleum where nothing can threaten or harm you. But that's not life; that's death.

## Destiny's Journey

I talk a lot about Destiny, which may sound like a rather abstract and philosophical concept, but to me it is very real and tangible. Your future, the one you experience either as a result of self-enforced and thoughtless actions (the consequence of allowing your looming threat to rule your life), or as a result of more generous and thoughtful actions (the consequence of discovering and following your guardian presence) is as real and tangible as the book you're reading.

Which would you prefer? The one you let take over, or the one you nurture by doing the soul-searching I've described in this chapter? To accomplish the latter, you cultivate balance and harmony, balance in all your personal and business endeavors, harmony with all the people who will benefit as you create a better future for yourself

Phil Overby, a young, upcoming division manager with Carstairs Computing, insists that the biggest lesson he has learned in his career so far is to pause frequently and concentrate on "the flow of things." He says that such a flow often runs counter to his original plan for a project, differs markedly from what he's conceived as the proper course of development for one of his subordinates, or argues against certain initiatives he's conceived for the division. "More and more," he says, "I've found that decisions don't always have to be made as fast as first specified, whether by my boss, my subordinates, even the customer, or me. I've learned that when I hurry a job, it often turns out that I have, in fact, slowed it down because I haven't had the right mechanism, or the right people working on it, or together, we still haven't asked the right question that points us in the right direction.

"When I'm pushing something hard and meeting resistance I didn't expect, it always helps me to slow down and see if I can figure what I'm truly feeling. Most of the time when this happens, I discover that my ambitions are out of line, and I'm restless. On the other hand, when I find the flow, or get it right from the start, I just know it."

Phil is talking about balance, harmony, and Destiny. To create a better future, to imbue his actions with balance and harmony, to, in a word, become and remain *grounded.* Phil has developed the wisdom to pause and think. He doesn't try to force his future through sheer, stubborn, selfish willfulness. He lets it flow naturally. Destiny enfolds and guides him.

This is a crucial point. The more you try to *force* a better future, the more it recedes; the less dominance you try to maintain, the more powerful it becomes.

"Come on," we seemingly hear, "our better future beckons." But as we go out to meet it, we'll wisely go forward with both faith and adaptability because, with our limited vision, we can't always see the big picture, and circumstances won't conform to our plan. What is *meant* to occur does so only when we fit our thoughts and actions to the picture; when we discover and act on being who we're meant to be.

Lisa Klimek, the CFO of Algonquin Forestry Management, loves to read Anne Lamott's books. In *Traveling Mercies*, Anne Lamott tells the captivating story of overcoming an early life of alcohol and drug abuse, and confronting the challenges of raising a beloved son, Sam, born to her out of wedlock. Lisa Klimek admires the way Lamott created a better future through faith and adaptability. She relies on God (Help me, Help me, Help me!), and she expresses her gratitude to God for all his gifts (Thank You, Thank You, Thank You!).

Although Lisa admits that she's not particularly religious herself, she finds Anne Lamott's attitude one worth emulating. She, too, feels she's been put here on earth for a reason. However, she has often come to crossroads in her career when she didn't know what she should do. Whenever that happens, she grows reflective, similar to Phil Overby.

Does the right path magically appear? Almost never. But it does gradually materialize as, in her words, "I put my head down, round up all the help I can get, and then go for it. If it doesn't work, I can ask forgiveness from anyone I may have offended or abused and acknowledge I didn't fully understand the situation—that I underrated the difficulties and oversold the case." She says these situations humble her, but don't intimidate her. "Overall, it's a good system. Most of the time, it works, and when it does I make sure I say thanks to all who helped. In either case, I'm a little bit smarter the next time around."

It takes courage to pause and reflect, to seek help, to acknowledge mistakes, and apologize. It takes courage to get grounded.

This whole business of free will (the freedom to create your own future, for better or worse) can get pretty complicated. So I will simplify it: there's *good* will, and there's *bad* will. Good will is authentic, grounded, balanced, and harmonious; bad will is dishonest, self-absorbed, precarious, and disruptive. Phil and Lisa practice good will. They slow things down. They harness their ambition in the service not only of themselves, but of all the important people in their lives.

Thus, they don't expect the world to support them, but offer support to the world as the best way to get to a better future reality, to their Destiny.

Wally Penrose, CEO of one of the oldest and largest apparel companies in the world, offers another instructive example of good will at work in the world. Wally is highly imaginative, determined, and droll, the sort of person I love to spend time with. When he came into his job a few years ago, he thought his background as a star marketer in consumer packaged goods with a couple of headliner companies had been his true Destiny. The new company, big, well-known, and admired, nonetheless had suffered a decline far greater than its board could stomach. Voila! In comes Wally on his white charger, avowed to conquer the problem. It didn't take long, however, for Wally to see that the issue for this enterprise was not fixing marketing, but getting control of its supply chain, which was hemorrhaging red ink.

Although Wally lacked any solid background for solving this problem, he rolled up his sleeves, called in a couple of savvy consultants, rejuvenated the spirits of a team gone flat, and returned the company to prosperity. At breakfast one morning he confided to me, "I've always wanted my work to be bigger than my job."

Wally had faith in himself, but he quickly adapted to the situation when it turned out to be different from what he expected. A less-grounded CEO would have forced his pre-conceived plan on the company, ultimately stumbling and failing to create a better future.

Recall from Chapter 1 the late Joseph Campbell's dark night of the soul. Remember how it can liberate you, how it can propel you to take courageous, big boundary crossing, Destiny-altering steps? That's what my friend Wally Penrose did. As you develop similar awareness, your looming threat begins to dissolve, and to reform as a guardian presence that lures you toward your Destiny. Bear in mind that the process never ends; your awareness continues to grow throughout your lifetime. It certainly has throughout mine. Yes, I gained valuable insights that evening in Philadelphia, but I've kept gaining them each and every day in my journey toward my own Destiny.

You've no doubt heard that all addicts are in constant recovery. Well, in my journey, I'm a recovering *angler*. I'm constantly crossing the boundary between the dark (looming threat) and the light (guardian presence). It's a lot like Zeno's Paradox: You walk halfway to the wall, then halfway again, and again, and again, and again....You never quite get there, but you get darned close.

One of my favorite crossing over stories comes from The Old Testament. Religious or not, you probably know part of the story of Jacob. Jacob is born a twin with Esau, following him out into the world, clutching Esau's heel. He grows up to be a slippery conniver who trades a bowl of soup for his somewhat slower-witted brother Esau's birthright, and then tricks their father into giving him the family blessing, which rightly belongs to Esau as first born.

When Esau, dim but physically powerful, vows to kill his brother, Jacob runs far away to Haran. One night on the way, he falls into a deep sleep, dreaming of a ladder that reaches from him to heaven, with angels ascending and descending. God stands beside him and speaks, promising that all the families of earth "shall be blessed in you and your offspring."

When Jacob awakes, he continues his journey to Haran where he meets Rachel, whose lightning shaft of beauty and love strike deep within his heart. Rachel is the daughter of Laban, the brother of Rebekah, Jacob and Esau's mother, who has sent Jacob to Laban for safety.

In Laban, Jacob meets his match as a conniver. To win young Rachel's hand, he first must give Laban seven years labor. Then Laban insists that Jacob first marry Leah, his homely, eldest daughter. Following these sequential weddings, Jacob agrees to work for Laban seven additional years.

After 14 long years, and due in no small measure to Jacob's shrewd efforts, Laban's modest fortunes multiply beyond anything he could have imagined. When Jacob asks for his freedom and recompense, his wily maneuvering around Laban's last-ditch chicanery, finally wins the reward. With his two wives, 11 children, servants, riches, and massive herds, Jacob sets off to return to his homeland and the terrifying prospect of meeting Esau.

On the night before their arrival, Jacob separates himself from the travelers' encampment and crosses the Jabbok River to a place where he can be alone to deal with his fear of Esau, a man who could destroy him in a moment with his bare hands. Early on, he meets a man (God) with whom he wrestles until daybreak.

"When the man saw that he did not prevail against Jacob, he struck him on the hip socket; and Jacob's hip was put out of joint as he wrestled with him. Then he said, 'Let me go, for the day is breaking.' But Jacob said, 'I will not let you go, unless you bless me.' So he said to him, 'What is your name?' And he said, 'Jacob.' Then the man said, 'You shall no longer be called Jacob, but Israel, for you have striven with God and with humans, and have prevailed.' Then Jacob asked him, 'Please tell me your name.' But he said, 'Why is it that you ask my name?' And there he blessed him."

In the end, Jacob's fear proves false. All is forgiven, and when Jacob arrives home, he does not receive a beating but, as the text in Genesis reads: "Esau ran to meet him, and embraced him, and fell upon his neck and kissed him, and they wept."

Why does Jacob's story enthrall me? Perhaps I see an unsettling connection between his "conniver" and my "angler." The story also illustrates the power of good will triumphing, in the end, over bad will. Sneaky Jacob cut corners, yet the Unnamable saw something special in him. He opened himself to Destiny's call to him and heeded it. He had suffered in life—Laban saw to that—and his continuing journey was not without great pain.

But he mustered the courage to return home, even though by doing so he might lose his life. Not until he spent his lonely night wrestling with the Unnamable did he become who he was meant to be. Displaying extraordinary strength, he *prevailed,* though not without consequence. His opponent threw his hip out of joint, and he limped the rest of his life. Ultimately, the Unnamable named *him.*

Similar to how Jacob's self-image as a conniver changed, my self-image lived out in a fog of self-absorption, and thoughtlessness and unawareness had to change. Could I give them the whole me, the full me, the straight story, for better or worse? Without direct transparency (nothing to hide, nothing to defend), authentic contact with people, and full immersion in life would elude me. Here was a boundary I had to cross: to risk directness at the expense of safety.

Similar to Jacob, I eventually came into myself. I rewrote my Style-of-Life.

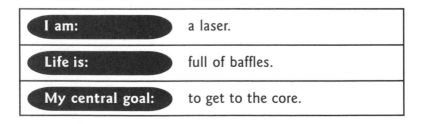

| I am: | a laser. |
| Life is: | full of baffles. |
| My central goal: | to get to the core. |

Understanding my exaggerated fear of vulnerability, and finally choosing to face, rather than ignore, that fear, I described myself as a powerful, focused beam of light, a penetrating light that could slice through all the baffles and obstacles in its way to strike the core of other people, of life, of myself. This metaphor, unrefined at first, propelled my journey toward a better future, a Destiny I grasped eagerly, as I shed my skin as a perceptive, but inconsistent darter.

You will walk your own crooked road across your own boundary of fear. It will meander, but it will move you forward, provided you name and face your fear. As Jacob found out, the crooked is often the shortest path. Whatever the course, the journey begins with one simple question: "Who am I?"

## The 2 a.m. I Am

Napoleon's remark that the true test of courage comes at 2 a.m., when you're least prepared to act, applies to discovering who you really are. The best insights often arrive when you've let your defenses down. That certainly applied to my close friend, Mark Madison, whose story parallels my own. Like me, he let vulnerability (or to use his word "safety"), govern his life. After I helped him travel through Joseph Campbell's dark night of the soul, Mark emerged with a clear agenda for change. To get there, he used what I call the I Am Questionnaire, a tool you can use on your own journey to identify your true self.

Joseph Campbell's study of myth and symbols convinced him that a person intent on living a free life can do so only by confronting and discarding what he called "the main obstruction." To pinpoint that barrier, you need to look for some dominant *symbol* in your life. We all have them. Mine was being the *adroit maneuverer* among aggressive groups, and winning kudos without getting wounded or killed. For my friend Mark, it was a dollar sign, or to put it another way, a *soaring net worth.*

Following Campbell, I then asked him "What center of thinking has produced your symbol?" "Money and security through my career and investing," he replied without hesitation. "Would your close friends and family agree that this symbol and the thinking that generated it pretty much runs your life?" I asked. "Oh, yeah, my wife in particular, thinks I've been obsessed with the business and now, more than ever, with my investments. You know what? I agree with her, but I don't seem to be able to stop," he said.

So then I asked, "Can you see a main obstruction in your life? Don't answer that question right now. Take some time. Think it through for a week. Don't force it. Let your mind flow."

When we met the following week, he said, "I think I've got it. My main obstruction is *seeking safety*."

Bullseye! And, Mark saw, that a once-bright central goal had tarnished into a dark and looming threat. Good will (a decision to provide safety for himself, his family, and his business associates) had turned into bad will (a blinding obsession with the almighty dollar).

Mark and I met because he wanted my counsel about two major events that had taken place in his life. First, he had lost his small business, Madison Milling Machine, an enterprise he had launched in 1980, and throughout the years had built into to a huge success. When he began to invest his profits in technology shares in the mid-1990s, he had grown his net worth to $12 million. Investing seemed so much easier than running the business, and he began to neglect it. When the tech bubble burst in 2001, he lost most of his capital, leaving him with too little to rescue his floundering business.

Disappointed and embarrassed that he neglected and lost the business, he took the money he salvaged and he began to reinvest in the market. He did well, but, as his wife observed, "He's so obsessed with the market now, it's all he thinks about."

He should, she thought, think a lot more about the second event that had occurred recently: an aggressive prostate cancer from which his doctors offered little hope of recovery.

When we got together after our week's hiatus, he had a little bounce in his step and a fresh gleam in his eye. His contemplation on the main obstruction in his life had inspired rather than depressed him. Once a fairly devout Methodist, he now confided that he thought his prostate cancer was a "notice" to his obsessed-with-safety self, to trust God in every moment, and to slow down and, as he put it, "count my blessings instead of my capital gains." He continued, "*A soaring net worth,* my false holy grail, precluded true safety and instead introduced real danger. Others saw it as a devil in me; for me, it was a suppressed god."

Mark was moved to make the necessary changes and journey down the road to "recovery," both from his obsession with financial security and his cancer. Today, there is serenity about him, and he spends much more time with family and friends. He is, for now I'm happy to say, cancer-free.

Spirituality and faith in a higher power played a role in Mark's decision to make some changes in his life. It will in yours, too, whether you practice an organized religion, believe in the laws of physics, or rely on a uniquely personal spirituality. Edmund Wilson (1895–1972), one of the most respected authors and literary critics of the 20th century, wrote, "No two people read the same book." I'll turn this just a bit and say to you that no two people worship the same God, and that's when *we're talking about the same God*. Journey on!

The 2 a.m. I Am Questionnaire below helps you begin your journey toward change by posing questions to uncover symbols that can lead to your central goal, be it a guardian presence or a looming threat.

On a scale of 1 to 5 (1 meaning "not at all important" and 5 meaning "very important"), rate yourself on the following items. Make your judgment based on your actual behavior, not your intentions. Remember, you want to discover not who you should, or want to be, but who you actually are.

For example, consider Question #1: *Do I want to own and wear fine apparel?* Do you dress casually or more formally at work? At a party, would you prefer to be the best-dressed person there, or would you feel more comfortable blending into the crowd? At home, alone or with those closest to you, do you choose a ragged old sweatshirt, or do you don a brand new track suit? Does a sloppily dressed person offend you? Do you admire a good-looking model wearing designer clothes in a magazine ad?

Don't make any value judgments while asking such questions. It's neither good nor bad to be a clothes horse or a ragamuffin. Just circle a number that most accurately describes your tendency/preference.

Keep a record of your questions and answers that lead to your final response for each item in the quiz. This way, you'll develop solid information that you can review in detail when you get around to composing your Style-of-Life. When you do, you'll want to ponder such answers slowly, remaining alert for symbols that reveal your real values, the ones you actually live by, not the ones you imagine you live by.

You'll notice that at the end of the questionnaire I've left space for you to add your own questions. I always find that my list doesn't capture key questions for a particular individual. Feel free to create your own, asking the same kinds of sub-questions for them as you do for the ones on my list.

## The 2 a.m. I AM Questionnaire

**Do I want to:**

1.  Own and wear fine apparel?

     1    2    3    4    5

2.  Enjoy fine food and drink?

     1    2    3    4    5

3.  Act poised and self-assured?

     1    2    3    4    5

4.  Display good taste?

     1    2    3    4    5

5.  Possess intellectual/emotional depth?

     1    2    3    4    5

6.  Travel widely?

     1    2    3    4    5

7.  Adapt easily to different circumstances?

     1    2    3    4    5

8.  Behave with warmth and intimacy?

     1    2    3    4    5

9.  Hold my own rather than submit to situations?

     1    2    3    4    5

10. Aim for perceptiveness?

     1    2    3    4    5

11. Collaborate with, rather than control, others?

    1      2      3      4      5

12. Take charge of my world?

    1      2      3      4      5

13. Be supporter or closer?

    1      2      3      4      5

14. Work to maintain my physical fitness?

    1      2      3      4      5

15. Emphasize fun in business and life?

    1      2      3      4      5

16. Strive for inclusion when dealing with people?

    1      2      3      4      5

17. Succeed at reuniting estranged people?

    1      2      3      4      5

18. Gravitate toward physically attractive people?

    1      2      3      4      5

19. Engage fully with significant others?

    1      2      3      4      5

20. Keep busy every moment of the day?

    1      2      3      4      5

21. Retire by age 55?

    1      2      3      4      5

22. Develop another career after retirement?

    1      2      3      4      5

23. Raise model children?

    1      2      3      4      5

24. Welcome "dumb" questions?

     1      2      3      4      5

25. Know how to tell funny or captivating stories?

     1      2      3      4      5

26. Extend forgiveness to someone who has wronged you?

     1      2      3      4      5

27. Be loved as a boss?

     1      2      3      4      5

28. Respected as a boss?

     1      2      3      4      5

29. Do all I can to make others' jobs easier/more effective?

     1      2      3      4      5

30. Declare my ideas/opinions to others vigorously?

     1      2      3      4      5

31. Poke fun at myself?

     1      2      3      4      5

Add a few questions of your own:

32. _____

_____

33. _____

_____

34. _____

_____

35. _____

_____

Once you have completed your first stab at honest answers, return to your Style-of-Life questions. A few weeks later, again several months later, and periodically throughout the years, visit both the 2 a.m. I Am questionnaire and the Style-of-Life questions, refining or revising your answers as your journey continues. Throughout time, you can *own* what I call the "ABCs of Change." "A" is your "At-First-I-Thought-I-Was Self," "B" is your "Better Self," and "C" is your matured "Creative Self."

The journey never ends, and the circle remains unbroken; you change and change and change yet again. You evolve, you "ripen," you flow more and more with, and create, a better Destiny.

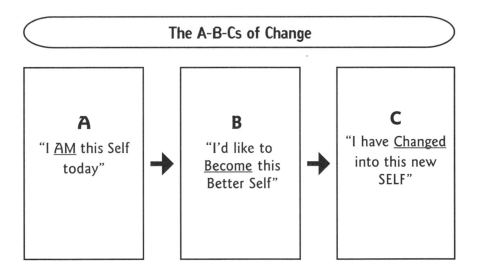

### The A-B-Cs of Change

**A**
"I <u>AM</u> this Self today"

➡

**B**
"I'd like to <u>Become</u> this Better Self"

➡

**C**
"I have <u>Changed</u> into this new SELF"

---

**In this chapter you have learned how to:**

➡ Answer penetrating questions about your deepest beliefs and desires.

➡ Connect your goals to those beliefs and desires.

➡ *Traverse* the boundary that separates fear and self-doubt from courage and conviction.

➡ Excavate the true Style-of-Life that matches your "inner CEO."

➡ Plan and track changes you want to make in your "Self."

**Your Inner CEO Punch List**

❑ Great CEOs are grounded. Are you grounded? If not, what changes can you make to become more grounded?

❑ Write down, file, think about, and rewrite periodically, answers to the following:

- Who am I *meant* to be?

- *What* do I fear?

- How does my fear *hold me back*?

❑ What kind of life has your Creative Self made? Is it a guardian presence or looming threat?

❑ How will you shape and flow with a better Destiny?

❑ What does it mean for you to "wrestle with God?"

# 3

# Facades

*The call to complete ourselves involves a remembering
that brings a 'shock of recognition,' the realization
that we have for years delayed living the essence of
who we are.*

—Marvin Hiles

Charlie Hunter, similar to Ted Engdall, the CEO we met in Chapter 1, ascended rapidly to his leadership position. CEO of a large manufacturing company, Obelisk, Inc., founded in the late 1800s, Charlie underwent the same personal exercise as Ted, except Charlie then applied that discovery process to his company. Sitting in his den on a Sunday afternoon, watching Phil Mickelson compete in the final round of the Masters, he jotted down his impressions:

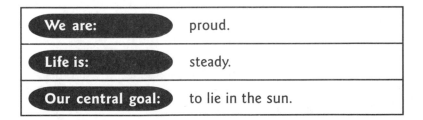

| **We are:** | proud. |
| **Life is:** | steady. |
| **Our central goal:** | to lie in the sun. |

In a scant seven words, Charlie had captured the essence of Obelisk. He had penetrated through the façade behind which the company had been hiding for a long time. Later, he confided to me, "For years, we've been basking in our glories of being the market leader and good citizen. Now, though, a competitor that didn't even exist 10 years ago is biting us in the ankles." Could he translate his insight into actions that his people would understand from the ground up?

Charlie took effective steps to wake up his slumbering company, and so can you, whether you wish to revitalize a partnership, a department, a division, a plant, a sales force, a research team, a front office, or any other team. You do what Charlie finally did: find ways to make changes from the bottom up, rather than from the top down. To help you do just that, to unleash your inner CEO, to serve as catalyst for organizational self-realization and reclamation, we'll apply the process Charlie used to an imaginary company, where you're the CEO. This is an examination that will help you pinpoint its looming threat or guardian presence, and apply what you learn to your own real corporation in your own real organization.

## Diagnosing Quest Music

Quest Music (QM) is a $100 million manufacturer of electronic musical keyboards that has reached a crossroads, where it has to either raise capital and innovate new products, or merge with a company that can give them the capital they need, and broaden the distribution of their products. Of course, the latter seems easiest, but that might entail the dumbing down of their exquisite product line; their best people would be heartbroken if that happened. Many would probably leave QM for greener fields. Before you do anything, however, you conclude that your first task is to figure out the true essence of your company.

To begin, you compare QM's stated "Ideal" self with its actual, or, "real" self. You do so by separating it into the two circles below. The left circle stands for what's ideal and the one on the right does the same for what's real. In doing this, you'll open your ears and eyes about QM the same way Charlie Hunter opened his about Obelisk. You'll find out about the power that resides in the right circle that you didn't know was there.

Let's set about sizing up your situation at Quest Music as shown on page 61.

The left-hand circle represents Quest's apparent side, the façade it offers the world, the self it wants people to see. The right-hand circle encompasses the company's concealed nature, what lies hidden behind the facade.

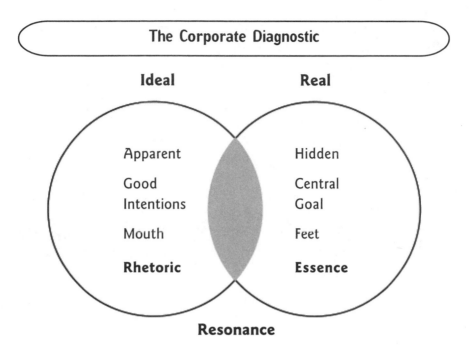

**The Corporate Diagnostic**

Ideal       Real

Apparent       Hidden

Good       Central
Intentions       Goal

Mouth       Feet

**Rhetoric**       **Essence**

**Resonance**

While QM's ideal self consists of all its good intentions (plans, advertising slogans, recruiting brochures, annual report, Website, training programs, policy manual, new Board of Director initiatives and the like), its real self embodies its central goal (the one that actually governs it). Already, you're beginning to get the picture, right? That Central Goal pulls all elements of your corporation into its service, much the same way your personal goal governs your life and work. Discovering that goal and assessing its potential for helping or harming your company is identical to the process you learned in Chapters 1 and 2.

Just as with an individual, this powerful goal can hover as a dark and destructive aura that infuses every organizational cell to damage Quest's health and viability, or it can nurture and sustain every cell to ensure vitality and longevity.

A company's ideal self lives in a world of "woulds, coulds, and shoulds," a world that can be as unreal as Oz. Karen Horney, another giant from the "social school" of psychology (she came into her own about a decade after Adler broke with Freud), coined the phrase, "The tyranny of the shoulds." That beautifully captures the danger of living in an unreal world. Think of how often we hear someone say, "I *would* have opened that door; I *could* have opened that door; I *should* have opened that door." They are describing *desirable* actions, ones that did not, and will not, come to pass. People who fall victim to the tyranny of the shoulds almost always go astray, and so do companies.

I often refer to an organization's ideal self as "mouth," because it utters all those good intentions that pave the road to ruin. It talks the talk. The real self, however, stands on two strong feet. It walks the walk.

| Ideal | Real |
|---|---|
| ‣ We're an industry innovator with an unassailable product line. | ‣ Leading product that's about to plateau. |
| ‣ Customer-focused. Recruit strong talent from outside. | ‣ Competitors more innovative than we are in providing service; we're overly dependent on our technology. |
| ‣ Top management is candid with each other, good at straight talk. | ‣ Our people talent emerges from the way we nurture them, not from outside stars. |
| ‣ Our marketing sets the standard for our industry. | ‣ Our bosses complain to us about their peers. |
| ‣ We drive to closure, stay on point, are determined accomplishers. | ‣ Our story to the outside, and even inside, lacks imagination and clarity. |
| ‣ We're smooth and polished. | ‣ We've lost "the long view" and grown complacent. |
| | ‣ What's made us great up till now is our grit. |

As you think about QM's ideal and real values, just jot down words and phrases you surmise that best describe them:

In the end, you struggle to capture the true essence of Quest Music the way Charlie did with Obelisk; in 10 words or less. Here's your first, preliminary assessment:

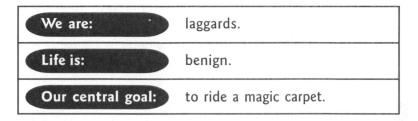

So what do you do with this insight? Look back at the Corporate Diagnostic: Notice the small area where the two circles overlap. That's the space where you might find an elemental harmony, where Quest takes its foot out of its mouth, walks its talk, and starts centering itself in an *unstoppable dense mass of authenticity*. The more overlap, the more resonance.

I've worked with executives when the overlap between their company's ideal and real selves are great, and when they're slight. (Total overlap would indicate perfection, and that's not part of the human equation; no overlap would mean complete discord, where an organization couldn't exist at all.) If you enjoy great overlap, congratulations, but I'm sure you realize you can't rest on your laurels, or you'll end up like Quest. So turn to the Diagnostic from time to time to gauge any new divergence. If you do, in fact, suffer the latter, you'll know you and your associates face a Herculean task of aligning your company's ideal self with its real self.

## Excavating Quest Music

Once you have done the diagnosis, what do you do next? How do you act on what's been revealed by your frank assessment of your company's selves?

Whether you're CEO of an organization, as you are in QM's case, or one of the many people seeking to take full responsibility for your slice of it in your actual company, effective action hinges on adapting to the *situation*, acknowledging that it, not you, controls your organization. That point may startle you, because, after all, if you should become a CEO, won't you be in charge of every situation? Consider a few events during just one day: Your husband comes down with the flu, so you have to take the kids to school; daughter Connie forgets her flute, you go back for it; Tommy tells you he has to stay late for a soccer game; your car gets a flat tire; your assistant must go on jury duty; your computer crashes, losing that important report; it rains, it pours, the pump goes out, your basement floods. And you thought you were in control! Repeat after me: "Control is an illusion." Ah, but hold on, you control *one* thing—how you treat these situations.

When you accept that simple fact, you yield to Destiny, finally able to be where you're meant to be. Like a ship on a vast ocean, you roll with the waves, moving forward even when buffeted by sometimes incomprehensible and enormous forces. You live and work with an eye open for a guiding star that illuminates the way to that Destiny. Of course, that's easier said than done.

Because you now appreciate the difficulty of plumbing the mysteries of your innermost self, it will come as no surprise that excavating a company's innermost self poses a huge challenge, especially when you take into account the complexity of an organization, and all your multiple relationships within and outside it.

"What, exactly is the real Quest Music?" It helps, I have found, to break this big question down into three smaller ones, the answers to which reveal how convolution actually behaves (moves), and how you might alter its movements (course) for the better.

## Questioning Corporate Identity

> ➤ What is our self-image?

> ➤ What's is our worldview?

> ➤ What central goal pulls us?

As we saw earlier, the façade of "we are innovators" masked the true answer: "We are laggards." Quest's worldview was not really "change-oriented" to which management gave lip service, but the belief that the environment surrounding the company was benign. And the organization's presumed goal? Not market dominance through spirited innovation, but the unwitting hope that they would somehow float above their significant challenges unscathed.

How will you answer these questions for your own team or company? As you work on that project, think about these two instructive models.

## Model I: USG

The first of two models I'll share with you is the United States Gypsum Corporation, founded in 1901 in Chicago. Consider a few salient facts about the company:

1. Through its operating units, it is the largest manufacturer of gypsum products in North America, the largest distributor of wallboard in the United States, and a leading manufacturer of ceiling panels and ceiling grid.

2. Serves four major markets: residential construction; non-residential construction; repair and remodel construction; and industrial processes.

3. Sales slightly more than $6 billion for 2007.

4. Ranked 433 among Fortune magazine's 500 largest U.S. companies based on annual sales in 2004.

5. Employs just under 14,000 people.

6. Reorganized on January 1, 1985, USG is the holding company for several subsidiaries in the building products industry.

7. Operates six principal subsidiaries: United States Gypsum Company; USG Interiors, Inc.; L&W Supply Corporation; CGC Inc. (Canada); USG International; and USG Mexico S.A. de C.V.

8. Operates a fully staffed research and technology center in Libertyville, Ill.

USG found itself in the news a lot during the past six years because it was one of several companies lumped together in a highly publicized, controversial, prolonged litigation over mammoth asbestos liability claims. USG's management, considering the claims exorbitant, sought protection by filing for bankruptcy in mid-2001, then, throughout the next five years, continued to operate in an extraordinarily successful manner. In the 10 years I have worked with the company, it has doubled its sales volume and maintained its dominant market share in its industry. Net profits have kept pace. Nonetheless, the company's stock price took a pummeling, plunging from a high of $63 in 1999, to as low as $2.80 shortly after declaring bankruptcy in 2001. By mid-December of that year, USG was the sixth most-heavily shorted stock on the New York Stock Exchange.

Arduous negations to reach a compromise settlement between the company and myriad litigants, including extensive discussions with key members of the Judiciary Committee of the U.S. Senate in hopes of winning congressional approval, failed until USG announced in Mid-January 2006 that it would settle the asbestos litigation by setting up a trust fund to pay off current and future claims.

A February 16, 2006, *Wall Street Journal* article entitled "Years Into Filing, USG is Smiling," quoted John D. Cooney, chairman of the Official Committee of Asbestos Personal-Injury Claimants, as saying the settlement was reached "in large part because USG was able to effectively grow as a company even though they were in bankruptcy."

The article also stated, "Even representatives of people who have asbestos suits pending against the company credit its management, led by Chief Executive William C. Foote, for figuring out how to keep that litigation from destroying the business." Amazingly, USG's stock price, after reaching its nadir of $2.80, continued to rise throughout the bankruptcy proceedings. According to James Barrett, an analyst at research firm C.L. King, "It's very atypical for a company like USG to emerge with its equity still intact." Warren Buffett, the second wealthiest person in America behind Bill Gates, held 15 percent of the company's stock at the time of the settlement, and as I write this, he has increased his stake to 19 percent. Why? As Buffet put it, "It's the most successful managerial performance in bankruptcy that I've ever seen."

I have detailed USG's recent history because it offers a stunning example of how a company with a solid, grounded understanding of itself can not only survive, but thrive, under circumstances that would ravage a less self-aware organization.

In 1997, after I had worked with USG CEO Bill Foote and his top team for a couple of years, he told me that given his firm's aggressive growth plans, he thought the company would benefit from rethinking its organization-wide mission. Could we, he asked, design an activity that would reach into all levels and operations of the company in order to review, understand afresh, and articulate the company's sense of purpose? Sure we could. I knew without a doubt that the personal and organizational self-discovery I had been espousing would lead to a mission that perfectly matched the company's resources. He agreed with me that mission development properly conceived and executed was, foremost, an exercise in organizational self-discovery, and that discovery should lead to a strategy that suits the true resources of the company.

Elated to retest my faith in applying Adler's principles to this situation, I helped plan a series of mission workshops. The first began with the executive committee (Bill and his direct reports), then extended to 10 identical groups of 25 to 30 people representing all operations and management levels throughout the company. The whole process, including analysis, took about seven months. Each of the offsite sessions that I planned and facilitated lasted two full days.

I introduced each workshop by outlining our agenda and focusing the group's attention on the word *value*. A positive *value*, I suggested, is more than a word or a vague concept. It's real and solid, a ball of gold in the sky that pulls our hearts and minds upward. It has a claim on our lives. If we appreciate its worth, we value it. The root *val* literally means worth. Think of the word *valentine* and you get the idea. However, if you claim something is a value, but you don't live by it, it's not a value at all, just a lump of lead.

Most people attach a positive moral tinge to the word value, but some of us also recognize that negative values exist. Hitler lived by negative values. His Holiness, the Dalai Lama, lives by positive values. We often hear people boast proudly, "We have forged a values-based corporate culture." Duh. All corporate cultures are values-based. But, are they bright ones (a guardian presence) or dark ones (a looming threat)? That, I told each workshop group, is what we want to figure out these next two days. By the end of the first day, I was able to ask that we rank the values most important to us, and see how we can craft a mission around them.

Believe it or not, each workshop was a lot of fun, providing four teams with a creative game they could play with enthusiasm. Occasionally, individuals rotated between teams in order to inject fresh blood into the exercise.

A couple of activities helped the groups excavate values without superficially asking, "What are our values?" That question tends to elicit the "party line." Instead, I invited each person to choose an animal that best symbolizes USG, outlining the characteristics of the animal that make it appropriate. "Inch worm," said one manager, and I asked why. "Because its head moves, then slowly each part of its body down to its tail—that's us! "Lizard," said another, because it takes great concentration to keep both eyes on the same goal." "Tasmanian Devil," said yet another, "because it spins crazily, but when it stops, it attacks well." And so it went. We laughed at the dozens of different images but soon engaged in lively discussion filled with rich insights. Later, analyzing the data, we were able to collect all the anologies and characteristics that allowed us to describe USG's behavior in terms of perceived strength, unresponsiveness, competitiveness, adaptability, family feeling-service-community, resourcefulness, teamwork, exploration, pride, and love of fun. Top honors went to lions (15), elephants (8), ostriches (7), tortoises (7), bears (6), turtles (6), whales (5), alligators, beavers, and hippos (4), and on down from there in a varied, and surprising, assortment of creatures.

A second activity simply asked participants to try their hand at completing the first of the Big Three Questions: "Who are we?" Responses included "family," "providers," "adaptors," "caterers," "listeners," "stewards," "pioneers," "gothic stone masons," "ants," "students," "nurturers," "long-distance runners," "tall oaks," and "fishermen."

All workshops required the participants to anonymously select the three most "critical-to-success" values culled from all those that people discussed and believed the company doesn't merely talk, but lives by. Votes from all the workshops were tallied, and the three most important values were: (1) integrity, (2) dependability, and (3) innovation. Sound pretty ordinary? Believe me, the romantic choices such as opportunistic, trend-setting, and swiftness were suggested and rejected: Nonetheless, a great corporation with staying power can be built around three key values like this.

At the end of two days, each group drafted its mission for the company, resulting in a grand total of 40 sample missions from 10 workshops. Not one of them stood up on its own as a suitable choice for the final mission, but each had elements that underscored values and themes we kept in mind before settling on a final draft.

The same was true of the various groups who crafted their versions of USG's Style-of-Life. None stood up by itself, but a few examples show how the three key values are present in how the people of USG gave answers to the Big Three Questions.

> → We are: listeners; life is: a challenge; central goal: to evolve.

> → We are: providers; life is: beyond; central goal: to serve expanding needs.

> → We are: oak trees; life is: new growth; central goal: to preserve, and expand our presence.

At the conclusion of the workshops, key staff fleshed out details of how the three values are expected in actual behavior. Admittedly, some of these admonitions may turn out to be ideal rather than real in practice; nonetheless, they stem from what the company has consistently shown by its past behavior. They are reminders more than oaths.

### Integrity

- Follow spirit and letter of law.
- Keep confidence/trust of all—us, customers, community.
- Business transactions at arm's length.
- Interests not in conflict with USG's interest.

### Dependability

- Word is bond.
- Do flawless work.
- Bring high energy to efforts.
- Promise only what you can deliver.
- Deliver what you promise.

### Innovation

- See what "wants to happen," and let it.
- Embrace change.
- Encourage and support informed risk-taking.
- Learn from successes and mistakes.

You might want to know how the company articulated its "final" Style-of-Life. Here it is:

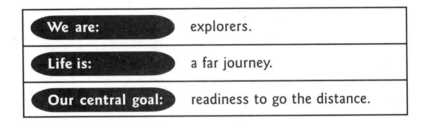

| **We are:** | explorers. |
| **Life is:** | a far journey. |
| **Our central goal:** | readiness to go the distance. |

Followed by their mission: We go the distance to provide the better way. Delivering building solutions for customers worldwide is our goal. Honoring relationships is our foundation. Integrity, dependability and innovation are the standards by which we live.

---

This Style-of-Life and mission fortified and enabled a besieged company to rise like a phoenix from Chapter XI. No member of top management left the company during this challenging period, and today USG remains poised to take itself to new heights.

## Model 2: Charlie Hunter

Let's revisit Charlie Hunter, that CEO of Obelisk sitting in his den on a Sunday afternoon, watching his favorite golfer, Phil Mickelson, sink an incredible 18-foot putt in the final round of the Masters. At that precise moment, a flashbulb goes off in Charlie's head. When he least expects it, all the work he and his team, like USG's, have invested in their Style-of-Life assessment pays off:

| | |
|---|---|
| **We are:** | proud |
| **Life is:** | steady |
| **Our central goal:** | to lie in the sun |

In truth, Charlie realized his company worships a bad goal, a dark goal, a looming threat. So why did Charlie leap to his feet and punch his fist in the air? Shouldn't he have slumped back in his chair in defeat? Not on your life. Charlie Hunter saw the situation clearly. He finally learned what he was dealing with, and the boundary he and his team had to cross, before Obelisk can reach its Destiny.

Knowing who Obelisk *is* and *where* it's headed gives Charlie the most valuable nugget of insight he's ever grasped. Now he can take informed action. If he hadn't gained this insight, or had let it depress and demoralize him, his future, and that of his corporation, would crash and burn.

When Charlie shared his visualization with his people, he heard a lot of muttering from the naysayers and play-it-safers within Obelisk, expressing attitudes that would once have matched his own. Gradually, however, honesty prevailed among many discontented old-timers and ambitious new recruits who felt that the company had really turned away from its once-shining path. They agreed with Charlie that Obelisk needs to return to its good values, ones that had been starved, and get back to its guardian passion that had somehow been crowded out. These natural strengths that had gone weak throughout a few short years included innovation, responsibility, and energetic movement.

How can Obelisk get back where it belongs? Well, they've already taken a huge step by waking up and facing reality. The company's new Style-of-Life will not merely mimic its original one because it has to reflect the new reality. Not only that, elements of the old one let Obelisk fall into its current state of disrepair, so the new Style-of-Life will avoid hollow words or vague philosophy, and be real and solid, a ball of gold in the sky.

After a good deal of discussion, his top team begins to track with him. They understand that beneath the looming threat of false pride, and the illusion of stability, beats a corporate heart that can pump life's blood into Obelisk. "All we need," observes one executive, "is a deft course correction." With enthusiasm, they compose an alternative Style-of-Life *that squares with who they are and where it's right for them to go!*

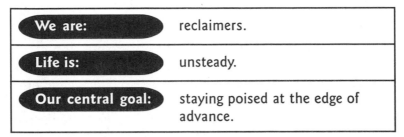

| We are: | reclaimers. |
|---|---|
| Life is: | unsteady. |
| Our central goal: | staying poised at the edge of advance. |

Now Obelisk can reclaim its Destiny, just as USG "explorers" did when they resolved to grow along their "far journey." Forgive me if I ask you to pause for a moment and consider this proposition: "No one can overstate the mass energy that gathers around a true reclamation of disowned strengths for a true cause."

As we go forward in this book, whether you're CEO, as you are in this hypothetical situation, or a member of one of the teams that makes your real organization tick, I'll ask you to reach back and speculate alone, and then later in concert with your team, as you strive to answer the Big Three Questions. Experiment with different combinations until one clicks. Use simple words, eschew business jargon. Play with figurative and metaphorical language, wax poetic. As I mentioned during our discussion of the USG situation, when people relax, get engaged, and make it fun, they can accomplish amazing things.

Recall now the Corporate Diagnostic chart we explored earlier. Your first stab at defining Quest's corporate personality, its culture, and its identity, resulted in a less-than-pleasant picture.

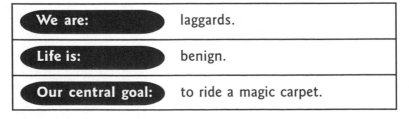

| We are: | laggards. |
|---|---|
| Life is: | benign. |
| Our central goal: | to ride a magic carpet. |

That's the real world. However, most of Quest's people are living in an ideal world—the world of facades and good intentions. Imagine, instead, that they could answer the Big Three Questions *positively,* and say,

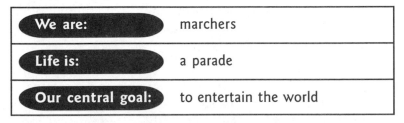

| **We are:** | marchers |
| **Life is:** | a parade |
| **Our central goal:** | to entertain the world |

As it is, Quest's people don't see what can be excavated, coughed up, and made to work for its life! As we saw earlier, it's more useful for them to see themselves like this:

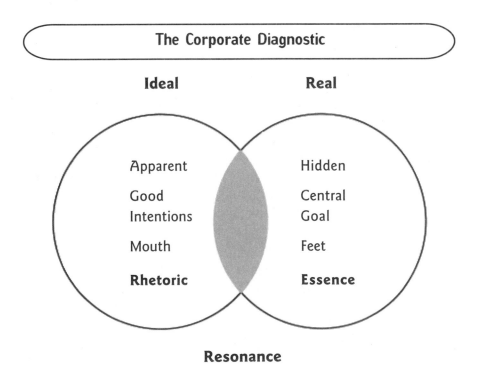

**The Corporate Diagnostic**

**Ideal**      **Real**

Apparent      Hidden

Good Intentions      Central Goal

Mouth      Feet

**Rhetoric**      **Essence**

**Resonance**

You see only a small overlap, but that little bit of harmony gives you something to work with.

You can also look at it this way. One corporate self-image (the one people *think* characterizes their culture) is expansive, while the other (the one that actually describes the culture) is limiting. Wouldn't it be nice if you could somehow make the more expansive self-image the true reality for your organization?

When he ran Intel in its glory years, the ever-perceptive Andrew Grove once said, "We learned that our people make strategy with their fingertips." To change Quest's outlook from a lagging, looming threat into a forward-marching force in the entertainment industry, you'll invest in a lot of sweat, toil, time, meeting, struggling, and speculating until you achieve a "group aha!" At that point, Quest won't just mouth their values; they'll display them with their feet, marching steadfast toward the right goal.

## Bringing It Home

In your own organization, group, or team, you'll do the same sort of work we just did at Quest. Even if what you and your associates generate at first doesn't completely please you, keep working at it. Eventually, you'll get there. More than ever, you'll know what you don't know, and what you need to know.

As more and more bull's-eye insights come to you, you'll learn which boundaries you'll need to cross over. If you keep refining your Corporate Diagnostic, you'll reveal the overlap, large or small, between the ideal and real. By crossing boundaries, you'll expand that overlap until the two circles come *closer* to becoming one; until the ideal and real merge into an unstoppable force.

It turned out in USG's case that the central goal was *a guardian presence*. But what if our workshops had unearthed *a looming threat?* In that case, articulating that goal in surgically precise terms would sound a clarion call to the responsible members of management to lead people across the boundary. This is exactly what Charlie Hunter and his team did so well at Obelisk, and what we did at Quest. All companies, in my experience, cannot avoid it from time to time as they face unanticipated changes.

All organizations, whether entrepreneurial start-ups, or century old or Fortune 500 giants, ride a life cycle that looks something like this:

**Phase 1:** **Birth and Creativity:** As the company struggles for survival, it is characterized by tremendous camaraderie, develops under a charismatic leader.

**Phase 2:** **Power and Growth:** As systems and procedures replace informality and randomness, administrators replace entrepreneurs, and conformity replaces spontaneity.

**Phase 3:** **Obsolescence and Decay:** As a company becomes less adept at responding to evolutionary change in the marketplace, corporate leaders are suspect for their motives, criticized for laxity in responding to opportunity, and search for cosmetic ways to repair their faltering organization.

**Phase 4:** **Rebirth or Death:** As matters worsen, a company either adapts to change or dies.

Of course, you can use the Style-of-Life assessment to see where your organization resides in this cycle, and take appropriate action. Obelisk was in the "obsolescence and decay" phase. It righted itself with new clarity and an adaptive self-image that stimulated rebirth. It embraced an authentic Destiny-oriented corporate strategy. Obelisk's rebirth strategy matched its natural endowments, the unique strengths already in place. Obelisk's people discovered who they were *meant* to be.

Now the company could climb back to where it belonged, in Phase 2 extending its power and growth. Whenever you put "natural resources" to use, whether in physical or human terms, you increase the odds of a successful outcome. As *Mind-Set* author John Naisbitt puts it, you ride a horse in the direction it's already going. This is what giant companies such as Procter & Gamble, 3M, and Caterpillar do as they amass great leverage. All three are more than 100 years old. Permanence is proof of adaptability.

That doesn't mean you just let the horse have its head. Keeping your hands loosely on the reins, you make necessary mid-course corrections, speeding up, slowing down, turning right, or turning left as the new situations demand. Nevertheless, even the most dramatic corporate turnarounds rely on tapping rich, dormant resources, albeit, riding the horse with a skillful leader in the saddle.

## The Significance of Essence

Skillful leaders look for façades masking realities, and they tear down the façades to expose those realities, the essences, good or bad, that truly characterize an organization.

I've always cherished this observation of playwright Eugene O'Neill: "If a person is to get the meaning of life, he must learn to like the facts about himself—ugly as they may seem to his sentimental vanity—before he can learn the truth behind the facts. And the truth is never ugly."

Excavating facts and harnessing truth to accomplish something beautiful requires deep thinking and meditation. Among all the people I've met or studied, three stand out as model meditators.

First is media pioneer and proud Scotsman David Ogilvy, who died in 1999, set the standards for taste and style in the field of advertising. The company he founded, Ogilvy & Mather, always ranked within the top five agencies in America.

In 1963, Ogilvy published his classic *Confessions of an Advertising Man.* In it he writes: "I hear a great deal of music. I am on friendly terms with John Barleycorn. I take long hot baths. I garden. I go into retreat among the Amish. I watch birds. I go for long walks in the country. I take frequent vacations, so that my brain can lie fallow— no golf, no cocktail parties, no tennis, no bridge, no concentrations; only a bicycle."

He goes on to say that while busy doing nothing, creative ideas for ads percolate in his brain. Once one bubbles to the surface, he takes action, knowing that he must buttress mental meandering with "hard work, an open mind, and ungovernable curiosity." This sounds a lot like what I'm suggesting, doesn't it?

Unfortunately, however, meditation is a foreign notion to most executives, who lack Ogilvy's unrelenting curiosity when it comes to thinking about their organizations; yet that's what I'm asking you to do—to think like a curious student of organizations. I have not found a better way to grasp the unarticulated central goal of an Obelisk or a USG. Our USG workshops used meditative exercises, as was Charlie Hunter's as he watched a golf tournament on TV. Once you achieve the sorts of insights these sessions stimulated, you can set performance goals in harmony with that central thrust, or, if necessary, alter the thrust and follow a better trajectory to success.

Second is symphony conductor Robert Shaw also died in 1999. He was the famed founder and conductor of The Robert Shaw Chorale and music director of The Atlanta Symphony Orchestra and Chorus, a post he held for more than 20 years.

I learned about Robert Shaw in my early 20s. My father hailed from Alabama, though he lived all his adult life in the north, and I made a hero of myself one year by buying him the Robert Shaw Chorale album of southern songs. How my father loved this music that captured Stephen Foster's respect for the pre-Civil War South. He and I listened to it again and again throughout the years.

Shaw's honors include seven Grammys; three ASCAP awards for service to contemporary music; honorary degrees and awards from more than 30 U.S. colleges, universities, and foundations; and the first Guggenheim Fellowship ever awarded to a conductor. In 1988, shortly before his retirement, he received the Gold Baton award, the nation's highest honor for distinguished service to music and the arts.

Some years ago in Chicago, I saw Shaw conduct a choir in Schubert's *Mass in G,* before which he delivered a lecture entitled "Worship and the Arts." His words and his music made an indelible impression.

In describing art, he emphasized four qualities: (1) purity of purpose, (2) historical perspective, (3) craftsmanship, and (4) revelation. As he spoke, I realized that his ideas applied not just to music or poetry, but to the art of management. It seemed so obvious to me that in the midst of our global existence, an evolutionary unfolding has been taking place in the world of work, from the CEO to the last drill press operator on the third shift. More than ever, people who work yearn to bring their unique gifts to bear on their own, and their company's enterprise. Shaw called that *purity of purpose.* Business people call it ethics, integrity, or character.

Historical perspective comes into play when you set about excavating any organization's "personality" to discern its Style-of-Life. You'll want to think long and hard about where you have been, and what that tells you about where you're headed.

By *revelation*, Shaw meant art as "the flesh-made word," a really nifty little twist on the revelations of Mohammed, Jesus, and Buddha, supreme global examples of truly living according to out their essences. The more we experience our work as a calling, as performance for its own sake and as a quality offering to others, be they colleagues or customers or family, we, too, live according to our essences.

Shaw's third quality of art, *craftsmanship,* embodies action, the tangible expression of our unique gifts. Craftsmanship enables us to refine and apply our gifts in a life-long undertaking we cannot sustain unless we unearth, name, and dedicate ourselves to our unique calling.

My final model may surprise you: rock star John Cougar Mellencamp. His current hit single as I write is "Our Country." You may have seen him perform it on TV at the second game of the 2006 World Series between the Detroit Tigers and St. Louis Cardinals.

Mellencamp lives in the small college town of Bloomington, Indiana, and grew up 40 miles southeast of there in the even smaller town of Seymour.

Bloomington is the home of Indiana University, while Seymour, population less than 16,000, would remain largely unknown to you unless you remember it as the subject of Mellencamp's hit single and video "Small Town" (from his CD *Scarecrow)*. One of the CD's other songs contains a relevant refrain: "You've got to stand for somethin', or you're gonna fall for anything." Values, principles, ethics, integrity, purity of purpose, you name it; without it you will fall for façades and never embrace essence. Your looming threat will annihilate your guardian presence.

Every company that has grown to any stature has done so because of a founder's commitment to an overwhelmingly affirmative idea. Whoever founded the company that employs you today believed against all odds in a product or service; overcame the physical, psychological, and financial obstacles of such an undertaking; launched the business; hired people; brought their products to market; and sold them by the millions because she *stood for something.*

If this company has lost touch with its values, similar to Obelisk, it courts ruin. Having forgotten who or where it is, it can't possibly figure out where it's going or needs to go.

To achieve, we say yes first. Then, oddly enough, to nurture and protect the yes, we have to learn how and when to say no. That can be difficult, but the yes coaches us. To put it another way, we have to say yes to something that matters before we can say no intelligently.

### In this chapter you have learned:

➡ The importance of continually excavating your organization's Style-of-Life.

➡ How to comprehending the *gap* between your organization's rhetoric and action; its good intentions and actual performance; its façade versus its essence.

➡ How to discover the *overlap* between your organization's ideal and real personality.

➡ How to craft a compelling organic mission around a "Guardian Presence" Style-of-Life.

➡ The importance of mastering the art of meditation.

### Your Inner CEO Punch List

☐ Begin your homework on discovery of your company's hidden goal. How have you seen your people making strategy with their fingertips? Write down some guesses.

☐ If you apply the *trust only movement* standard to your relationships and company right now, how might that change your outlook?

☐ What did you learn when you contemplated Quest's Corporate Diagnostic?

☐ Have any positive values in your company languished?

☐ How can you best ride your company's horse in the direction it's already going?

# 4

# Boundaries

*One's range of choices is ordinarily limited by one's vision.*

—David R. Hawkins

Curt McCauley, president of the plumbing products subsidiary of Lassiter Corportion, addresses his team: "Hey, guys, I'm really sorry. Building that $25 million plant three years ago seemed like a terrific idea. Now we've got to shut it down. Lousy local schools, a stagnant local economy, a sputtering infrastructure. We just can't get talented people to stay there. Our quality there stinks, we've had two product recalls. We're bleeding red ink. Boy, did I screw up."

Nodding to his VP of operations, he continues. "Steve, where were you when I really needed you? When I kept insisting that we build this damn thing you kept saying it was the dumbest idea you ever heard. You should have stopped me!" Everyone chuckles at this tongue-in-cheek rebuke.

Seriously, though, everyone had played a part in the fiasco, but Curt, unlike many executives, put the blame squarely on his own shoulders. When the boss takes the heat at the "error boundary," even though others share responsibility for a bad decision, respect replaces angry accusations and responsibility negates finger pointing.

Boundaries. Where reality comes to life. A mistake, a kiss, a handshake, a snub, laughter, a shouting match, a funeral, a celebration, an invitation, or a report. All involve a boundary that separates people, ideas and objects. In Curt's case, he saw his mistake as a boundary between blaming others and accepting full responsibility.

How do you recognize boundaries? What risks lie on one side, what opportunities on the other? How do you cross from the negative to the positive? The answers hinge on an insightful reading of human beings, the good, the bad, and the ugly. When you develop a firm grasp of boundaries, you will take action based on their affect on people—the good, the bad, and the ugly.

Permit a brief digression: In the 1960s, I was a graduate student in sociology. As one of my electives I chose a course in the psychology department called Theories of Personality. In that course, I learned that a group of psychologists had arisen (not as a formal alliance, but simply as a collection of thinkers, scholars, and practitioners) in opposition to Freudian orthodoxy. Dubbed the "social school," the group's luminaries included Alfred Adler, Karen Horney, Eric Fromm, and Harry Stack Sullivan.

Their thinking impressed me so much, I became committed to their ideas, especially those of Alfred Adler. The social school didn't neglect the study of the individual, but from a theoretical and practical standpoint, they focused more on connections between individuals and the world that surrounds them. Connections. That's another word for boundaries.

## The A-T-A Question

Adler's colleague, Karen Horney, also captured my attention, with an elegant, unforgettable proposition that complements Adler's concept of the central goal. She said that "in every interaction with someone or something, you are moving either away from, toward or against that contact." Away-Toward-Against. A-T-A.

Consider a simple interaction between Karen and Jason:

    **A.**  Karen asks Jason to help her move a sofa. Jason says he's busy reading the paper; she should ask Tom to help her instead.

    **T.**  When Karen asks Jason for help he asks her to wait a minute, until he can finish the paragraph he's reading.

    **A.**  Jason responds to Karen's plea for help by saying she should forget moving the sofa; it's fine where it is.

In the first instance, Jason moves *away* from his relationship with Karen; in the second he moves *toward* her; and in the third he moves *against* her. A greater awareness of his actions, and how they affect Karen, might help him to alter his behavior. Does he really want her to replace him with Tom? Does he want to deepen his relationship with her? Does he want to make her angry and start an unnecessary argument?

Horney's simple proposition encourages us to consider our relationships in a new way. When we do so, we increase our awareness of the boundaries that serve as important *events* on the path to our Destiny.

Throughout this chapter, we'll discuss how you can boost your "boundary competence," a skill that will help you spot and face all the ever-present boundaries at work and in life, whether they present hurdles between you and others, between you and yourself, or between you and your Destiny.

Think about it. What separates you from that high-performing, but irritating, colleague at work? From discovering how others really perceive you? And on a mundane level, what separates you from a long, straight drive off the sixth tee? In each case, success depends on you first identifying, then crossing, a boundary.

It's an unusual phenomenon that applies to something as simple as housebreaking a golden retriever puppy, pausing to absorb the beauty of a dew drop on a yellow rose in an open field one morning, or feeling joy at the sight of a dozen pelicans flying in formation, high in the sky, making their swoop and dive, hunting, streaking, skimming inches over the sea, then becoming instantly savage in a final dip to devour their prey.

From the momentous to the mundane, a boundary separates depression and boredom from exhilaration and joy, the ordinary blahs of a dull life from the extraordinary purity of Destiny fulfilled. Every boundary matters, whether it involves your wife, tears streaming down her face, blurting out, "How could you forget our anniversary?" or the world-changing decision to invade Iraq. Great and small, obvious or subtle, life-sustaining or dangerous, look for them. Welcome them. Cross them wisely. I've never met a first-class CEO who didn't do that each and every day; but my point is just that each day is loaded with circuits and contact points, whose significance cannot always be known at first sight.

Think about any person or event in your life. Pause to ask if you're moving *away from, toward,* or *against* that person or event. Does your position make you happy? Unhappy? Does it harm or help the person or situation? If you could approach it differently, what, exactly, would you do?

If you incorporate these questions into your encounters, that is, ponder the A-T-A question, you'll find yourself more adept at seeing the importance of your answers, and successfully negotiating all the boundaries that separate ordinary performance from extraordinary accomplishment. Only those who become *aware* of their boundaries can develop the mastery on which such accomplishment depends.

Throughout the years, I have found this BAM (Boundaries Awareness Mastery) Grid quite useful:

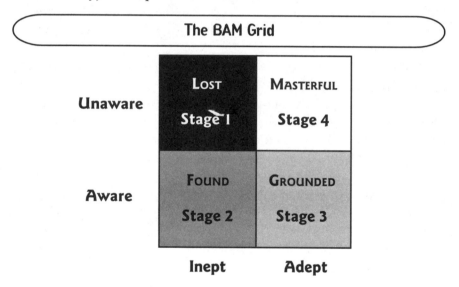

**The BAM Grid**

|  | Inept | Adept |
|---|---|---|
| **Unaware** | Lost<br>Stage 1 | Masterful<br>Stage 4 |
| **Aware** | Found<br>Stage 2 | Grounded<br>Stage 3 |

Stage 1: Lost people are inept and unaware.

Stage 2: Found people are inept and aware.

Stage 3: Grounded people are adept and aware.

Stage 4: Masterful people are adept and unaware.

Similar to most people I have coached, you take one look at this grid and exclaim, "Whoa! Hold on a minute, Allan. The most masterful people (the most effective CEOs) are adept and *unaware?* That doesn't make sense."

Ah, but it does, actually. Once you have reached the stage where you are grounded, when you easily detect and deal with boundaries, you'll be moved further still to work toward a higher degree of mastery when, as you encounter a boundary, you behave fluidly and effortlessly to cross it, not pausing even a second to think about it.

That sort of almost automatic behavior inspired this ancient Chinese gem from the *Tao Te Ching*:

> The master arrives without leaving,
> sees the light without looking,
> achieves without doing a thing.

Let's go back to Karen and Jason. When he told her to forget about moving the sofa, he was behaving in Stage 1 (unaware and inept); when he told her to ask Tom instead, he was operating in stage 2 (aware and inept); and when he asked her to wait a minute, he was responding in a classic Stage 3 manner (aware and adept). But consider the fourth possibility: Karen asks for help, and Jason, without pausing a nanosecond to think about it, sets aside the paper and enthusiastically grabs one end of the sofa. Voila! He just automatically behaved in a way that delighted Karen and strengthened their relationship.

You see this sort of effortless, unthinking acuity every day. If you follow professional football, you've no doubt seen clips of LaDanian Tomlinson, the truly incredible halfback with The San Diego Chargers. He glides through holes or around ends to gallop down the field for a touchdown. He doesn't look for holes in the defensive line; he just finds them automatically. His mastery during the 2006/07 NFL season matches Eric Dickerson's record of rushing for 1,200 yards in each of his first six seasons. He broke Shaun Alexander's all-time NFL scoring record of 30 touchdowns—and not one of those touchdowns did he celebrate with end-zone choreography! For the record, he scored 28 rushing, one receiving, and passed for two. He rushed for a league-high 1,815 yards on 348 carries, had 58 receptions of 508 yards, and was 2-for-3 as a passer, two, as I said, for touchdowns. This is a performance to match, and perhaps surpass, such greats as Jim Brown, O.J. Simpson, and Walter Payton. Topping it all off, he won the National Football League's MVP award. Tomlinson is so good, he doesn't know it. If you ask him how he does it, he can't tell you. That's mastery.

In a less-exalted setting, Nicole Parsons, the "Dervish of the Coffee Stand," offers a down-to-earth example of "natural" mastery. Nicole works for AJ's Fine Foods, a subsidiary of Basha's Markets, which is a 12-store chain in the greater Phoenix area. At the beautiful upscale store on the northeast corner of Central Avenue and Camelback Road, Nicole presides over the coffee stand in a small cubicle that serves a three stool indoor counter and an outside walk-up window.

Nicole knows all regulars by name, enquires about important events in their lives, and remembers every detail she hears, while continuously pouring coffee, lattes, cappuccinos, and wrapping pastries for a steady flow of customers. Watch her work on Thanksgiving morning in her Pilgrim dress and bonnet. Outside stands a line of a dozen people while I, a stranger, occupy an inside stool with two other customers. It's like watching Tomlinson run for daylight: effortless, joyful, a fan's (or customer's) delight.

"Hi, Beth," she says to the woman beside me, offering her radiant smile as her hands move with amazing swiftness and grace. "How did it go with Amy's wisdom tooth and the trip to the dentist?" "Oh, fine," says the proud mom, "she took it much better than I did." The friend who has brought me here laughs, drawing Nicole's attention. "Hi, Ted, the usual? And your friend, here, he likes double espresso with water, right?" Right, even though she's only seen me once before. "Bye, Allan," she says with a wink as we depart.

She makes it all look easy. She's a natural. She's so good she doesn't know it.

Getting back to Jason, his Stage 4 behavior obviously works best in his situation, but some situations are not what they seem at first glance. For example, you may seem to be moving away from your CFO at a critical moment, but the boundary you face stems from a project he's asked you to approve, which you don't believe in. In this case, you're moving away from the project, not your CFO. Other times, you may appear to be moving away from or against a project, but it's really the timing that bothers you. Remember Karen and Jason? Suppose they moved the sofa yesterday and expect delivery of a new one today. Jason might rightly suggest they wait for it to arrive before they do more heavy lifting. Sometimes it makes no sense to do something in a relationship, even automatically, just because it would make the other person happy.

You may also encounter the approach-avoidance syndrome. Suppose a young man (let's pretend he's your son, Arthur) can't make up his mind about marriage. He alternates between two women he says he loves. He moves toward one, then away from her and toward the other, then away from her, and back to the first, repeating the process again and again. When the psychologist Rudolph Dreikurs treated a client in therapy who'd caught himself in this sort of approach-avoidance pattern, the incisive Dreikurs pointed out to his client that "Two women are fewer than one." Obviously, your son and Dreikurs's client needed to do a lot more work on discovering who they really are, and where they're heading in the long run.

If one of your subordinates should face some trade-off the way Arthur makes choices in matters of the opposite sex, you'll now be inclined to wonder if he may not be moving away from Option A or Option B, but rather away from making any decision, because he's fearful that any choice he makes will be a mistake.

When you routinely ask the A-T-A question and apply the BAM Grid to a situation, search relentlessly for the direction or method of movement. Pierce beneath the surface of stated intentions: Don't listen to their words. Watch their feet. Trust only movement.

## The Lost CEO

An emphasis on trusting your own actions rather than your words will help you discover any gap between how you view yourself (who you think you are) and how others see you (who you really are, in their eyes, at least). Take, for instance, this story about a CEO at a prestigious, Frankfurt-based global financial services firm I'll call Labyrinth. Gordon Parker, Managing Partner (CEO) of the firm's western hemisphere, needed to learn a lot about boundaries and his actions. He began by listening to honest feedback from his subordinates. He knew his behavior displeased his peers and subordinates, but he could not figure out exactly how his own actions caused that displeasure. The comments he elicited from his people convinced him that he needed to make some changes in his behavior, and, as he scanned their comments, I urged him to look for "boundary flags," points at which he could ask the A-T-A question and apply the BAM Grid:

| Feedback on Gordon's Performance | |
|---|---|
| **Subordinate's Dissatisfaction** | **Gordon's Boundary Flag** |
| He's super smart, but has a short attention span; tunes out fast. | Moving *away*. |
| I wonder what he does. What's his focus? | Moving *away*. |
| He often wastes my time. | Moving *against*. |
| He's not in command of the important details he should know about the business as a whole. | Moving *away* |
| He seldom uses his power to break logjams. | Moving *away* and *against*. |
| He's not always clear when he needs to be. | Moving *away*. |
| He needs to think twice before falling for the next "sexy new thing." | Moving *away*. |
| He's actually proud of his style, which he calls "organized chaos." | Moving *against*. |
| He waits out conflict situations hoping they'll just go away. | Moving *away*. |

Applying the BAM Grid, Gordon had to admit he was *unaware* of the seriousness and vehemence of the complaints against him, and that he does little to reverse the poor opinions *(inept)*. That put him squarely in Stage 1 as a lost CEO.

Each comment, he realized, highlighted a boundary, an opportunity for contact that needed his urgent attention. Because he had lacked awareness of these boundaries, he had gotten himself into deep trouble, and had put his promising career in jeopardy. Could he turn this situation around and get back on track toward his Destiny? As Gordon and I worked together, I was pleased to see him take the bad news courageously. He would, he promised himself, battle through the boundaries by moving *toward,* rather than away from or against his people:

| Gordon's Boundary Plan | |
| --- | --- |
| Short Attention Span | Take time to listen carefully and ask probing questions when addressing any issue. |
| Lack of Focus | Make Labyrinth's and my priorities clear in every conversation. |
| Wasting People's Time | Intervene only when absolutely necessary. |
| Inattention to Details | Create and revise lists of the pieces of every puzzle. |
| Logjams | Deal decisively with all threats, respect subordinates' authority on personnel issues. |
| Lack of Clarity | Choose a few simple, powerful words to explain convictions and priorities. |
| Infatuated with New Ideas | Turn a gimlet eye on unbridled enthusiasm. |
| Pride | Practice humility. |
| Procrastination | Make contact with people who need support and decisiveness. |

These action items entailed little more than Gordon's making contact with his *own* convictions and sharing them with his people—moving *toward* them. Quite naturally, his people responded to his new movement toward them by moving toward him. The gap narrowed and then closed. Gordon had crossed crucial boundaries so successfully that individual, team, and organization-wide performance increased dramatically.

Earlier, I cited longshoreman-philosopher Eric Hoffer, whose insights I greatly admire. As Gordon engaged in his boundary crossing, I gave him this Hoffer quote about spreading himself too thin: "The feeling of being hurried is not usually the result of living a full life and having no time. It is on the contrary born of a vague fear that we are wasting our life. When we do not do the one thing we ought to do, we have no time for anything else—we are the busiest people in the world." Putting it another way, when you're so busy moving *away* or *against* somebody or something, inept and without awareness, you're letting some significant boundary endanger you. That's when you need to ask the right questions about your movement and create a plan to move from lost to found.

In the end, Gordon yielded most of his duties to an internal successor eager and able to handle them, and then applied his brilliance to where it made the biggest difference for Labyrinth: deal-conceiving and closing. He huddled with his boss in Frankfurt, and hammered out an agreement for him to create and head a new business unit, which became a major engine of profitability for the global enterprise.

## Exploring the Land Between

What does your mind's eye picture when you hear the word *boundary*? A shoreline? The point where meadow meets tree-line? A "No Trespassing" sign? A door to a room that may hold a treasure or a tiger? The imaginary line that separates the U.S. from Canada?

"Good fences make good neighbors," wrote Robert Frost, a line that reminds us that a fence makes us aware of the possibilities for turning our neighbors into friends or enemies.

In the context of leadership, I have borrowed from the new behavioral and organizational meanings of the word, which describe "lines in the sand" in families, communities, economies, and various organizations including educational institutions, government, law enforcement, houses of worship, hospitals and, of course, the corporation. And look at the *playing field* of sports; bounded by lines, it has become a generic term for all of life.

Boundaries, whether visible or not, divide and differentiate. They invite the imagination. If you cross the line, will you meet danger or opportunity, the tiger or the treasure? The possibilities ignite our emotions, from fear and loathing to exhilaration and delight. Once you open the door, cross the line, or navigate across a turbulent river, you may mutter, "Boy, I didn't see *that* coming." Or you may insist that you just felt something was "up."

So. What do you do when you see a "line in the sand," when you identify that contact point that separates success from failure?

In most cases, you might wisely step back for a moment to reconsider the consequences of crossing it now. Should you wait? Should you flee? Human emotions usually prompt fear, fight-or-flight, or dependency. What makes sense here? Ask the A-T-A question: If I move toward it I may make a friend or find a mentor; if I move away from it, I may save myself from danger (or risk losing a friend or mentor); and if I move against it, I may have a big fight on my hands.

A boundary is not a line, it's a space, a large span of opportunity and danger. It contains vast possibilities: a new lease on life or death; today and tomorrow (we couldn't get it done then, today we can); here and there (this will bring a laugh in Madrid, a frown in Berlin), success and failure (detail works on this project, broad brush won't); antagonism and support (she fought with me for years, now supports me 100 percent); acceptance and rejection (he always said no, now says yes) and so on, *ad infinitum.*

All that lies in "the land between" represents the risk gap you can choose to enter with initiative and adaptability to gain clarity for moving forward, or withdraw from all together to maintain a level of comfort, albeit often false comfort. You can stare at it with clear eyes, or you can bury your head in the sand.

The "two parties" inhabiting "the land between" can be friendly or adversarial. They may be external (your board of advisors, your competitors, your suppliers) or they may be internal (competing chorus, conflicting desires, warring options). Life is full of boundaries. Martin Buber said it nicely: "All real living is meeting."

Meeting takes place in "the land *between*." It gives you space into which you can step and begin a dialogue or negotiation, out of which can arise authentic *contact,* and the highest level of human relationship. This can occur even when the boundary arises from competition, conflict, and war.

Your boundaries will change shape and priority constantly, as will the space constituting either a confronting foreground (do it now) or a receding background (give it more time and reflection).

Regardless of their nature, however, as you cross, honor, or avoid them, you'll find that you measure your movement, not only in direction, but also by ticks of the clock and pages of the calendar turning. You're likely to ask yourself: Am I moving toward, away from or against this boundary? What, exactly, am I doing? Should I do more? What? How much time have I been given? How long will it take? What is its significance?

Consciously contemplating your movement, its direction, its benefits, its costs, and the time it consumes, you may make minor or major adjustments along the way.

Here's what I mean. Curt McCauley's boundary was a *mistake.* But he made a dramatic course correction and got himself back on track. Think of a decision you made or an action you took, where despite all your thoughtful planning and good intentions, things just didn't work out as you wanted. Perhaps you were wrong or perhaps you weren't wrong at all, but simply in the wrong place at the wrong time. Effective CEOs often convert failures into successes. Sometimes, too, you end up knowing all too well the meaning of the old expression, "Be careful what you wish for." Finally, no mistake is chiseled in granite. A good friend once observed, "Just because you made a mistake doesn't mean you are one."

I've compiled this list of boundaries shown on page 93, just the tiny tip of a gigantic iceberg, to help you pinpoint your own boundaries.

## The A-B-Cs of Boundaries

| | | | |
|---|---|---|---|
| ‣ Advice | ‣ Gratefulness | ‣ Nurture | ‣ Urgency |
| ‣ Boss | ‣ Habit | ‣ Obligation | ‣ Volatility |
| ‣ Conflict | ‣ Illness | ‣ Prestige | ‣ Waiting |
| ‣ Deadline | ‣ Joy | ‣ Quiet | ‣ 2X this year |
| ‣ Education | ‣ Kindness | ‣ Reduction | ‣ Yielding |
| ‣ Failure | ‣ Long-term | ‣ Speech | ‣ Zero |
| | ‣ Memory | ‣ Tradeoff | |

Back in Chapter 1 I introduced a boundary as a circle with a line drawn down the middle, the black left side representing a looming threat; the bright right side standing for a guardian presence.

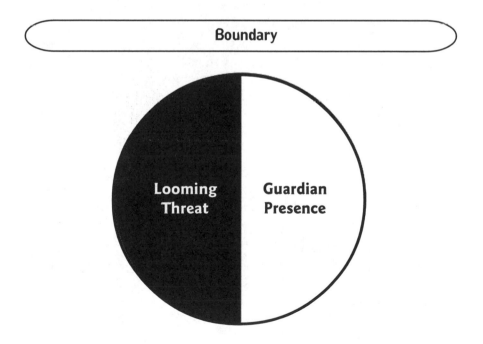

**Boundary**

**Looming Threat**  **Guardian Presence**

On the dark side of the boundary, you encounter a personal looming threat that ignites fear and self-doubt. Here you feel unhappy and disappointed. On the bright side, you discover courage and conviction. Here you feel grounded, focused, unfettered, balanced, centered, authentic, and powerful. Here you generate high octane performance.

Once again, pretend it is 2 a.m.:

▶  Define a boundary.

▶  Describe its dark side (looming threat).

▶  Detail its bright side (guardian presence).

▶  Set a specific date to cross to the bright side.

You will probably find yourself completing this exercise more wisely now that you have delved more deeply into the anatomy of boundaries. That's what Len Filkin did. I've worked with Len, a gifted hospital administrator, for the past six years. CEO of Alliance Care, headquartered in a southwestern state, Len presided over this multi-location, specialty practice hospital system that *US News & World Report* ranked number one in its category for 13 straight years.

Alliance's Board expected great things from Len, whose predecessor had led the hospital to the pinnacle of its industry. Though Len lacked a background in Alliance's specialty, his skills and experience fit beautifully into Alliance's expansion plans. He had amassed a long, distinguished record in public health, and had recently masterminded and executed a complex merger between two large acute care hospitals in the far west.

For seven years he performed well, surpassing all the key measures of hospital growth in a difficult national healthcare environment, and maintaining Alliance's number one standing with *US News & World Report.*

About a year ago at lunch, he shared with me his enthusiasm for a new chief financial officer he'd hired with the expectation that he might eventually succeed him as CEO. "I might even exit sooner than planned. I'm thinking about running a smaller hospital in our community. My wife and I love it here. I'd relish turning around an institution our community really needs."

Some months later, however, Len's expectations hit the fan when the new CFO uncovered major accounting irregularities engineered by the former CFO. Despite the fact that Len had not known about the fraud, he felt compelled to resign because the fiasco had occurred on his watch.

Of course, the media attention drawn to alliance's problems and Len's resignation produced a certain amount of "collateral damage," tarnishing Len's sterling reputation and making it impossible for him to undertake the "dream job" of turning around that troubled smaller hospital.

Throughout the next six months, he confronted this unanticipated boundary:

| | |
|---|---|
| He defined it: | An unfair fall from grace. |
| He described its dark side: | Early retirement under a cloud of disgrace. |
| He detailed its bright side: | Renewed humility and a rededication to community service. |
| He set a specific date to cross to the bright side: | One year. |

Participation in state hospital association activities and a host of charitable causes in the community led, seven months into that year, to a surprise invitation from a small Catholic acute care hospital that needed an acting CEO to guide it through the troubled waters of publicly funded healthcare. "I'm having the time of my life," Len told me recently. "But I have to admit, earlier in my career I doubt I could have dealt with the setback. Our focus on boundaries throughout the past few years makes all the difference in the world."

The good sisters who run this hospital wanted Len all along. You wouldn't be surprised, given his new joy at work, that has elevated his status from "acting," and fully owns his title of CEO.

It takes a lifetime to master all th e subtleties of boundaries.

What should be clear to you at this point is that boundaries are ubiquitous. Most often, we don't see them for what they are: *specifiable* choice points for contact across the full range of life. Though we may not see them, we still have to live with them, and understand the affect they have on us. If you're willing to learn how to read boundaries, you'll better learn how to read life itself. To *not* do so is to bypass wisdom that's available, which will enlighten each step you take.

To illustrate this point, I'd like to quote this passage from *The Book of Qualities* by Ruth Gendler:

> Wisdom wears an indigo jacket. She takes long walks in the purple hills at twilight, pausing to meditate at an old temple near the crossroads. She was sick as a young child so she learned to be alone with herself at an early age. Wisdom has a quiet mind. She likes to think about the edges where things spill into each other and become their opposites. She knows how to look at things inside and out. Sometimes her eyes go out to the thing she's looking at, and sometimes the thing she is looking at enters through her eyes. Questions of time, depth, and balance interest her. She is not looking for answers.

## Living and Working the Authentic Life

If you'll ponder the A-B-Cs of Boundaries, you'll see that as well as ubiquitous, boundaries frequently overlap, creating yet another layer of complexity. For example, take the case of a CEO considering Mr. A and Ms. B for promotion to a higher level job.

Suppose Mr. A has been distracted by a daughter with a drug problem. Then imagine Ms. B has been suffering from a chronic health problem that could grow worse, but probably will pass with time. Clearly, you'll find it to your advantage to weigh more than merely talent and the job itself as you contrast the two options.

A boundary seldom involves only one variable ("Am I going to invest two years obtaining an MBA?") or *between* one person and another person ("My husband needs to generate more income while I attend Wharton). The MBA option also includes, "Do we want to delay having children? Does the MBA give us the right return on investment? What aspects of our lifestyle should we cut back while I'm in school?"

If one of your subsidiary presidents, such as Curt McCauley earlier in this chapter, has made a costly decision or two, the ramifications cascade throughout the organization, affecting his subordinates, his superior, the overall performance of his subsidiary, and other units that depend on McCauley's operation for their output. The land between boundaries sports as many blades of grass as a championship golf course, some smooth as a putting green, some rough as the red Fescue at the U.S. Open., but it becomes ever more apparent that they're anything but simple!

Intangibles often outnumber the tangibles. Ideas, values, philosophies, principles, emotions, even spirituality and religion, further complicate any boundary, one as straightforward as selecting the right person for the right job in New Delhi.

When dealing with all the variables, the best CEO never withdraws from others, either physically (behind closed doors and a legion of lackeys), or emotionally (behind a wall of aloofness, lack of candor, and inflexibility). Withdrawal is *acceptable* only in rare instances, such as when someone demands an immediate decision you're not prepared to make.

In my experience, people always prefer a CEO who's *real,* even if she isn't off-the-charts brilliant, or blessed with an ideal management style free from all foibles and inconsistencies. As the Tex-Mex music legend Doug Sahm put it, "Baby, be real." Be authentic. Provide a model for establishing and maintaining *contact* with people.

When you make contact with another, with yourself, or with any boundary, authenticity more than anything else, should guide your movement. For example, one executive says to another, "Mike, when we began haggling over who was going to manage the new venture, your guy or my guy, we were just sniping, trying to beat the other guy and win for ourselves. When we turned our attention to who would be best to run business, the decision made itself, and the right person was neither of our first choices." Authenticity trumps gamesmanship every time.

Authenticity. Another intangible. But similar to beauty and truth, you know it when you see it. When clients ask me how to achieve it, I often quote this statement from Miller Williams in his book, *The Ways We Touch*:

> Have compassion for everyone you meet even if they don't want it. What seems conceit, bad manners, or cynicism is always a sign of things no ears have heard, no eyes have seen. You do not know what wars are going on down there where the spirit meets the bone.

Another executive, Norman Zastrov, wrestled with boundaries not unlike those that confronted Gordon Parker, the CEO we met earlier in this chapter. For a couple of years, Zastrov served as CEO of a well-known electronics security products manufacturing company headquartered in the Pacific Northwest. He was recommended by an executive search firm that had collected grand references for this candidate. Later, as it turned out, all that praise should have raised a red flag: During the last 10 years, Zastrov had held four jobs with four different companies. At the time, though, no one on the Board wondered why their top candidate had so frequently flitted from one position to another. Was he fleeing from something?

The answer came within two years, as it became increasingly evident that Zastrov couldn't negotiate the boundaries presented by his job, and displayed no interest in learning to do so. The following chart contains abbreviated comments gathered from subordinates at the time.

| Bridgebuilding | Teambuilding | Self Esteem |
|---|---|---|
| ‣ Negative internal "press." | ‣ Doesn't create contact. | ‣ Not clear to others on strategy and vision. |
| ‣ His paranoia divides people. | ‣ Avoids real confrontation. | ‣ Blows up/anger at self for inadequate clarity of expression. |
| ‣ Poor use of corporate staff. | ‣ Teams work in silos. | |
| ‣ Not a good listener. | ‣ Many meetings/not effective. | ‣ Impulsive, often pulls his "big play" trigger to overcome string of failures/ double-or-nothing style. |
| ‣ Lacks know-how of organizational steps. | ‣ He won't accept a COO under him. | |
| | ‣ Doesn't trust; won't delegate. | |
| ‣ Has enemies, not allies, within company. | ‣ Can't get us into orbit. | ‣ Indiscriminate vulnerability displays; loses confidence in self; "cry for help"? |
| ‣ His explosions keep distance, hides fears of inadequacy. | ‣ Not a coach, or developer. | |
| | ‣ Sales force short on total value concept. | |

Similar to Gordon Parker's feedback chart, Zastrov's reveals a lot of boundary flags. They suggest a central goal that was a major looming threat. Zastrov's fleeing of previous jobs was just a form of hiding, hoping he could disguise his incompetence by keeping one step ahead of his mistakes bearing down on him. To this day I consider this lost CEO one of the most tragic figures I've encountered in my long consulting career.

While Gordon Parker acknowledged his boundary flags, Zastrov ignored them. The former marshaled the inner resources to take remedial action and gain authenticity, while the latter went to hell in a hand-basket of illusion and false pride.

Gordon came to understand that he acted the way he did because he *believed* he could excel without intrusion or interruption. His central goal: *to roam at will.* Zastrov never did grasp the fact that he avoided contact, because even though he had come this far, he *believed* he didn't deserve it and was hiding. Gordon solved his problem by acknowledging his avoidance, setting new boundaries that radically improved his contact with his associates, moving courageously forward to apply his gifts, and enhance the performance of his firm. Zastrov continued to hide, felt life closing in more and more and, sure enough, found himself back at the headhunter's office.

Why such radically different outcomes? For one thing, they charted different paths with respect to their Styles-of-Life, one altering his wisely, the other sticking to his rather blindly.

When describing his concept of the central goal, Adler also sometimes called it "the final fictional goal," a definition influenced by the philosopher Hans Vaihinger (1852 to 1933). Vaihinger argued that we can never completely know the underlying reality of the world, and as a result we construct systems of thought, which we falsely assume match reality. We behave "as if" the world matches our models. Even the Style-of-Life is an "as if" construction. If I'm not, intrinsically, "a loser," but the "I am" part of my Style-of-Life calls me one, as Zastrov's did, then I live my life "as if" I am destined to fail.

Zastrov's Style-of-Life, his looming threat, his fiction, caused him to run as a loser from the boundaries he needed to traverse. Gordon exercised the same fidelity to his Style-of-Life as Zastrov, but his was a new one, no longer hidden, and it was not a fiction. He reclaimed himself and scaled new heights. No longer living as if he were a maverick, darting from daylight (world view) in order to roam at will (hidden goal), he became the pioneer he always was, still growing, on track with Destiny.

## Mastering Boundaries

The art of examining boundaries is the art of examining all of life. Recognizing, negotiating, and navigating boundaries superbly leads to living life superbly, on and off the job. Whether you are an engineer, musician, architect, teacher, mother, soldier, house-husband, CEO, widow, lifeguard, gardener, philosopher, mathematician, cabinet-maker, pilot, athlete, saleswoman, retiree, or CIA operative, mastering boundaries and clarifying the contact points in your world will open up a sense of fulfillment rather than feelings of sadness and disappointment.

Permit me to quote a little more poetry on this point. Written by Maria Rainer Rilke (1875–1926), these lines are the last three stanzas of his poem, *The Man Watching,* translated by Robert Bly. The son of a Czech army officer, Rilke was secretary to Rodin, the master sculptor in Paris. These lines that I've committed to memory beautifully capture the importance of mastering boundaries:

> What we choose to fight is so tiny:
> What fights with us is so great!
> If only we would let ourselves be dominated
> as things do by some immense storm,
> we would become strong too, and not need names.
> When we win it's with small things,
> and the triumph itself makes us small.
> What is extraordinary and eternal
> does not *want* to be bent by us
> I mean the Angel who appeared
> to the wrestlers of the Old Testament:
> Whoever was beaten by this Angel
> (who often simply declined the fight)
> went away proud and strengthened
> and great from that harsh hand,
> that kneaded him as if to change his shape.

Winning does not tempt that man.

This is how he grows: by being defeated, decisively,

by constantly greater beings.

## Piercing the Wizard's Curtain

What makes boundaries both inevitable and indispensable? They define every situation, even though you often have to peer behind the facade to get it.

As Dorothy and her companions discovered when they finally pulled away the curtain to see the Wizard of Oz, things often aren't what they seem. And as we discussed when we talked about the "fictional" nature of our constructions of reality, discovering a boundary's true nature, and determining if it is a real or imagined one, takes *mastery*.

Look for this clue: the boundary's *purpose,* "good" or "bad." If you can't identify the purpose behind whatever situation you're examining, you'll never know its true nature, and if you don't know its true nature, it will continue to baffle you. "Purpose" is just another word for the central goal of a person's Style-of-Life. However, the true purpose of even a simple, everyday object may lie far beneath your initial understanding of it.

Take a humble meeting room chair, for example. You know its purpose: to provide you with a seat at the conference. But that's only the *apparent* purpose.

Look more closely at it. Can you appreciate its structure and the materials used to manufacture it? The all-too-familiar non-breathing upholstery and tubular stainless steel legs? That chair wasn't built for you, it was built for the hotel management that needs to stack and store hundreds of chairs in a compact space. It's lightweight, sturdy, durable, and stackable; it can be transported easily, stored with others in a closet, and it can work as well in a dining room as in a conference room. That's reality.

However, at the "comfort boundary," the chair fails to achieve its *apparent* purpose. After an all-day meeting, a tired Linda stands up, aching from sitting so long in a contraption that fails to give her the back support she needs.

Now think of a rationalization. It's the reason given by someone for an action, but not the real reason; a boundary's purpose can be like that. And just as with a rationalization, you may not be aware of a boundary's true purpose when your actions or words declare it. Even when, in complete sincerity, you set or recognize a boundary, you can still be blindsided by unintended consequences. When this happens, you can be sure a purpose more powerful than the one you first visualized or announced is brewing.

This more powerful purpose is no more "good" or "bad" than yours, but it does let you know that what you have in mind isn't going to work. You need to abandon the idea, go at it in a different way or time, or peer deeply into people's counter reaction to see what it says about the situation's needs. Their behavior may block your intentions in ways that are just as misguided as yours in this situation, but their message, perverse as it may seem, is that you better choose a different alternative.

Consider this starter list of boundaries shown on page 103 that typically pop up on the yellow brick road to organizational success. All show that the stated purpose is not the real one. You'll see that some executives establish boundaries in complete sincerity, yet their avowed purposes do not come about. In other cases, they declare purposes, but from the start, people don't accept them as credible. As you'll see in #13, management starts out with good intentions. They see their purpose foiled, but then learn from the experience, and turn their lemon into lemonade.

All these organizational examples prove that the art of managing is the art of managing boundaries. Superb managers manage them superbly, mastering them by mastering contact. Find the point of contact, define the boundary, determine its potential for a good or bad result, and think and act as best you can to get a good result.

If you can't find a boundary, trying to solve a problem is an exercise in futility. Things *are* as they *are*, but you won't have figured them out.

For instance, suppose you face a crucial deadline for a team report. Obviously, you needed to set a deadline to get the job done, and so you set a comfortable one. But then, you can't understand all the floundering, bickering, procrastination, and evasion that besets the project. Well, that comfortable deadline just allowed one of Parkinson's Laws to work its magic: "Work expands to fill the available time."

## Boundary Reality Check

| Apparent Purpose | Real Purpose |
|---|---|
| 1. The performance review verifies my accomplishments this year. | It emphasizes what's required of me in the future. |
| 2. A progress report is a report on what we've done on a project. | More often a tracking mechanism for our bosses to highlight what hasn't been accomplished so far. |
| 3. A management conference is designed to keep the team abreast of developments in the industry and add to their skills. | Most often corporate recreation & reward masked as education—attendance at trade shows builds contacts for executives who may need to change jobs in the future. |
| 4. A colleague asks me a question to get an answer. | Often asks me a question to make a statement or imply criticism. |
| 5. A request for more information leads to making a more informed decision. | Such requests frequently made to slow down or kill a project. |
| 6. Leaderless teams are egalitarian and generate superior ideas. | Such teams generate confusion, lack of clarity, endless checking and politicking while our competitor makes progress. |
| 7. Setting up a "horse race" between two executives for a promotion gets the best out of both. | Assures competition and hoarding of information by subordinates of each who need to collaborate with each other for the good of the business. |
| 8. We acquired Hendrik Glove to make ourselves stronger. | We acquired them to make ourselves bigger. |
| 9. Quality is Job #1! | Really? Perhaps something else is. What is it? |
| 10. We seek consensus to create full participation by all. | We seek consensus to avoid conflict and straight talk. |
| 11. I'm promoting Karen into that job because she's the most qualified. | He's promoting Karen because she's the most loyal. |
| 12. The primary audience for our mission is our own people. | The primary audience for our so-called mission is our customers. |
| 13. We funded a cultural arts center for our community because we thought it was needed. | It failed, was closed, was converted to a seniors center that has thrived. *That's* what was needed. |
| 14. I praise my subordinates to make them perform better. | He praises us because he wants us to like him. |
| 15. Let's table that decision for further consideration. | An indirect way to say No. |

While the apparent purpose of the deadline was to give people plenty of time to do their work, giving it was allowing them time they didn't need, or, perhaps, the project is much bigger than you envisioned, and their stalling gives *you* time to see that, and give them the time and resources they need to really do it right.

Now, *rethink* the deadline situation as a boundary:

▶ Define the boundary: The report, and deadline as assigned, is realistic.

▶ Describe its dark side: Wasting valuable time evading a job that some think is more complicated than it is.

▶ Describe its bright side: A quick summing up of how past work was the right building blocks to move smoothly to the next stage.

▶ Set a specific time to reach the bright side: Report is due tomorrow at 4 p.m. rather than in two weeks.

By thinking about the report as a boundary, you create an atmosphere in which you can lead people from Stage 2 (aware and inept) to Stage 3 (aware and adept) where the team has become enlightened in a way that they weren't. Your meeting with them to reset the deadline included a good-natured explanation that your rethinking generated. This was a missing link you acknowledged to them, and it got everybody on board. They saw you as the natural you are, and you helped them move along the continuum toward Stage 4.

It all starts with making contact, engaging people in a meaningful dialogue, and conducting necessary negotiations. After your explanation, it goes something like this: You ask Bill how long he thinks it will take to *write* the report. He allows ample time, say two days. You then ask if the team could set a world's record and do it in two hours. "Why not, then?" Bill offers. When the team tries to break a record, it probably will.

This same principle applies to a boundary within yourself. Make contact with your authentic self, engage in dialogue, conduct a necessary negotiation, then GET IT DONE.

Do that successfully, as Gordon Parker did, and you'll become a boundary master, comfortable in your own skin, effective in your relationships with others, and successful as a best-in-class CEO in your corner of the world. You'll conquer the business task at hand; you'll bring an open mind to every problem and opportunity; you'll never force issues because you know that simply doesn't work; you'll successfully negotiate with all stakeholders; you'll find the *and* in the situation; not the *but*; you won't play bully or know-it-all; won't pull rank; and you'll become the consummate listener. Your mastery will shine through and you won't be able to explain that fully, no matter how hard you try. You'll be so good, you won't know it.

### In this chapter, you have learned how to:

➡ Recognize that you are *always* moving away, toward or against someone or something, and that knowledge has great significance for you and your world.

➡ Measure yourself, as Gordon Parker did, against the standard of the BAM Grid to achieve mastery in any area of performance that concerns you.

➡ Make boundaries (those ubiquitous dividers you seldom see) concrete, and the events by which you create authentic contact with the significant people in your work and life.

➡ Distinguish between the apparent and the real purpose of a boundary, thereby giving you the means to define accurately any situation you face.

### Your Inner CEO Punch List

☐ Look at some areas where you claim to have drawn your line in the sand. How firm are these lines? Are there any habits or comforts you need to shed? Which ones are there, but faint, where you need to redeclare?

☐ Take a few moments to wonder if there's a boundary flag waving at you that you've ignored, or put off and need to address now.

☐ No? Move on to the fourth bullet. Yes? Pick one. Look at it closely in its three-dimensional aspect. What space is there, waiting for you to step into, with whom? What's between you and where you need to be?

☐ Make sure you're in contact with your people. Yes, your schedule is horrendous, and the time pressures are great, but get to *know* these folks. Care about them and their families. Let them see and know you. Let them know what you like and don't like. Taking time is saving time.

☐ Name an "as if" in your life that has had you fooled.

# 5

# Boards

*Teach us to care and not to care. Teach us to sit still.*

—T.S. Eliot

Everyone, including every CEO, has to deal with people both above and below them. For you, it may be a boss and your assistant. For a CEO, it's the board of directors and the executive team. Who sits on your board?

My client and good friend Arch Wardlaw is a warm, gifted man who cherishes the image of his top team striding down the road, eight-abreast, arm-in-arm, heads thrown back, laughing, feeling good about themselves and each other. It's a perfect portrait of a winning team.

It didn't start out this way. It took time, patience, and constant effort, with a lot of missteps along the way. Lately, he's been wondering how he can create a similar portrait of himself and the board of directors, and of the board and his top team. How can he get those immediately above and below him to share the easy camaraderie of a winning team? That's a tall order no one else can fill. How will he do it? Not as a controller, but as a skilled collaborator.

In relationship to his top team, Arch currently straddles Stages 3 and 4 on the BAM Grid shown on page 108. In his relationship with his board he occupies Stage 3. To improve that position he'll turn full bore to developing Stage 4 mastery.

Grounded CEOs understand the *concept* of CEO-as-collaborator, supplying the energy source for building trust and candor at the boundaries between these two groups. To govern with distinction, boards need exposure to the gifts of the top team; to produce the right outcomes, the top team needs engagement with a board made up of wise heads and big hearts. It's up to the grounded CEO, ever the learner, to convert concept to action, and serve as alchemist to produce this essential, intricate bonding.

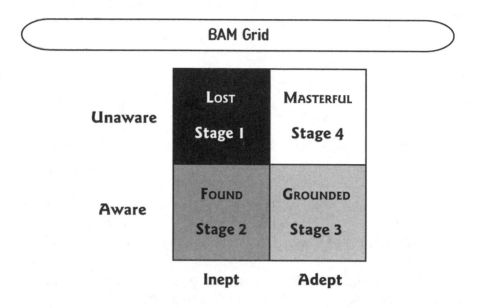

**BAM Grid**

|  | **Inept** | **Adept** |
|---|---|---|
| **Unaware** | LOST  Stage 1 | MASTERFUL  Stage 4 |
| **Aware** | FOUND  Stage 2 | GROUNDED  Stage 3 |

Your Inner CEO needs to interact effectively with your own board, be it an actual board of directors, a superior, or an informal board you can assemble from peers, associates, mentors, family members, or anyone else who can serve as your advisors. You can treat your boss and her peers as your board, and you can get on a board yourself, perhaps with a local not-for-profit organization or structured committee in your community (a house of worship, a social organization, a humane society, a school board, etc.) Inserting yourself into any situation that parallels the structure and process of a board will help you release that "executive within."

## Fly-on-the-Wall Coaching

I think almost anyone could learn a lot about career success through "fly-on-the wall coaching" when you observe a CEO coaching session just as it takes place during one of my consulting projects. That holds true especially for interaction with boards, because only a small percentage of executives ever experience them firsthand. The fly-on-the-wall experience will also benefit you if you ever serve on a board yourself, even if its only your local conservation commission.

The skills you acquire can only add to your range of competence "back at the office" among your associates and superiors as you move up your company's corporate ladder.

That's what happened to Bill Wallace, a client of mine who works as senior vice president of human resources for Gaylord InterScience. He'd served for a couple of years on the board of the Red Cross chapter in his large Bay Area city with such distinction that the other members asked him to become chairman when the current chairman's term expired. Even though this position would entail many volunteer hours of hard work for two years, Bill gladly accepted the invitation to accomplish even more for a cause in which he believed deeply. In the end, however, he gained something he had not expected: greater poise and *gravitas* at Gaylord InterScience. Forgive me for this excursion into Latin, but I've never found a better word to describe the "weightiness" that prompts other people to take you seriously. Dealing with fund-raising strategy, executive recruitment, ethical issues and personnel problems of the Red Cross sensitized Bill to similar situations confronting the Board at Gaylord, particularly its lead director and the chairman of the compensation committee. Although he does not wish to become a CEO, his deep involvement with the Red Cross added immeasurably to his community network and his value as a colleague and advisor to Gaylord's CEO. As a result, he's become an A-Player at the top of his game, and at the top of his company.

Another vicarious board experience you might explore is "armchair coaching," when you scour business books, newspapers, and magazine for cases and stories featuring board subjects, including those where boards have drawn attention to themselves for either negligent or admirable behavior. As a very first step, I recommend you read "What Makes Great Boards Great" by Jeffrey A. Sonnenfeld from the September–October, 2002 *Harvard Business Review*.

You might also consider ponying up the $475 annual dues to join the National Association of Corporate Directors (NACD). If you do so, you'll learn a lot about boards through monthly chapter meetings, an annual national meeting, workshops run by top-of-the-line resource people (that your company might pay for), and outstanding publications. Check it out at *www.NACDonline.com*. This investment in your future will greatly expand your network, your knowledge, your poise, and your gravitas.

Let's pause here a moment to consider 8 Rules of Engagement that will help you build fruitful board relations:

# 8 Rules of Engagement

1. Engage in activities that can help you become a better collaborator on your current job (your main priority). This can be any activity that requires team effort, perhaps a building project or a team sport such as doubles tennis and racquet ball, or touch football.

2. Volunteer to serve on task forces, or suggest creating one that might open a window of opportunity or shed light on a nettlesome issue, such as effective diversity hiring or alternatives for affordable workforce housing. The interdisciplinary, cross-functional nature of a task force parallels board work.

3. Think of your boss and her peers as *your* board, your peers, and/or the people who report to you as your team. Voila! You've created another situation that parallels board work, where you supply the energy source for two key groups, just like a CEO.

4. Find some local government committee that needs new blood (they all do!) on their advisory board. Perhaps your boss, or your company's head of external affairs, could make some introductions. You might also consult Board Source, a terrific organization that does for not-for-profits ($99 annual dues) what NACD does for its members. Log onto *www.boardsource.org*.

5. Follow press and news accounts of corporations and organizations whose boards show you how to do it, and how *not* to do it (Motorola and Qualcomm on the positive side; New York Stock Exchange and Hewlett-Packard on the negative side—though H-P CEO Mark Hurd deserves high praise for the way he rose above the fray to recover

the dignity of this great company in this ludicrous situation). If you're a minority or a woman, follow the stories and careers of people such as Carlos Gutierrez, Sam Scott, Valerie Jarrett, and Indra Nooyi. They're models for you. Carlos Gutierrez, Hispanic, rose through the ranks at cereal giant Kellogg to become board chairman and the youngest CEO in that company's nearly 100-year history. He left that post to become U.S. Secretary of Commerce. Scott, African-American, is president and CEO of Corn Products International, lead director of Motorola's Board, and serves on the Boards of Bank of New York and Accion International, a not for profit that makes business micro-loans to underprivileged populations throughout the world. Jarrett is an African-American woman who is CEO of Habitat Company, a residential real estate firm headquartered in Chicago. She's also chairman of the board of University of Chicago Hospitals and a board member of USG. She's included in the 2007 class of 10 model directors by the prestigious *Outstanding Directors* of New York City. Indra Nooyi, born in India, is chairman and CEO of PepsiCo. She had a distinguished background in strategy and finance with the international giant ABB Group and Motorola before joining PepsiCo as a senior executive. She is also a director of Motorola., and the Federal Reserve Bank of New York.

6. Observe your boss's interactions with your company's board, listening for their off-hand comments about their own exposure or presentations to the board. You might be surprised by what you learn if you just ask, discreetly and diplomatically, "Gee, what's it really like in there? I'd give anything to be a fly-on-the-wall."

7. Volunteer your assistance to some executive putting a report or presentation together for the board. Even if you play a modest role in a routine project, you'll gain valuable exposure and learn a lot about the process.

8. Know the names of your company's directors and follow their careers. Again, a little diplomatic investigation can pay off. Most board members are fairly well-known public figures who may appear in *Who's Who in America*, or

*Who's Who in Finance and Business*. Even if they don't, they probably held big jobs earlier, and may well serve as directors of other companies as well. (Don Lennox, a client of mine when he was CEO of Navistar, told me once about attending an annual meeting where a shareholder asked one of his fellow directors, a retired as a CEO of a Fortune 500 company, "Mr. Jones, I see you're chairman of the executive committee of the board. What does that mean?" Mr. Jones replied, "It means I'm on my way down, but I've been there.")

Knowing about your organization's directors adds to your knowledge about your company; knowledge, more than anything else, unleashes the executive within.

## New Era Catalysts

Every enterprise, from building a townhouse to the invasion of Normandy, from a string quartet to the Boston Symphony Orchestra, requires one effective executive. None can survive two different managements. In whatever kind of organization you can name, that central figure functions as a catalyst at the boundary between two factions (the board and the top team). Do I even need to *whisper* the word *boundary*?

The master catalysts not only acknowledge the necessity of this age-old boundary between the factions, but they also draw new boundaries that accommodate equally necessary change. These new boundaries define a creative tension that is held in place only by the deft practice of (1) trust and (2) candor by both factions in relation to each other. Without both in equal weight, our vaunted "new era of governance," characterized by "open book" management and scrupulous observation of legal and ethical principles, will come apart at the seams. The emphasis on *control* that characterized the old catalyst got a lot of executives, their boards, and their companies into trouble. On the other hand, a board that approaches its stewardship in an adversarial fashion, courts trouble as well. New players on both sides of this boundary will shun control in favor of trust and candor.

The new era catalyst bears the major responsibility to provide energy for melding trust and candor between the two factions. This job matters more than any other. Fortunately, as business continues to ramp up in speed and complexity, exponentially expanding the demands on you, you'll spread the burden across an energized and *integrated* board and top team.

The outside board, no matter how accomplished, diverse, and committed to the two chief duties of *care* and *loyalty*, consists of part-timers. They come together four to six times a year, most often for one day's onsite work, including board committee responsibilities. Fortunately, many do their homework and come to meetings well-prepared for discussions and decisions.

Many, too, have themselves served as CEOs. Historically, they've accepted invitations to join boards for a variety of reasons: to reap honor and prestige, to obtain insights that may benefit them in their day job, to protect and represent the interests of large investors in the company, to support the CEO as friend and advisor, to enjoy intellectual stimulation and confront the challenge of the business proposition, and, of course, to receive compensation in the form of fees for service and stock opportunities.

Regardless of their motivation, their responsibilities include feedback to the CEO. As catalysts, CEOs *need* ample, candid, trust-based feedback.

I once consulted with several members of top management at Rexford Brands, a $12 billion household-name consumer products company, among them Bill Youngren, the CFO, who told me that in his 14 years with this corporation, he had never received a performance appraisal from his boss, CEO Harry Fineman.

I bring this up because it's not at all unusual for CEOs to grow lax in giving straight, regular feedback, negative and positive, to their direct reports. Sometimes that derives from their own reluctance to receive such feedback themselves, no matter what the source.

Imagine, also, how hard it is for members serving on a board with other CEOs, to evaluate the board's performance as a whole, the performance of each individual member, and, of course, their own performance. Yet, the new era of corporate governance mandates higher standards for candor, which, properly delivered and received, actually promotes trust.

When it comes to evaluating their own performance, boards have been making great strides forward. However, while some have worked hard at developing methods for evaluating their overall performance, and even some directors conduct candid self-assessment, few boards conduct anonymous peer reviews, where every director evaluates all other directors, one-by-one, in confidence, and in accordance with a written standard. The information gleaned from such an effort and fed back to each director, also in confidence, can do a lot to enhance candor and trust between board members, between top executives, and *between these two groups themselves.* Hello CEO as catalyst! Hello boundaries!

How do you apply principles of new era trust and candor to your informal workplace "board" or "outside-activity" board, or any significant exchange you conduct with others? Regardless of your situation, you want to avoid the "Emperor's New Clothes" syndrome or the "Mom loves you no matter what" effect. If those around you always tell you what they think you want to hear, or praise everything you do unconditionally, you'll not only cease growing professionally and personally, you'll run the risk of letting your dark side expand at the expense of your bright side. Demand candor, promise you'll accept it without anger or retribution, and provide candor yourself. Do this and you'll both bestow and receive trust.

If you doubt the value and power of trust and candor at the boundary, consider this brief example that illustrates the positive shift taking place between today's boards and top teams:

A client I'll call Neal Farley is CEO of Halsey-Frickert, a New England heavy manufacturing company. Recently, he shared his views with me on working with his board. "Basically, the board's job is to stop me from going where I don't want to go." Apparently, that appealed to the board because they take their jobs as skeptics to heart.

"Not only do I not mind, I appreciate their doing their homework to really critique some of my ideas that would be big investments financially and a redirection of the workforce away from what we think of as tried and true. We're in a mature business and we have to find and fund new avenues."

This attitude has won Neal a reputation in the industry as a "wild hare," a somewhat over-stated way to describe his penchant for risk. The board helps restrain that penchant at times.

"When the board shoots down an idea that the team and I have worked up carefully, we usually see the wisdom in their counter position. After all, we have some real winners on our board who know their stuff and that's what I mean when I say they stop me from going where I don't want to go."

On one occasion, though, Neal needed to provide similar candor to one of the company's new directors. "At a meeting when four of our top team and I presented a projected new plant in Arizona, this fellow would ask questions meant to challenge our assumptions, and that's good, but this time there was just too much edge to them. He looked around the table two or three times that afternoon and said, 'My job is to keep Neal honest.' I accept that, but it has to work both ways. In this case we challenged him, and all the other directors bought in on our capital investment and we've gone ahead with the program and it has turned out really well." Candor engendered trust. Trust engendered candor.

After the meeting, Neal and his four associates discussed the meeting and asked their lead director what he thought. The director said he would speak with the new member to let him know his behavior, if not his intention, had gone over the edge. "I said I appreciated his support, but I'm the one who asked to be stopped from going where I don't want to go, and I'd like meet with him personally to clarify what I mean by that and what I consider the ground rules for candor and trust."

Neal set up a breakfast date with the new director the following week. "I told him that his comments rankled me and that I'd appreciate it if we could just get better acquainted so he could share with me where he was coming from. He said he'd given thought to his actions because he sensed he offended not only the team but also his fellow directors. He said he appreciated the feedback and looked forward to our next 'strategy dust-up.'"

Long story short, that episode took place three years ago, and now the new director has become the board's lead director; he has played a vital role in keeping Neal from going where he doesn't want to go. As for Neal, he proved himself a master catalyst in the new era.

While most executives adhere to the legal requirements in the new era, (symbolized mainly by Sarbanes-Oxley regulations, legislation passed as a response to corporate abuses of the late 1990s), you can't legislate the sort of honest, caring communication I'm advocating here. Collaboration depends not on laws, but on trust and candor at the boundary.

Only deftly balanced trust and candor between board and the top team can overcome the "club mentality," the "Emperor's New Clothes" syndrome, and the "mom loves you no matter what" effect that infects too many boards. They also help boards learn how to ask the right questions that help CEOs and their top teams find the right answers to daunting problems. As they engage in the joint quest, all players (board, CEO-as-catalyst, top team) become cognizant of each other's gifts and limitations without embarrassment or apology.

## Idea Exchange

As Arch Wardlaw and I worked on his challenge to forge a stronger relationship at the top team-board boundary, he began to see solid results. Here's how we did it.

First, we began emphasizing collaboration in the bi-monthly board meetings. Arch took the lead. As CEO, he knew he could be the catalyst who helps both groups cross over the boundary to make contact with each other.

The board often comes into a meeting cold, with a burdensome amount of factual information to digest, and not enough warm, informal prior feedback that a CEO could have provided in a variety of ways: phone calls, e-mails, and informal meetings away from the office between top executives whose responsibilities for performance match the board members' responsibilities for oversight.

Because Arch knew that most CEOs and top teams haven't distilled enough pointed direction about specific issues and problems, he provided that guidance in order to stimulate the board's best judgment. Gradually, the board went beyond the old armchair analysis and frequent preoccupation with trivial details. Arch also replaced the old system of detailed written reports with meetings designed to generate the exchange of ideas. Idea exchange became the centerpiece of the board meeting.

Now, a new director, brought in for his gifts and experience, feels eager to brainstorm in meetings, not just to prove how smart he is, but to help the company achieve its goals.

So what, exactly, did the New Catalyst CEO do?

He kept it as simple as A-B-C:

A. Limit your top team's *presentations,* keeping them bright and on-point. In this case, less is usually more.

B. Insist that every presentation begin with a headline that clearly states management's point of view from a WE standpoint.

C. Follow the headline with concise supporting detail that gives the board the essential data it needs to think through an issue or opportunity.

For example, suppose you are responsible for a five-minute presentation to the board on the subject of Globe Tech's Asian presence. Your headline reads: "Globe Tech Should Sell Off Its Asian Operation."

"Throughout the past 90 days, Phil, George, Linda, and I have done research on the appropriateness of selling off our Asian Operation, and have concluded we should do so for four reasons.

1. Except for our general manager, we're thin on management over there.

2. After developing some great new products that have won design and usability awards, our distribution limitations leave us struggling a distant third in the market.

3. We can bring our general manager back to the home office to head up all our global operations, a development opportunity for him, and a chance for us to evaluate him as a candidate for top management. Our number two over there is a national capable woman, whose presence makes the business an attractive purchase.

4. We have received two strong offers to buy the business, and we can use the cash better elsewhere.

This leaves us with two options: (1) sell to Ducat, the number two share company, headquartered in Singapore, and (2) sell to Rapunzel, our major domestic competitor who wants to get into this region with a running start.

We'd like your thoughts on the best way to go. Does anyone see any options we've overlooked?

Notice how this:

▶ States the top team's forged agreement on a point of view.

- Offers a headline that expresses it compellingly.

- Offers concise supporting data.

- Stresses what you want from board.

I cannot overemphasize the first item, your top team's agreement on a point of view. It represents *collaboration,* the same sort of collaboration you want to establish with the board. That's one reason the presentation opened with a statement and concluded with a *question.* It invites candor and opens the door to a team-board WE built on the foundation of your top team's WE.

This WE builds confidence and trust within the board. They feel inclined to think freely and speak candidly. Now it's not us (the board) and them (the top team), it's "we're all in this together." Collaboration arises, a boundary gets crossed, the road to results becomes clear.

Even though directors who do their job right are independent from, and candid with, management, there's no conflict of interest in the perfectly normal human feeling of wanting to belong. Work and the feeling are not mutually exclusive, but when the vital components of any endeavor, and the spirit of belonging takes place amid an environment of candor, clarity, and collaboration, everyone wins: the board, management, the company, its customers, and its shareholders.

These additional tips for improving team-board relations will help you create that win-win-win situation:

### All Aboard

- Prepare the board for management changes and surprise. Informal lead-up announcements can reduce the discomfort that often arises when people and plans appear on the scene.

- Make sure any printed material sent to the board contains the all-important *top team's point of view.* This allows the board to focus on issues and do the sort of homework that ignites productive idea exchanges.

- Eliminate words and phrases that imply control, such as "we want your buy-in" or, "we're assuming you'll approve the new provision."

- Incorporate words and phrases that emphasize collaboration, such as, "We look forward to a joint review of our proposed diversity hiring practices" or, "We're appreciative of your insights from our board retreat that set us in a fresh new direction."

- Activate a long-term, top team-board relationship building plan, which might include a less task-oriented annual board retreat.

- Consider engaging the help of a skilled facilitator or coach.

My client, Pat Canavan of Motorola, builds team-board relations like a master craftsman. We have been working together and exchanging ideas for almost 20 years. As Motorola's senior vice president of global governance and member of CEO Ed Zander's top team, Pat plays a key role in reviving Motorola's fortunes. When we first worked together, he was senior vice president of global organizational and management development. He spent a great deal of his time then (as he does now) serving as liaison between the board and top management and supplying his strong voice to the company's initiatives in the area of corporate social responsibility around the world. It's a tough job, particularly in a complex $40 billion organization that's spread around the world. But Pat does it skillfully, and with a great sense of humor.

Throughout dinner not long ago, as I was sharing my views on board performance, I asked him for his thoughts on what could turn a good board into a great board. Borrowing my pen, he jotted down the following:

### Pat's Paradigm

- Board needs to see selves (as a body) as architect or interior designer.

- Board meetings (arrangements/procedures/agendas) are "set up" by top management in the company "house." How can the board make its own space, create a "home"?

- Board members need to conduct "out-of-body" evaluations of who we are, how we stack up as shareholder representatives.

- If called upon, what would we as board and management say about us?

- How can we as humans make this (being the company's directors) a more fulfilling experience?

I honestly believe that any board that went about its business this way would do a great job. Pat's advice clearly emphasizes the crucial questions: Who are we? Where do we want to go? How will we get there? His approach also paves the way for the CEO to fulfill the role of catalyst, creating an environment where collaboration rules.

After re-tooling your board meetings along the lines I've suggested, and once you begin seeing the positive results and "warming up" that occurs, try using Pat's Paradigm with your board. Meet with your non-executive chairman or lead director, confiding that you and your team would love to work with the board in a new way; she'll probably love the idea. Of course, you can adapt Pat's Paradigm to any board, formal or informal, in either your work or personal realm.

## Out of Control

Great CEOs think outside the control box. They're out of control in the same way the corner grocer is out of onions. "Sorry, we don't do that anymore." Many directors, even the most conscientious and hard-headed, will welcome a non-adversarial game change. A couple of years ago, Nate Witherspoon, the non-executive chairman of Laidlaw Cement, called me to arrange a meeting—a private luncheon he hosted at his Midtown Manhattan Club.

As it turned out, Nate and his board were concerned about the performance of their CEO, Av Wolsley, who had held the job for about two years. Laidlaw had recruited Av from the outside. As Nate revealed the board's concerns, I was impressed by his calm, articulate, and objective assessment of a puzzling situation. In Nate's own words:

Something is going on in Laidlaw that's not quite right and I'm concerned, over our possible consequences. I can't quite put my finger on it, though.

Our top management team is dysfunctional. We could just fire Av and hope someone new will straighten it out. But there are problems with that: We'd have to pay Av a big severance package. We'd mount an expensive and time-consuming search for his replacement and lose time. A new CEO will cost us a third more, and he might not succeed either. He'll terminate at least two or three top people before we even know if he's any good. That will require more costly severance packages, and we'll have to conduct more expensive searches for their replacements; they'll each cost us a third more. Finally, if Av's replacement's not good, we have to start over. I figure this will all cost us perhaps 15 to 20 times Av's current package.

I like Av a lot, and there's no question in my mind that he's loaded with talent and has the kind of strength I like in somebody with his kind of responsibility. My feeling, shared by a couple of our directors, is that we ought to retain somebody like you to work with Av and the team to uncover the real problems and address them quickly. Could you do a little detective work and maybe such coaching?

I took the assignment. To make a long story short, I met and interviewed all members of top management and some board members. I agreed with Witherspoon's assessment of Av Wolsley's talent and suitability for the job, a view I shared with the whole Board. Av, I agreed, is a winner, and just needs a little support building his interpersonal skills and making some difficult organizational decisions. In particular, he needed to deal with a couple of executives on the team who feared change and blocked innovative initiatives by a talented subordinate who represented the future of the business. Although Av knew this, he had delayed taking action for so long that he worried he looked weak to people who also recognized the problem.

Why had he tolerated this situation so long? Because more delay could only add to others' negative perception, I urged Av to solve the problem immediately. He did, sending the executives on their way humanely and generously, thereby signaling his strength. After he promoted two of the younger, innovative managers to fill their shoes, we embarked on a team-building project for the whole team. We also set in motion the same kind of discipline for board work that Arch Wardlaw instituted. In fairly short order, the board came to appreciate Av's talent, and stepped up their support for their CEO.

For his part, Nate Witherspoon, a model non-executive chairman, has forged a strong, candid relationship with Av, which has spread across the boundary between board and team with remarkable financial results and customer satisfaction. It all happened because Nate, the board, Av, and the executive team shunned control and embraced collaboration.

To succeed in the current corporate climate, more boards and CEOs are accepting the fact that they cannot achieve admirable performance through control. Control blocks the sort of candor, good will, and trust that enables people to help each other out when their organizations face inevitable crises. Control breeds adversarial relationships, and adversaries breed escalating conflict. Collaboration resolves conflict, and builds respectful bonds, and respectful bonds breed peak performance.

Given this fact of corporate life in the new era, board members should be chosen for a track record of collaboration, not solely for their titles, awards, and participation in the "old boy network." Apply this principle to your own formal and informal boards. Bring onto your board people who can collaborate with you on your growth and development as an executive. Don't rely too much on high-status powerful people, and minimize your inclusion of friends and family.

The same holds true for boards searching for a new CEO, for a CEO searching for new top team members, for any executive looking to promote prime prospects from a crop of high-potential subordinates, for the greenest recruit from Wharton, and the most seasoned veteran on the sales force.

In the previous era of management, executives thought control not only gave them power, but reduced the pressure that comes with the top job. Ironically, however, collaboration, not control, lessens the pressure on you, and makes you easier on yourself and everyone around you. People enjoy your company more than they would if you constantly try to keep them under your thumb, and they appreciate your talent more when you act like a teammate rather than a dictator. Results improve and morale soars. Your top team feels safe with you because they now know where you stand, and they, too, grow more candid. The board finds you a guiding light, not an obstructionist, and revels in the fact that you honestly seek their ideas and trust their judgment.

How do you make the transition from controller to collaborator? First and foremost, you cultivate the four skills star collaborators always cultivate:

## The Four Skills of a Star Collaborator

1. Astute selector (of executive and board talent).

2. Invisible initiator (let them do it their way).

3. Willing worker (bring your gift to the party).

4. Life-long learner (use it or lose it).

**Astute selector.** None of your activities ranks higher than building a superior team with high-performing, talented people. Note the stress on *performance.* Top performers love their work, tackle it with relish, and grow steadily into better performers each day. If you can't easily size up people or get distracted by their titles or credentials, rather than their fitness for the work, they won't get the work done, and you'll end up with an unhappy team. Perhaps you can rely on someone on the team who excels at selection. Watch and learn how she does it.

**Invisible initiator.** Control freaks need not apply. Once you select the talent, what do you do with it? Respect it. Even if you've selected a trainee, you did that because the trainee displayed tremendous potential. If he needs hands-on training to get launched, provide it, but bear in mind that you enhance the future of the team by letting him arrive on his own steam at a destination you (or the team) defined. An effective initiator bestows the gift of autonomy.

**Willing worker.** Invisible initiators delegate, delegate, delegate. But that doesn't mean you deliberately withhold your gift from the team. Talent is talent only when it works. Make yours work. Separate your unique strength from your routine strengths, and offer that unstintingly to the team. I've always liked this observation from Emmett Murphy, author of *Talent IQ:* "Every worker leads, every leader works."

**Life-long learner.** Nothing disheartens and frustrates us as much as a CEO, or anyone in a leadership position who starts coasting. Avoid deadening routines that offer little more than comfort. At least once a year, take on a significant task that scares you. Doing so will keep your synapses snapping, make you dependent on other talent for guidance, and enlarge your respect among your subordinates.

People who develop these skills operate most effectively at the boundary where leaders, board, and teams make contact. Each skill, as you can see, depends on letting go of control.

- Let the board's responsibility grow.
- Let them chart their own makeup.
- Let them review your performance with candor.
- Let them express their independence.
- Let the board chose your successor.
- Let them exercise their judgment.
- Let them make their mistakes.
- Let them learn and grow in their incisiveness.
- Let them be good at what they do.
- Let them ask all their questions.
- Let them question your answers.
- Let them know what you think.
- Let them know what you want.
- Let them learn how good you are on their own.
- Let them see you at ease.
- Let them choose your guidance.
- Let them get to know your top team.
- Let their light shine.
- Let it go.

Power is a funny thing; the more you hoard it, the more it diminishes, the more you give it away, the more it increases. Real power comes not from dictatorial control, but from confident collaboration. Real power is power over yourself, the hardest power to acquire and apply. Can you "let it happen" when you feel tempted to "make it happen"? Oh, there's nothing wrong with trying to "make it happen," provided you realize that like all of us with our limitations and biases, you often strive for the wrong things.

This poem by Stephen Crane says it all:

### A Man Saw a Ball of Gold in the Sky

A man saw a ball of gold in the sky;
He climbed for it,
And eventually he achieved it—
It was clay.
Now this is the strange part:
When the man went to the earth
And looked again,
Lo, there was the ball of gold.
Now this is the strange part:
It was a ball of gold.

When "make it happen" becomes "control it," you pull a looming threat out of Pandora's Box. When "let it happen" means "collaborate on it," you stimulate a guardian presence to emerge.

## The CEO Boundary Quiz

A catalyst stimulates collaboration, facilitating decision-reaching rather than arbitrarily imposing decisions on others. However, let me make it crystal clear that I'm not arguing in favor of consensus. Consensus is a watered-down decision, the lowest common denominator, often reached when everyone on the team has been manipulated or cowed into saying yes to something they don't agree with, but feel compelled to endorse. The leader, eager for agreement, pushes for something on which everyone can agree, and ends up with something in which no one fully agrees. In the end, consensus makes a poor umbrella: whenever it rains, consensus dissolves into a puddle of nothing.

Collaboration, on the other hand, arises between a leader and team who practice "full voices and superior choices." Collaboration requires candor and trust, which means it's inevitable that talented people with strong convictions will often differ in their evaluation of a situation. *We want that!* The collaborative leader makes sure people will eagerly put forth all possible options in a climate of openness, but when serious differences occur and decision time arrives, the leader makes the decision in accordance with which option she believes will generate superior results. Remember: You are a facilitator who *makes decisions.* "The Decision" is why you are where you are: at the head of the table. But by the time you make it, you've traveled a swift test track with the best hearts and minds at your disposal. Such collaboration between the CEO and the top team leads to the "headline" the team presents to the board when it wants the board's best thinking on the subject.

Great governance of any enterprise arises from collaboration between you, your board, and your top team. Your board, perhaps a formal corporate one, perhaps your informal personal one, convenes to:

- Establish trust and candor between the board and the top team.

- Exchange ideas.

- Clarify individual and collective expectations.

- Examine options for governance.

- Conduct joint review of decisions and actions.

- Review and revise performance standards for individual and the group.

Similar to a good marriage, sessions occur in an environment of love and respect, even when disagreements, debates, and even arguments break out. Governance without tension and dissonance is governance by control, not collaboration. A good catalyst champions candor and the discussion it engenders. A good catalyst banishes anger and resentment.

You handle dissonance by keeping the focus on authentic commitment to the mission of the business, commitment generated by boundary-crossing collaboration. Arch Wardlaw has built this competence. Av Wolsley has built this competence. So can you.

To help build your boundary competence, I suggest you take this short CEO Boundaries Quiz. Please keep in mind that the results suggest only a *general level* of competence, and provide just one basis for thinking about the ways you might improve managing in the land between. If you score high, don't feel smug. You can always do better. If you score low, don't slit your wrists. This may indicate a new beginning, your first steps toward a better Destiny.

Try to answer these 20 questions the way someone who knows you well, such as a board member, might answer on your behalf. That can enhance your objectivity. Circle the number that most accurately describes your behavior for each question. Ignore the small heart symbol (♥) for now. I'll explain this in a moment.

1. Are you comfortable when you're not in control of a situation?

| 4 | 3 | 2 | 1 |
|---|---|---|---|
| Usually | Often | Sometimes | Seldom |

2. In discussions with associates, do you hold your tongue until they complete their sentences?

| 4 | 3 | 2 | 1 |
|---|---|---|---|
| Usually | Often | Sometimes | Seldom |

3. Do you invest your vitality in collaborations with others?

| 4 | 3 | 2 | 1 |
|---|---|---|---|
| Usually | Often | Sometimes | Seldom |

4. Do you make use of your unique gift? ♥

| 4 | 3 | 2 | 1 |
|---|---|---|---|
| Usually | Often | Sometimes | Seldom |

5. Do you listen to your "inner voice" to learn what you care about down deep?

| 4 | 3 | 2 | 1 |
|---|---|---|---|
| Usually | Often | Sometimes | Seldom |

6. Are you able to give and receive "bad news" with good will?

| 4 | 3 | 2 | 1 |
|---|---|---|---|
| Usually | Often | Sometimes | Seldom |

7. Rather than consensus, do you seek the one option likely to produce distinctive results?

|   4    |   3   |     2     |    1   |
|--------|-------|-----------|--------|
| Usually | Often | Sometimes | Seldom |

8. Do you rid yourself of habitual behaviors that seem to get in your way?

|   4    |   3   |     2     |    1   |
|--------|-------|-----------|--------|
| Usually | Often | Sometimes | Seldom |

9. Do you have the patience to wait until the time is right?

|   4    |   3   |     2     |    1   |
|--------|-------|-----------|--------|
| Usually | Often | Sometimes | Seldom |

10. Do you remove or reassign mediocre performers in a timely fashion?

|   4    |   3   |     2     |    1   |
|--------|-------|-----------|--------|
| Usually | Often | Sometimes | Seldom |

11. Do you see value in people who disagree with you?

|   4    |   3   |     2     |    1   |
|--------|-------|-----------|--------|
| Usually | Often | Sometimes | Seldom |

12. Do you see your critics as your teachers?

|   4    |   3   |     2     |    1   |
|--------|-------|-----------|--------|
| Usually | Often | Sometimes | Seldom |

13. Do you treat failure as learning?

|   4    |   3   |     2     |    1   |
|--------|-------|-----------|--------|
| Usually | Often | Sometimes | Seldom |

14. Can you work and grow subject to an independent board?

|   4    |   3   |     2     |    1   |
|--------|-------|-----------|--------|
| Usually | Often | Sometimes | Seldom |

15. Do you have respect for your competitor?

| 4 | 3 | 2 | 1 |
|---|---|---|---|
| Usually | Often | Sometimes | Seldom |

16. Do you avoid bullying behavior?

| 4 | 3 | 2 | 1 |
|---|---|---|---|
| Usually | Often | Sometimes | Seldom |

17. Do you declare yes decisions without gloating and no decisions without apology?

| 4 | 3 | 2 | 1 |
|---|---|---|---|
| Usually | Often | Sometimes | Seldom |

18. Do you cultivate independence by your board members?

| 4 | 3 | 2 | 1 |
|---|---|---|---|
| Usually | Often | Sometimes | Seldom |

19. Do you believe yourself worthy of intervening in an associate's life? ♥

| 4 | 3 | 2 | 1 |
|---|---|---|---|
| Usually | Often | Sometimes | Seldom |

20. Are you at ease with others and yourself? ♥

| 4 | 3 | 2 | 1 |
|---|---|---|---|
| Usually | Often | Sometimes | Seldom |

| 20 to 29 | Stage 1 (Lost) Unaware and Inept. |
|---|---|
| 30 to 59 | Stage 2 (Found) Aware and Inept. |
| 60 to 69 | Stage 3 (Grounded) Aware and Adept. |
| 70 to 80 | Stage 4 (Masterful) Unaware and Adept. |

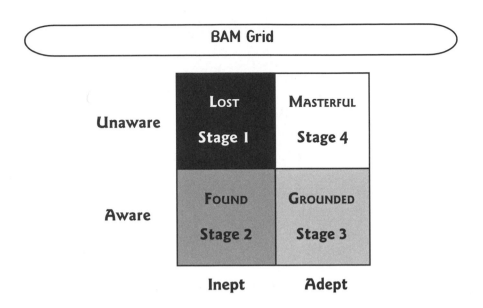

Total your score and then determine where it falls on the chart below:

Now what about those little ♥ symbols? These questions address the less tangible and harder to quantify subjective and emotional aspects of leadership; the ones that engage your heart more than your head. Let's explore each one a bit further.

♥**#4** *Do you make use of your unique gift?* The exploration of this question leads us into a brief foreshadowing of the subject of Chapter 8.

By models, I mean people who we want to emulate in some way. Models are naturals. They've connected with something authentic and unique inside themselves. We're fascinated just by the way they carry themselves. We learn more from what we see in them than from what we hear from them. Even if we do love to listen to them, we do so not just because of their wisdom, but the *way* in which they convey it.

Thirteenth century Persian poet, Rumi, wrote these two lines that capture the significance of the gift you have to give: *Be your note.*

I'll show you how it's enough.

The model is someone who has found her note and sings it to the world. Assuming you have done your homework and have discovered your Style-of-Life, and concluded that it constitutes a guardian presence, rather than a looming threat, you are already a model! You possess a gift you're already giving, often without even fully realizing the benefit others enjoy by making contact with you. You answered this question by circling 3 or 4. However, if you don't know your unique gift, you can't answer the question at a level above 1 or 2.

Models exist in all walks of life. I consider Paul McCartney an excellent one. I saw him perform live for the first time in Phoenix on his US 2005 Tour.

Was he good? Oh my, yes; absolutely superb, in fact. But think about it: He's not the best guitar player, piano player, or even songwriter in the world. He doesn't sing like an angel. But he fronts a drummer who eats the scenery and envelops the audience, two brilliant young guitar players who stoke the performance with stirring theatrics, and a genius of a musical director at the keyboard who plays a host of other instruments as well. He employs a manager, of course, and 120 staff behind, below, and in front of the concert stage, making sure everything down to the last incendiary detail comes off flawlessly.

The respect and comfort he and his fellow musicians enjoy with each other, the contact he and they make with the audience, and his soft, even boyish, understated charm pull us to him as he reaches out to us.

He connects. He's been there, seen it all, and knows what to make of it. He's a vision of mirthful, unequaled poise, a pop-performer. A natural? So good he doesn't know it? You bet.

♥ **#19** Do you believe yourself worthy of intervening in an associate's life?

Mentoring provides life-long learning in corporate life, though it often fails to provide all it could. Good mentors care for people and guide them without trying to control or micromanage their behavior and attitudes. Control or manipulation can only injure the learner's true self. However, many otherwise good mentors sometimes make the mistake of believing they're not qualified to intervene in an associate's life. This story of a desperately ill woman illustrates what I mean:

131

When I was in the hospital, the one person whose presence I welcomed was a woman who came to sweep the floors with a large push broom. Of the 50 or so people that made contact with me in any given day, she was the only one who wasn't trying to change me. One night she reached out and put her hand on the top of my shoulder. On her next visit, she looked at me. No evaluation, no trying to figure me out. She just looked and saw me. Then she said simply, "You're more than the sickness in that body." I kept mumbling those words to myself throughout the following day. I remember her voice clearly. "You're not the fear in that body. You're more than that fear. Float on it. Float above it. You're more than that pain." I remembered floating in Lake George when I was five, floating in the Atlantic Ocean at Coney Island when I was seven, floating in the Indian Ocean off the coast of Africa when I was 28. Without any instruction from me, this Jamaican guide had led me to a source of comfort that was wider and deeper than pain or fear. It's been 15 years since I've seen the woman with the broom. I've never been able to find her. No one could remember her name; but she touched my soul with her compassionate presence and her fingerprints are there still.

—From *No Enemies Within,*
Dawna Markova,
Conari Press, 1994.

♥ **#20** *Are you at ease with yourself and others?* Do you feel comfortable with your true self? If you do, others will, too. How do I know this? Because I experience it firsthand. Do I experience it all the time? No; sometimes I'm not at ease with some people, but that says more about me than it does about them. But I can say truthfully I experience it every day, and most of my days entail meeting strangers, as well as people, whom I've known for decades.

Knowing my personal pilgrimage from earlier pages, it will come as no surprise to anyone who asks how to gain ease with their self that I say: "Meet your real self first." When that happens, as I've tried to show in discussing these three "intangible" questions, you naturally present yourself more authentically, and people appreciate sharing that self. The Jamaican guide beautifully presented herself, and that self helped heal another.

In my endless quest for my real self, late one night in an open air bar in St. Barts, I turned to my wife, Cher, and said, "I don't give comfort." I thought I'd discovered a second looming threat. I was referring to a shortcoming I'd excavated as a CEO coach. A few days later, I realized it wasn't a second looming threat, just a sub-set of the one I shared earlier: *to be safe.*

I didn't give comfort because I was withholding. I wasn't transparent, letting the chips fall where they may. I found that "giving comfort" meant giving myself. Hints don't work. The "angler" self at the time meant my sharp eye saw my way into situations. "Life is tricky" meant I was sophisticated on complexity and tradeoffs. "To be safe" meant I sought to play the odds expertly, without getting killed, and come out a survivor, if not a true champion. Bottom line: I lived a compromised life. I was far from *at ease.*

### In this chapter you have learned that:

➡ As a younger person, you can take eight specific steps *today* to prepare yourself to become a CEO who provides the energy source between your board and top team.

➡ A new era of accountability has emerged, and along with it, the need for you as CEO to serve as the catalyst between your board and top team in a way that prevents an adversarial climate.

➡ Your board meetings offer a genuine idea exchange opportunity for boards and top teams.

➡ You can invite your board to revise their self-image, climate, and housing by examining a template from an expert (Pat Canavan of Motorola).

➡ You will accomplish more with less control, by relinquishing the *illusion* of control.

**Your Inner CEO Punch List**

❐ Establish in your mind if, for the most part, the changes I've described in this chapter require you to assume a new role as catalyst between your board and top team. If you don't think so, skip #2 and #3.

❐ Review the Let It Happen list. Do they seem weak to you? Strong? If they strike you as strong, you will make a good catalyst.

❐ Learn to operate as a star collaborator. It doesn't come easily to most CEOs, or anybody else. Don't beat yourself up if you feel you don't know where to start. Get help. You'll be in good company.

❐ Are you a bully? If so, how does that abuse power?

❐ What role will you play to make sure your team forges its point of view in preparation for board meetings?

# 6

# Visions

*We may be lost, but we're making good time.*

—Yogi Berra

Some years ago, I delivered a keynote speech at the annual management meeting of one of our leading east coast pharmaceuticals companies. Although I was scheduled to appear in the afternoon, the company's CEO asked me to arrive the night before so I could eavesdrop on the morning session to get more of a feel for the company, and to hear the senior vice president of strategic planning present the firm's "New Vision." I welcomed the invitation, but couldn't work up enthusiasm for what I assumed would turn into little more than a cheerleader's pep talk.

Sure enough, this is what came up on the screen:

> ➤ **Slide 1:** What drives our company?
>
> ➤ **Slide 2:** Who do we want to be?
>
> ➤ **Slide 3:** How do we get there?

When thinking about the future of their businesses, CEOs and their teams most often start with these three questions. There's nothing wrong with them, but they don't strike at the heart of "the vision thing." Real vision depends on asking two deeper questions first: "Who are we?" and "Where are we headed right now?" If the goal revealed by these questions serves as a guardian presence, then the company can switch on the hyper drive. However, if it's a looming threat, the company can take corrective action.

Sadly, my pharmaceutical client failed to ask the right questions first, and ended up an acquisition of a much larger, but unsuitable partner that eventually devalued the whole enterprise with its own poor vision. As you know by now, you have to do a lot of painstaking homework before you and your associates can confidently answer the basic questions that rightly precede all others. Otherwise, you will never develop 20/20 vision.

## Corporate Magnetism

In Chapters 1 and 3, I describe how, as individuals and corporations, we're governed by a central goal. In particular, in Chapter 3 I urged you to begin ascertaining your company's central goal by observing two models, USG and Obelisk, then pretending to apply your CEO skills to the fictitious Quest Music. In this chapter and the next, you'll finish that task by focusing on the organization that currently employs you.

All goals lie at the end of the playing field. As we play the game, as we take action (or contemplate taking action), that goal looms in the future, whether we see it or not.

It doesn't matter if the payoff takes one second or 10 years. Whether I quickly step aside to avoid an out-of-control skateboarder, zooming toward me down the slight incline of the sidewalk on Chicago's Michigan Avenue, or your CEO spends a decade carefully nurturing, three executives so that at least one of them will qualify to succeed him, both actions seek their purpose—their goal—in the future. I use the verb *seek* deliberately, because it suggests *consciously* stepping into the future with your eyes fixed on the true goal.

I cringe whenever I hear someone talking about what drives them or their company. That's the wrong word, the wrong way of thinking about the future. The force acting on you or your company is not a wind at your back, but rather a magnet on the horizon, *pulling you forward into the future*. Everything you and your associates *do* today, or ever have *done* in all the days and years past, drew you inexorably toward some goal.

When asked to state their goals, most people describe little more than their good intentions, which usually go the way of most New Year's resolutions: nowhere fast. However, if you accept my proposition that individuals and organizations are governed by a central goal they may not even know exists, a central one that controls all intermediate ones, and that you and your associates endorse it by virtue of your actions, then you have to find a way to see it clearly. Only then can you decide whether it's a looming threat or a guardian presence.

Now we're going to play a little game where we explore how you, yourself, and your company ("YC") can use vision to isolate your central goal and the future toward which it pulls you. Who you want to be as a company (be it a company of one or a multinational) produces who you are now. But here's the trick: does who you *say* you want to be match who you really *are*? If you honestly examine and name your *actions,* your actual behavior and decisions, you'll stand a much better chance of figuring out the goal. If you *know* who you want to be, then you can determine *if it is right* or *wrong* for you.

I don't want to dismiss YC's past, however, because looking at the past does force you to appreciate what actions you took in YC's history to meet *goals* back then. What you wanted to accomplish at that time, good or bad, told you who you were and where you were headed *then.* Those goals may or may not support YC's central goal today.

Remember Karen and Jason from Chapter 4? They belong to a "company of two," a marriage. Sadly, Jason's habit of ignoring Karen's requests for communication, and his stalling whenever she asked him to do something for their marriage resulted in a separation. When Jason tallies and dates examples of distancing himself from his wife, he realizes that his behavior reflected the magnetic pull of a dark, unknown, and distasteful goal: separation. When he turns and replaces it with a bright goal true to his heart's desire (reconciliation), he also replaces the way he defines himself, "Distancer," with "Partner," a designation that conforms to the pull of the brighter goal.

Hidden goals, revealed goals; old self (past), new self (future); it all depends on clear vision of both who and where you were yesterday, serving what goal, and who and where you will go tomorrow; again, serving what goal. If you gain such vision, you may, with a lot of concentrated effort, transform a looming threat into a guardian presence.

No, your company is perfect. Jason will suffer setbacks, but at least his vision has cleared. For example, it's likely he'll discover from this exercise that he distances himself from other people as well, with somewhat the same result: separation or termination of a boss, job, or an old friendship. No corporation is perfect either, but in the pages ahead we'll imagine that the hypothetical Angus Corporation practices almost perfect vision. The exaggeration simplifies our exercise in the early going, and allows us to grasp Angus's Style-of-Life, and what values have prevailed throughout its past. Bear in mind, though, that YC may have started off with exemplary values, just as Angus did, but got lost, just like Jason did, somewhere between the altar and a single bed in a lonely apartment.

## Angus Corporation

**1933:** In the depths of the Depression, 27-year-old Harold Angus and his younger brother, Morton, quit their jobs with a coal mine in West Virginia in order to promote a conveyor system for coal and ores that Harold had been tinkering with in his garage for more than two years. Patent in hand, the brothers envisioned a rich future, especially when their former employer bought their contraption for $2,000.

**1935:** Finally, after several lengthy car and train trips, and a raft of promising, but ultimately disappointing sales calls, and reaching the point where they grew increasingly worried about their future, they sold a second machine to a large company with far-flung operations. Two weeks later, the customer ordered 10 more.

**1935:** The Angus brothers hired five employees, rented a small shop, and with a loan from their local bank, bought used manufacturing and assembly equipment.

**1936:** The brothers developed a reputation for honest dealing and willingness to experiment, and adapt their equipment to industries and plants outside of mining, eagerly re-engineering their products for new applications.

**1938:** Angus Brothers Corporation moves its headquarters to Charleston, West Virginia, where it built a new plant from scratch. With the company employing 90 people, Harold oversees the manufacturing operation as president, earning a reputation in the industry as a product engineering genius. Morton takes charge of sales and crisscrosses the country, endlessly writing orders and opening new doors. The company impresses customers with its extraordinary field service staff and rapid distribution of new and replacement parts.

**1941:** The war effort generates record sales, propelling spectacular growth. By 1945, the company employs 3,000 people in eight plants nationwide, 30 percent of them women. Everyone loves working at Angus Brothers.

**1948:** Angus Brothers Corporation becomes Angus Corporation. When Morton dies of a sudden heart attack, Harold replaces him with Les Garton, a non-family member, rather than either of his two sons or Morton's son, all three of whom work in the business.

**1955:** The company exceeds $1.5 billion in sales, having now diversified into the construction equipment business by buying a top quality back-hoe maker, Jupiter Task-Master, and a large company, Road Rock, that makes highway paving machinery.

**1961:** When the company goes public, Harold becomes chairman and CEO, and Les Garton, president, seems his likely successor. The three Angus sons leave the business, wealthy with Angus Corporation stock.

**1966:** At the age of 59, Harold, wealthy beyond the wildest youthful vision of a high-school dropout, now serves as chairman of the board of trustees of West Virginia University, and proves to be a remarkable fund-raiser. Retiring to become assistant secretary of defense in President Lyndon Johnson's administration, he leaves behind a company that *Business Week* has declared one the 100 "Best Companies to Work For," and *Forbes* ranks it 16th in the nation's fastest growth, big cap companies. He's also the featured interview in the July-August issue of *Harvard Business Review* under the headline "Big Business Leader Leads the Balanced Life: How Does He Do It?" *Fortune* calls Angus Corporation a model of social responsibility. Les Garton replaces Harold as chairman and CEO.

**2007:** A portrait of the late Harold Angus hangs in the Angus boardroom, an inspiration to all who gaze upon it. The company he founded and built first through his own efforts, then through others who shared his estimable values, has grown into a global leader known favorably throughout the world. Unlike so many entrepreneurs, Harold knew how to let go, to trust others to get the job done.

Angus Corporation was Harold Angus's YC. What made it tick?

**Possible Angus Corporation Style-of-Life**

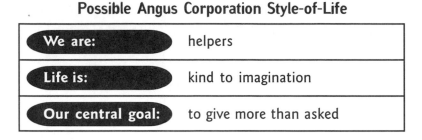

| We are: | helpers |
|---|---|
| Life is: | kind to imagination |
| Our central goal: | to give more than asked |

Likely Angus values: courage, tenacity, industry, innovation, service-mindedness, flexibility, optimism, trustworthiness, gratefulness, resourcefulness, decisiveness, experimentation, and warmth.

———

While no individual or company, no YC, can practice such positive values 24/7, 365 a year, they regularly diminish any negative values such as hypocrisy, manipulation, and arrogance that may pop up from time to time. When dark forms arise as looming threats, bright forms as a guardian presence usually confront and conquer them.

## Getting to the Kitchen

Remember questions two and three (Who do we want to be? How do we get there?) asked by the company I visited at the opening of this chapter? They are not wrong in themselves, but they mislead us if we ask them before we have gathered the information to answer them accurately. Because they're normally the first questions top management asks when they convene to formulate and articulate YC's vision, and because nobody can supply truly accurate answers, they lead the team to make up stuff that sounds good: "We want to be #1, we'll get there with top talent." Sometimes "vision teams" do this just to please their CEO; they don't believe it in their hearts either, yet it ends up dominating their company's rhetoric. Illusion replaces reality, creating fertile soil for the growth of looming threats.

So let's take YC back to the two more fundamental questions:

- Who are we?
- Where are we headed?

Are we #1? No, we're #5. Will we get to #1 with top talent? Not unless we recruit more talent. Until then we're headed for #6 or #7. See the difference? The two wrong questions lead to illusion and poor vision, the two more fundamental ones lead to reality and clear vision. It takes a lot of good, honest effort for you and your associates to answer the right questions with precision, but, trust me, it's worth it. Your future depends on it.

Suppose YC has successfully built and marketed fine furniture for 75 years. Envisioning growth, you think you might easily double your net profit by acquiring a large *casual* furniture company. However, since the distribution channels, manufacturing processes, customer outlook, marketing mindset, and sales force requirements for casual products differ so markedly from those for fine products, such a takeover might conflict with who you are (not who you want to be, but who you actually are). The wrong questions might tempt you to plunge ahead, while the right questions might make you pause for deeper reflection.

If you discover (and believe in) who YC is, and where YC is really heading, blow the bugle. Plunge ahead. If you don't, blow the whistle. Pause for deeper reflection. Sounds like a boundary doesn't it? If you carefully follow this sequence, you'll place yourself in a select group of executives who, literally, *know* their business. You'll possess clear vision.

As you've seen, the "Who do we want to be and how do we get there?" questions represent the second half of the vision equation. Philip Roth puts it nicely: when you're writing a novel, he observes:

> You're sort of like a busboy in a restaurant, loaded up with dirty dishes—and blindfolded. The guy says, "Find the kitchen." Well, you may or may not have an accident on the way. If you get to the kitchen and get to the dishwasher, it's an enormous feat.

That captures the plight of the captain of YC, or the CEO and his team.

You're trying to see where you're going while blindfolded; you want to get to the desired destination, you're burdened with baggage and have to navigate a crooked path through dangerous and unseen obstacles.

141

How will you get to your own kitchen, to that place where you know who you are, where you're headed, who you want to be, and how you can get there? You might just do it by heeding a Chinese proverb.

## Wisdom of a Chinese Proverb

In my work I use a lot of metaphors when I talk about vision, but two of my favorites are the microscope and the telescope.

Whenever leaders ask the two wrong questions first (Who do we want to be? and, How do we get there?) they're looking at YC through a telescope, a scanning from here to "out there" over the horizon, to the rainbow. Whatever answers they see always sound so good, they rush to make them public.

Don't get me wrong. Vision "out there" plays a critical role in leading YC to greatness. But vision "in-here," what you see peering through a microscope, comes first. If it doesn't, the rhetoric won't match or sufficiently overlap the company's essence. If essence prevails (it always does), top management ends up wondering what the hell happened! Remember our left-hand, right-hand circles?

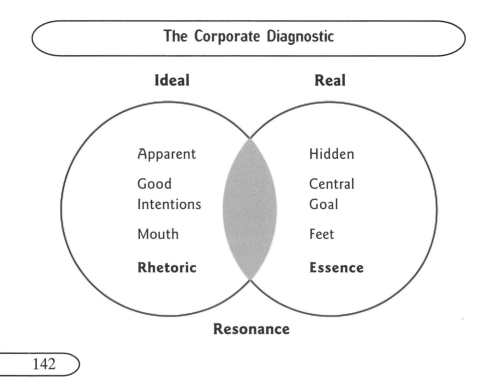

The microscopic view, the one that studies what's inside and you and YC, provides the foundation for figuring out the "who are we" and "where are we headed" questions, the first ones you ask. Only then can you fully appreciate the telescopic view. The one that searches out there rather than in here. Looking deep inside, not across valleys, you begin to discern an excruciating level of detail, focused on the here-and-now, the way it is, for better or worse. It's an unblinking, detached reading of actions and, in turn, of values. Our actions, and the accurate articulation of values that we glean from those actions, tell us who we are and where we're headed. I call this *Vision Here-and-Now.* Though it gets short shrift, it's at least as important as the telescopic follow-through vision that I call *Vision There-and-Then.*

Meditate for a moment on this ancient Chinese proverb: "Unless we change our direction, we are likely to end up where we are headed."

Sounds a little like Yogi Berra doesn't it? "When you come to a fork in the road, take it!" However, the proverb contains a lot of wisdom. It makes no judgment as to whether the direction is good or bad. It is just what it is. It also expresses the fact that your present action will take you to a certain destination, whether you realize it or not. You are going somewhere, perhaps in a direction you think you're *not* going, but are. The more you think about it, the more complicated it gets.

You can see how confusion, dissonance, and wasted motion can occur in YC when you believe you're going one way, while in fact, you are heading in another, slightly off-course direction. Eventually, you wind up totally lost. Whatever the width of divergence, it contradicts the official rhetoric and makes you feel ill at ease, even if you cannot put your finger on just what makes you uncomfortable.

You are well aware that most people find it hard to see themselves as clearly as others do, thus outsiders can sometimes see this unease more clearly than we can. We just row merrily along, carried in the stream, never heeding the uneasy feeling that a steep waterfall lies around the next bend. At the conclusion of World War II, the world's citizens gasped in shock when they learned about Hitler's holocaust in Germany and Stalin's genocide in Russia. Citizens in those two nations apologized profusely, all the while wondering, "What were we *thinking?!*" As you sail toward your future, you want to make sure you know what you're thinking.

## Fourth Presbyterian Church of Chicago

YCs come in all shapes and sizes: individuals, small businesses, global conglomerates, government, and not-for-profit organizations. Fourth Presbyterian, a large, complex, urban church in downtown Chicago, provides a fascinating example of the last category. Some years ago, I undertook a *pro-bono* assignment with this congregation, helping them re-craft their mission and chart a new future.

Fourth Presbyterian Church (FPC) opened its doors for its first worship service on Sunday morning October 8, 1871. That night it burned to the ground, consumed in the historic Great Chicago Fire, a conflagration that destroyed 2,124 acres, or very nearly 3 1/3 square miles, and turned 17,450 buildings into ashes, leaving 98,500 people homeless, and killing more than 100 people. The congregation rebuilt the church, then in 1914, moved to its current location on North Michigan Avenue in the heart of Chicago's "Gold Coast." Since then, this church has had only four senior pastors, an amazing average tenure of 23 years per each. The current pastor, John Buchanan, who has now served 22 years, wanted to build the Church's future on the foundation of its distinguished history.

Since 1985, when Buchanan came on board, FPC boasted these achievements:

 ▶ Membership more than doubled from 2,600 to 5,400 (from 1996 to 2006 the Presbyterian Church, USA membership declined by 13 percent from 2.6 million to 2.3 million).

 ▶ Endowment grew 3.5 times its 1986 value.

 ▶ Giving by members to annual operations quadrupled.

 ▶ A major building renovation and expansion project came in on-time and on-budget.

 ▶ A successful $14 million capital campaign completely paid for renovation.

 ▶ Partners in Education, created in 1992, raised funds from corporations and foundations that had not formerly donated to religious institutions. Renamed Chicago Lights with expanded programming, this undertaking operates with a $1.6 million budget, with 20 percent coming from corporate and foundation sources.

- A current capital campaign has raised $ 25 million in cash and pledges to date.

- A parcel of land purchased in the Cabrini Green neighborhood will be used to build a community center for residents of the Chicago Housing Authority.

- A newly created Academy for Faith and Life to enhance the education of church members.

John Buchanan, a gifted leader and preacher, does not get all the credit for these accomplishments. Rather, he, with his gifts and capable leadership, has confirmed, strengthened, and extended the values that have always ruled this great historic congregation. To learn more about the church's ministry as a neighbor in Chicago, and as a force around the world, go to *www.fourthchurch.org*.

When I consulted with John Buchanan, I used many of the procedures described in Chapter 3 when I unfolded the story of USG. However, in addition to asking the program staff (Buchanan's "top team") for their "animal analogies," I asked them to capture their perceptions of the church in a single word. Their responses included: encouragement, interaction, organism, catalyst, growth, treasure, continuity, coalescence, care, substantive, strength, WORD, trust, urban.

**Keel-of-Boat Values**

**Keel**

Then I asked them what themes these words suggested to them. Did they shed light on the organization's behavior and offer clues to deep-seated values? I wanted them to think about FPC's "keel-of-the-boat" values. "Think of a sailboat," I said. "You don't see its keel because it is underwater, but it gives the boat direction." It looks something like the upside-down tip of an iceberg.

The themes identified by FPC's top team gave clues to the values that serve as "keel" to this ministry: continuous and dynamic movement, stability in troubled water, immersion in urban issues, grassroots community involvements, empowerment for change, true to Christ's teaching, energizing and fulfilling care, confident place in community/ability to minister (self-esteem).

These phrases painted a rosy picture, but John Buchanan felt the organization's actions did not match the rhetoric; that is why he approached me. Who are we? Where are we headed? Who do we want to be? How will we get there? By asking these questions in the proper order, the FPC team began to see some unfulfilled expectations, a treasure not fully opened.

As we worked together, the organization's real values began to emerge above the surface, including a vague sense of concern for lack of results in some areas, and not living up to all the positive rhetoric. Bringing this line of investigation to a close, I asked them *what these themes help explain* about their relationship with the church. Some of their answers surprised us. The themes, some said, explain: Why I'm tired; why members walk away; why staff is so intensely involved; why we don't trust members more for performance; why we're not just one body, but a collection of "power-filled" churches; why trust between staff/members is increasing; why we're not petty; why we're all here; why we have a heavy sense of responsibility; why we're not always willing to share it; why we feel tension between being "pastoral' and "practical." You get the picture: There are some gaps between who we are and who we think we are.

FPC's strong lay committees meet as an entire body once every other month. A few weeks after my retreat with the top team, about 125 people met one night to hear a report on our mission deliberations and offer their thoughts on some rudimentary new mission statements; the discussion proved lively and productive.

Eventually, the staff appointed a seven-member task-force to draft a final mission. John Buchanan chaired the meeting, which I attended as an advisor. The final draft, completed in an hour, captured FPC's clarified vision:

> We are a light in the city reflecting the inclusive love of God. Comforted and challenged by the Gospel of Christ, we strive to be a welcoming, serving community. At the intersection of faith and life, we share God's grace through worship, preaching, education and ministries of healing, reconciliation and justice. We affirm

the worth of all and nurture each individual's spiritual pilgrimage. Inspired by our heritage, we confront our future with hope and confidence in God's purpose.

## Clarifying YC's Vision

Every savvy YC will do what John Buchanan did: take a blank sheet of paper and draw a grid like the one below. In the left column you'll fill out the blanks with single words that describe YC. Try to come up with many alternatives on your own, and ask friends, family, associates, and colleagues for contributions. As you fill in that one-word description on the left side, complement it on the right with phrases that support that one-word description; for example, one staff member at Fourth Presbyterian Church, who offered the word *yeast* for the bread of change. One, who chose *substantive,* supported that choice with "Weight/presence/resources to feed." The one who responded with *urban* said, "We're a real city church."

### YC Identity Kit

| One-Word Identity | What Justifies That Choice? |
|---|---|
|  |  |
|  |  |
|  |  |
|  |  |
|  |  |
|  |  |
|  |  |

I'll ask for a little patience at this point. I know you're anxious to chart a brighter future for YC, but before you can do that in the next chapter, you first need to carefully examine YC's current focus and decide whether or not it's the right one. To do this, you can use a simple tool I learned about 15 years ago from Wally Olins's book *Corporate Identity.* Olins's firm, Saffron, is a London-based, leader-of-the pack, global reach consultancy, that helps corporations and nations comprehend and declare their identities, *most importantly to their own people,* as well as to external audiences such as suppliers, customers, the general public, and world neighbors. I felt a kinship with Olins when I read his words, because they so closely paralleled my own. In a nutshell, he proposed that the best corporate mission assures self-discovery. Sounds like vintage Allan Cox doesn't it?

Olins goes on to say that all corporations that succeed have to be capable and resourceful in four areas: (1) product or service *distinction*; (2) environment; (3) *communication* of their product or service; and (4) behavior. Any company that falters in being proficient *in all four* will finally fail.

But here's the catch: To excel, a company will achieve superiority in *one* of these four areas, above all others. It will know it, declare it, and build its structures and systems around that knowledge and declaration. To say it another way, for a company to shine, it can't neglect any of these four areas, but it will be dominant as the acknowledged leader in its industry by mastering one of these four.

Porsche offers a shining example of *product distinction*. Some sports cars cost more than a Porsche, some less. Some, such as a Maserati, are even more exclusive, but a Porsche stands as a car recognized by most people as a symbol of quality. The feel and smell of the leather seats, the tightness and responsiveness of its handling, and the firm design all combine to make it a unique, rich partnership with its owner. A few years back, I remember the president of Porsche, Peter Schutz, stating that the company views its competition more like second homes and sailboats than as other sports cars. Porsche could not succeed without providing customers with a good environment in the car itself, its showrooms, and repair shops; effective communications and promotions about the product itself; and the behavior of its employees with each other and its customers. Yet without the superior product (the Porsche), the company would be just another car company.

Porsche stands out on the product side. A distinctive service organization, one that provides a service unmatched by any other in its category, is Caltech. Caltech stands alone as a tight, brilliant engineering school.

Starbucks is an example of a "Killer Category." It possesses all the four qualities, too, but its extraordinary success stems primarily from the singular *environment* it provides its customers. The Starbucks handheld cup has become such a status symbol that when a customer carries it into the workplace, she carries some of that environment with her.

For a wonderful example of world-class *communication,* take a look at Coca-Cola. Basically, this one-of-a-kind global company sells little more than flavored water. But Coke displays amazing skill of making us think Coke is "it" and "the real thing," and that by consuming it we can "teach the world to sing." This past Christmas, my wife said to me, "You know that Santa Claus I saw in Coke commercials when I was a child? To me, that's the real Santa!"

Harley-Davidson also communicates splendidly. Even non-bikers recognize the aura and culture surrounding their "hogs." Resplendent with tattoos of the company's logo on their arms, their riders dominate a macho national bikers rally in Sturgis, South Dakota each summer. Said one conventioneer a couple of years ago, "If you're not living on the edge, you're taking up too much room!"

When it comes to superior *behavior,* Southwest Airlines has overhauled its industry and created numerous copiers. The company that promises we're free to move about the country, at very reasonable fares, succeeds because of the behavior of its people, who stand ready to make the flying experience as satisfactory as possible.

Can an elephant sprint and glide like a gazelle? Not in a million years, right? But companies, like people, and perhaps like YC, often try to be who they're not, trying to do something they can't (or hope to) do, going in the wrong direction. Think of a Kentucky Derby thoroughbred bolting from the stall, only to have his jockey turn him around and race off in the opposite direction. Seems absurd, but companies do it all the time.

No matter how well you and your associates know your company, search for *revelation* as you try to define your "here-and-now" vision. *Revelation can clear the mist from your eyes.* Then, if you pay attention to what's revealed, you'll less likely embark on a misguided "there-and-then" visionary quest. You'll know what you're thinking.

If you want to redefine vision to ensure that it's authentic and compelling, you have to work hard work to cross boundaries with vulnerability and courage. You are an elephant? Get used to it. Rely on your true strength.

I doubt you'll be surprised that articulating both "here-and-now" and "there-and-then" vision takes more than a little haggling, even heated, good-faith collaboration. Nobody's smart enough or has cornered enough intuition and judgment to achieve revelation alone. However, you can make a good start by considering to what degree you possess the four necessary qualities listed by Wally Olins. Does anything you discover help you name *one* as the quality in which YC excels? Yes? How will you nurture that natural tendency and skillfully use it to support the other three? Elephants may not be gazelles, but that doesn't mean gazelles are *better* than elephants (and vice versa).

Think and feel alone. Think and feel together. Head and heart. Heart and head.

Then complete the YC Qualities Chart.

| YC Qualities Chart | |
|---|---|
| **Quality (Choose One)** | **The Degree to Which You Display It** |
| Superior Product or Service? | |
| Environment? | |
| Communication? | |
| Behavior? | |

Which, if any, of these stands out from the rest? Circle the one that seems most dominant, then try to rank the others 2, 3, and 4. Don't expect a perfectly clear picture, but do look for clues that will help you detect your true identity—elephant, gazelle, or some other image, such as a scrabble board. Though it may require Olympian effort, the payoff will be worth it.

## An Olympian Effort

I've found that achieving true corporate self-discovery almost always requires an Olympian effort and the endurance of a marathon. But I've also found that every YC who does it reaps a terrific benefit.

If it came easily, everyone would have done it by now, and we'd be living in a heaven on earth. You'll remember the late David Ogilvy, my favorite advertising icon who appeared in Chapter 3. If he could look over our shoulders, he would say, "Grasp the nettle!" A little pain? A lot of gain!

You can scarcely discern your corporation's true essence (the vitality that's lodged in the right circle) by using rhetorical methods (the ideal, perhaps the illusion lodged in the left circle). For example, if you and your associates try to uncover who you are by listing your "corporate values," you'll probably end up with, pardon me, pure blather. All the usual "wannabe" stuff is just that: woulda, coulda, shoulda, blah, blah, blah. It's ideal, not real.

Now do this: For the time being, pull yourself away from championing and defending YC. Yield your attachments to the past, your traditional blinders, your house slogans, all the *fictions* you've manufactured about your identity, qualities, and purpose.

Instead, become a detached participant, a well-wishing mentor, an "identity doctor" accurately diagnosing YC's behavior and actions. This will help elicit clues about your *true* values, your *lived* values, your *actual* behavior.

Some will be positive. Others will be negative.

*We are what we do.*

If you and your associates will commit yourselves to this sort of detached diagnosis—discovering YC's actual behavior—you'll stand a much better chance of developing the best prescription for a healthier future. Ask these questions:

▶ What do we *do* here?

▶ What worrisome decisions have we made?

▶ How often do we make decisions *like this*? Do they fit a pattern? Who makes them?

▶ What decisions have we avoided or refused to make?

▶ Which decisions do we make quickly? Which ones take longer? Why?

▶ How do we treat outsiders, visitors, consultants, new hires? How long does it take them before they feel welcomed?

▶ What frightens us?

▶ Do we talk the talk, but fail to walk the walk?

▶ Do we walk the walk, but fail to talk the talk?

▶ Who gets hired/fired/promoted/ignored?

▶ Have we created taboos here? What gets you written off, fired, or sent to Siberia without a hearing?

▶ What brings out our best?

▶ What brings out our worst?

Of course, you could dream up hundreds of such questions. Create your own list. Put some dispassionate people (people who want real answers, even discomforting ones) to work drafting a tailor-made questionnaire for YC. Relax. Get playful. Have fun. There's no law that says introspection has to be painful, boring, and distasteful. If YC answers the questions with humility and candor, you'll create an x-ray of your company, the sort of evaluative tool a good surgeon would use before making an incision.

When discussing and answering your particular questions, keep our picture of the two circles in mind. What's ideal? What's not? What's apparent? What's hidden? What represents rhetoric and good intention? What reveals YC's central issue? When do the ideal and real overlap? Tread carefully, though: don't listen to your words, watch your feet.

| Mouth | Feet |
|---|---|
| We're committed to new products! | The truth? We're harvesters. We haven't brought a new product to market in three years. |
| Our return on equity looks great. | Honestly? We've cut R&D 30 percent the last two years; and haven't built a new plant in the last decade. We're robbing Peter to pay Paul. |
| We're bold! | Reality? We bluster because we're scared to death! |
| Or... | |
| We're duller than dirt. We haven't done anything innovative in years! | Actually? Our industry is more than a hundred years old. We started it, and we've navigated through three major industry shifts in that time. We led the way every time, and all our competitors ate our dust. Dull? Make that permanent! Solid. Indestructible. Adaptable. |

By carefully sorting out disparities between what your mouth says and where your feet tread, between positive and negative values, and by not recoiling from what you see that you don't like, you can begin to feed your malnourished strengths until they crowd out your overfed limitations. In my experience, when a great company has gone astray, you can always find people in the wings with a healthy appetite for rejuvenation. With the first credible signal, they stand ready to recapture lost excellence. It's *your* job to feed them.

**In this chapter you have learned:**

→ That true vision comes in two phases: first, vision here-and-now, and second, vision there-and-then.

→ The force acting on your company (YC) does not drive from behind you, but pulls you forward like a magnet.

→ Who we are as a company now is the single best indicator of who we're going to be.

→ Keel-of-boat values lie beneath the waterline where we can't see them, but they control direction nonetheless.

→ For YC to excel, it will become pre-eminent in one of four key qualities: product or service, environment, communication, or behavior.

**Your Inner CEO Punch List**

☐ Ask yourself if what you truly want for your company is right or wrong.

☐ Shy away from hollow rhetoric. Dig for some values in your company you know are right, helped your company survive, but now live only on life support. Also dig for values that are wrong, that have led you astray.

☐ Conduct a dispassionate diagnosis of your company's identity and values. Plot how you can begin to crowd out overfed limitations with replenished strengths.

# 7

# Futures

*The real voyage of discovery consists not in seeking*
*new landscapes, but in having new eyes.*

—Marcel Proust

I believe wholeheartedly in Ockham's Razor, the philosophical principle that for any complicated situation, the simplest explanation is the best one to choose. Consider the power of simple ideas captured in a few words: Winston Churchill's admonition to all Britons that the war effort required "blood, sweat, and tears." That image rallied a nation.

In education and the world of training and development, the expression is: Repetition is the key to learning. The quality movement in business insists that you "do it right the first time." And most basic, people honor the maxim "time is money."

When it comes to crafting the actual Style-of-Life, visualize your mission for your company (YC). I respect architect Louis Sullivan's observation "Form ever follows function." In biology the shape of a wing, a fin, a tooth, and a claw grows out of its owner's need to fly, swim, bite, or scratch. In your application of YC's mission, you'll look at how its visible form (a wing) emerges from a need to accomplish something (to fly).

Sullivan, a genius who mentored Frank Lloyd Wright, and himself the father of the skyscraper, created buildings that weren't just works of art to the eye, but marvels of human engineering. He and Alfred Adler would have gotten along well, I think. Sullivan called it "function," Adler called it "goal." They both meant purpose.

In his own field, Sullivan didn't mean that architects always design structures that correctly anticipate their use, but that no matter how you design a building, its *form* would undergo change to serve its actual *purpose.* This actual *use,* to which people put the structure (function), whether properly foreseen or not, whether good or bad, would eventually affect its form, not sometimes, but, in Sullivan's view, *always:* "Form ever follows function." Each word counts, the four together express a powerful idea.

Reflect, a moment on your hypothetical experience at Quest Music, where, as CEO, you served as the company's "architect." Think about its structure. It may not have been a sprawling multinational conglomerate, but it did have its complexities: several operating locations, a variety of products and customers, and a serious marketing challenge.

Picture Quest's people, each with an ax to grind, and with a stake in the events. Imagine its history, its competitive environment, and its internal structure, the machinations of which defy easy understanding. When you came aboard, you didn't know at all how to turn this dysfunctional organization around. From working with the Corporate Diagnostic model, you know that when someone says "things didn't go according to plan," someone made the wrong call on function. It also happened back in Chapter 4 (see item #13 on the Boundary Reality Check), when the company that funded a cultural center for its community, saw it fail, then reopen successfully as a senior center. Purpose emerged, form changed. Forgive me if I repeat myself, but in the spirit of Ockham's Razor: purpose, goal, function—they all mean the same thing.

## The Future "Causes" the Present

Back in Chapter 1, I said that *the future gives birth to the present.* Did that puzzle you at the time? It runs counter to our conventional belief that the past gives birth to the present, and the present gives birth to the future. However, when you think of the future as a magnet, you realize that it *pulls* you toward it. The past doesn't drive you to the present; the future pulled you here. This is crucial because the mental shift it requires does more than anything else to release your inner CEO.

The Chinese proverb from the last chapter holds that YC's present situation foretells its future: "Unless we change our direction, we are likely to end up where we are headed."

Does this mean that the past gives birth to the future? Not if you accept the fact that YC's people are being pulled toward a goal that defines a particular future. The question then arises: Will that future shine brightly, or will it cast YC into darkness and despair?

Try this mental game. Suppose you're relaxing on the deck of a luxury cruise ship when you hear the hull creaking and suddenly think, "Titanic!" Without even thinking consciously about it, you'll automatically locate the lifeboats. Your gut-level belief (not the captain's placating rhetoric) about the future determines present actions: the future gives birth to the present.

If you don't like the *who* in the "who we are today," you don't like the goal, purpose, or function that's pulling you off course. If so, change it, and replace it with one that taps into YC's malnourished positive values. Such values Charley Hunter revived at Obelisk. *You can revive them at YC.*

Once you find and name that new goal, YC's direction automatically will change as a new magnet pulls it forward. Who will you be? Who you *are.* Change your goal and you will change who you need to be in order to be a better you in the future. To put it another way, a better future gives birth to a better present. Does this make your head hurt? Don't worry about it; it made my head hurt when I first discovered it too.

If the luxury cruise passenger senses no danger, he won't go looking for lifeboats. He'll keep relaxing in the hot tub, gazing contentedly at the horizon. In your work where organization horizons may lie much further away than on a pleasure trip, the same rule applies. The central goal of YC shapes who YC is, and how it acts in the present.

Earlier, we saw USG take action through affirming itself as an explorer, constantly adding knowledge and strengthening itself to cover great "distances" in both miles and time, discovering significant alternatives all along the way.

USG, YC, or any individual can take action only in the present. Yesterday has vanished, and tomorrow has not yet arrived. USG's guardian presence goal shapes the day-by-day actions that add up over time, and leads it to a future payoff. Their goal is their magnet that pulls them to a green field instead of a wasteland. Get the goal right, and you'll get yourself and your business right.

Many YC's lack the full awareness of that's where they *are*, right *there*, in a position where they are being pulled relentlessly *to the unknown destination*. Will they arrive at a green field or a wasteland? Who knows? No one understood this better than CalTech's late Richard Feynman, a dean among Nobel Prize winning physicists, who once wrote, "Physicists like to think that all you have to do is say, these are the conditions, now what happens next?" In other words, they assume you can see the whole (the future) by examining all the parts (the present).

However, as I've pointed out, *the parts emerge in anticipation of the whole* (where we've got it wrong). Look at the parts—they reveal the *nature* of the whole. Look at the whole; it tells you what the parts *mean*. This brings us back to the Corporate Diagnostic:

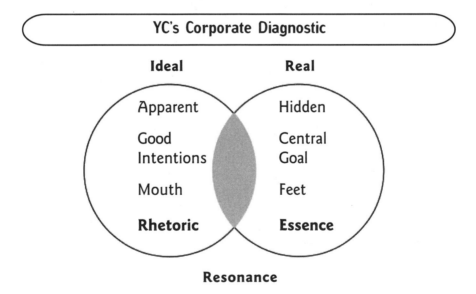

**YC's Corporate Diagnostic**

| Ideal | Real |
|---|---|
| Apparent | Hidden |
| Good Intentions | Central Goal |
| Mouth | Feet |
| **Rhetoric** | **Essence** |

**Resonance**

Here again, the left circle contains YC's good intentions. The right encircles its central goal. The central goal pulls all elements, no matter how seemingly insignificant, into its service. *This goal, then, in reality, is YC's governing purpose,* its function. The goal lives for tomorrow, and, like a shepherd hen, gathers its brood of today's actions.

Rainer Maria Rilke, the poet's poet I quoted earlier, put it this way:

> The future enters into us,
>
> in order to transform itself in us,
>
> long before it happens.

At this point, Adler's *central goal* meets Sullivan's theory of *form ever follows function*. If you apply Sullivan's deep insight to the articulation of your company's two-part vision (here-and-now/there-and-then), you discover:

- YC's *function*, its purpose, its central goal, comes first.

- YC acts in conformity with this goal, and those acts produce *forms*. Without exception, they *ever follow* the goal.

- YC's forms can be clarified and translated into everyday language by articulating its self-image and world view.

- YC's day-by-day decisions and actions point to its central goal.

If you adopt this perspective, believing that the future gives birth to the present, you can build YC upon a foundation of strength, a strength you may only have suspected or hoped for in the past.

Let's look at how this applies to a hypothetical YC, the 75-person headquarters accounting department of a large consumer financial services firm, Reserve Resources. Gary Summers, Reserve's CFO, heads up this department and wonders why so many of his bright people go about their work in a rote and unimaginative way. They plod because they find their daily work plodding: number crunching for the 12 regional vice presidents around the country who make credit decisions for their regions.

Those regional vice presidents are basically sales types who could benefit from more imaginative counsel on how to earn a better return on the millions of dollars the parent company makes available to them. With this in mind, Gary goes off on a retreat with the seven financial executives who report directly to him, and after a lot of soul-searching, this bright team concludes that they've been serving the wrong goal: producing timely, sophisticated, exhaustive financial reports.

Halfway through the second day, Art Gramley, a team member who serves the vice presidents in the northeastern region, blurts out: "We need to add value, not just numbers!" Bingo. Everybody's jaw drops. This simply stated new goal rejuvenates everyone as they resume their jobs with gusto. It's a goal that even harmonizes with the corporation's name.

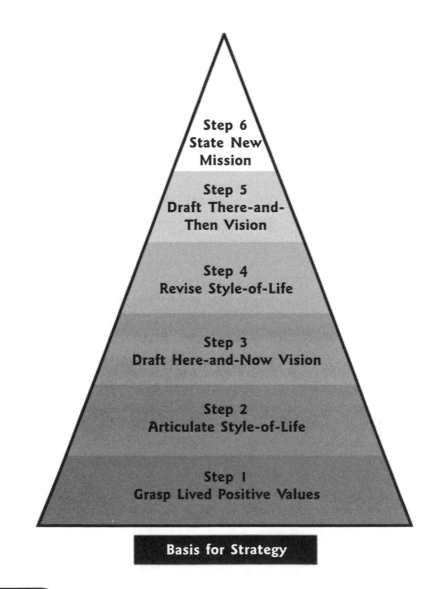

Step 6
State New
Mission

Step 5
Draft There-and-
Then Vision

Step 4
Revise Style-of-Life

Step 3
Draft Here-and-Now Vision

Step 2
Articulate Style-of-Life

Step 1
Grasp Lived Positive Values

**Basis for Strategy**

Now, suppose Gary Summers wants to take his fledgling break-through insight and translate it to his peers and his boss, Mary Flanagan, the CEO of Reserve Resources. How do they all walk a new path? Let's suppose Mary listens to Gary's story and says, "I'm with you. Let's go." The journey starts with six steps as shown on page 160.

Step 1. Get a firm grasp on YC's lived *positive* values.

Step 2. Articulate Style-of-Life.

Step 3. Draft "here-and-now" vision ("Who we are and where headed?").

Step 4. Revise Style-of-Life, if necessary.

Step 5. Craft the "there-and-then vision ("Who we want to be and how to get there?").

Step 6. State the new mission based on values and this two-part vision.

Reserve Resources takes these six steps of self-discovery, and receives the same benefits as USG and Fourth Presbyterian Church did. The new mission of Reserve Resources is the basis for a newly conceived strategy and its authentic message is aimed straight at its own people. They are a party to the firm's clarified purpose, unique-ness, and method. Join me now as we apply this self-discovery pro-cess to YC.

## Step 1: Grasp YC's Lived Positive Values

As you begin to get a handle on YC's values, remember that the sort of positive *values* that help make an organization great are more than words or vague concepts. Real and solid, like a ball of gold in the sky, such values pull our hearts and minds upward. They stake a claim on our lives. We most appreciate them; we most value them. The root *val* literally means worth. Just think of the word *value* for a moment. It derives from the Latin *valore* (to be strong). Strength. Positive values exert their strengths in our lives. They are worth some-thing. They are *valuable.* They are *valid.* They make us *valiant.* They mail us a *valentine* from the future.

Most people attach a positive moral meaning to the word, but most of us also recognize that negative values exist. In order to isolate YC's positive values, you'll want to know its negative ones as well. Whichever values you list, rank them in terms of relative importance, as primary or secondary forces. As you do your homework, you may find, for example, that YC pays a lot of rhetorical attention to innovation, but you notice that your superiors rarely mention that value in staff meetings, and it never comes up in your performance reviews.

As always, in your quest for precision and clarity, you want to boil each value down to a one-word noun. Nouns carry a sense of substance: innovation, not innovative; talent, talented; dominance, not dominant. Make a distinction between qualities and outcomes of qualities. "Safety" is an outcome of a quality, perhaps "care" or "responsibility." See the grid on page 163, then draw and complete one like it on a blank sheet of paper. You'll notice that the upper left-hand space is shaded. This is what I call the "Power Box," because if YC can find a way to give these values their "head," like that Derby winner, in every respect, it will be a beautiful beast!

If you find it difficult coming up with a lot of nouns, try stating behaviors first. They often provide clues to traits or qualities or values. For instance:

- Don't trust anyone who seems sincere = Distrust
- Don't enjoy the work; complain a lot = Boredom
- Laugh at those who suggest new ways of doing things = Disrespect
- Look busy when you're not = Busywork
- Don't make norms explicit = Vagueness
- Don't trust other groups = Isolationism
- Put down your group = Arrogance
- Treat women as second class citizens = Bias

Now play with the animal analogies I presented when we discussed USG and the Fourth Presbyterian Church. For the previous list, you might write down: cat, crow, hyena, hummingbird, amoeba, clam, cobra, and wolf. These images help bring an abstraction (defensiveness) to life (porcupine). They help you get a grasp of the concept.

| YC's *Lived* Values Grid | | |
|---|---|---|
| | **Positive** | **Negative** |
| **Primary** | Creativity<br>Analysis<br>Consistency<br>Aritculateness<br>Brilliance<br>Integrity<br>Candor<br>Reliability<br>Predictability<br>Trustworthiness<br>Generosity<br>Principle | Criticism<br>Glamour<br>Slowness<br>Rigidity<br>Arrogance<br>Narcissism<br>Vanity<br>Vision<br>Pride |
| **Secondary** | Openness<br>People-sensitivity<br>Commitment<br>Initiative<br>Tradition<br>Compassion<br>Opportunism<br>Enthusiasm | Tardiness<br>Harshness<br>Brusqueness<br>Image<br>Coldness<br>Encouragement<br>Detachment |

Do the same with one-word identities if you didn't do it earlier. Keep working on this exercise until you feel satisfied that you have boiled it all down to the essence of YC. Extend your effort to include others, associates, teammates, family, and friends, your formal or informal board. Go about the task cheerfully, playfully. Make it fun.

Finally, before you take a stab at composing YC's Style-of-Life, try your hand at completing the chart on page 165. I've supplied some examples to get you started.

## Step 2: Articulating YC's Style-of-Life

You now possess a full tool box for articulating YC's Style-of-Life: classifying YC's values, creating animal analogies, stating one-word identities, surfacing negative values, and sketching how YC compares to other companies. Keep in mind, too, these exercises from previous chapters, particularly the Corporate Diagnostic, the MRI of corporate innards, keel-of-boat values, and the four-stage corporate life cycle. All this homework will prepare you for the ultimate final exam: YC's Style-of-Life.

Before we tackle that project head-on, however, I'd like to offer a surprising suggestion: As much as YC's milestones (its high points and, for better or worse, its *big* decisions) reveal what makes YC tick, you can learn just as much from the "little decisions," those routine, mundane day-to-day activities that telegraph attitudes, and actions and contribute greatly to the big decisions.

All decisions require sound judgment, little ones no less than big ones. If you take little ones less seriously than the big ones, you'll usually end up making a big mistake.

Here's a good example of what I mean. A cavalry captain decides to put off re-shoeing his horse because the blacksmith can't get the right-sized nails. Riding to warn the general of an ambush, the captain falls into a ravine when his horse's loose shoe snags on a tree root. The horse drowns with its rider, the message never arrives, the general leads his troops into a massacre, and that catastrophe forces the general's army to surrender. I know it's a well-worn cliché, "For want of a nail, the war was lost," but for any YC, the "nails" play as big a role in outcomes as all the king's horses and all the king's men.

Of course, little decisions, though seemingly less crucial at the time, accrue over time, and, at a later date, seem collectively to have

| YC's Comparative Positioning Chart | | |
|---|---|---|
| **Like All Other Companies** | **Like Most Other Companies** | **Like No Other Company** |
| Typical public company structure with separate HQ and divisions/subs spread around the country. | Male oriented. | Only US company with 2 plants in Madagascar. |
| Advertise in trade magazines. | Reasonably profitable. | First company to incorporate in Idaho. |
| Have an annual planning and budgeting cycle. | Think we're better than our competitors. | Have never recruited a top executive from the outside. |
| Pockets of inertia. | Offer adequate health care coverage. | Brightest group of top executives I've ever seen in one place. |
| Involved in many community charities. | Hire some women and minorities in key spots. | An incredibly great cafeteria. |
| We do job-posting internally. | We are better at talking the walk than walking the talk. | I can't remember when any meeting started on time. |
| We employ our share of mediocre performers. | Our CEO is fairly isolated. | We've never been sued. |
| | | |
| | | |
| | | |
| | | |
| | | |
| | | |
| | | |

*anticipated* what lay ahead. The magnet draws them forward as powerfully as it does the life-or-death decisions. They have an ax to grind. They color our vision, they help shape the issues that will embroil us, and they influence later options. In other words, they often set or *confirm* a hidden agenda!

James Gleick, former *New York Times* science writer published an exquisite book, *Chaos,* in the late 1980s that made the growing field of chaos theory more accessible to lay people like you and me. Gleick notes that among the world's most prominent physicists in the 1960s, the concept of "sensitive dependence on initial conditions" took on great significance. What these brainy physicists meant by the term was that tiny differences in input could rapidly escalate to overwhelming differences in output. Gleick writes, "In weather, for example, this translates into what is only half-jokingly known as the butterfly effect—the notion that a butterfly stirring the air today in Peking can transform storm systems next month in New York."

Your inner voice can warn you of the implications of the little "nail and butterfly" decisions you (or others at YC) choose to make. Do those tiny decisions conform to hidden purpose, drawn forward by a looming threat, or do they flow toward a guardian presence? Try this thought experiment: Retrace the steps leading up to your last "big" decision, and pinpoint the little decisions you made along the way. You'll probably find that they harmonized with the big decision, for little decisions constitute clear signs. Pay attention to them.

> A little neglect may breed great mischief, for want of
> a nail the shoe was lost, for want of a shoe the horse
> was lost, and for want of a horse the rider was lost.
>
> —*Poor Richard's Almanack*, Ben Franklin

Obviously, I know nothing about YC, but you do. You're your own best expert. Yet, I can still guide you to a brighter future. By the end of this exercise, you will have sketched a clear picture of how YC *lives today* in 10 words or less. By the end of this chapter, you'll have painted an accurate (though tentative) view of the landscape surrounding YC, and whether it poses a looming threat or guardian presence. Then, and only then, can you decide what, if any, action to take.

Now take a few minutes to study the YC *Lived* Values Grid you filled out a few pages ago. I'll do the same with the one I filled out, helping you travel down your own unique path.

Take particular notice of the box on the upper left, and concentrate on it. Isn't it wonderful? If you could just wipe away the other three boxes and adopt the shaded one, you'd find yourself living in Nirvana. Unfortunately, the other boxes do exist, and they represent competing focus for YC's heart. Almost assuredly, the real YC doesn't live in Nirvana, nor does it suffer in Hell, but probably languishes in some purgatory between the two. The trick is moving up to the clouds and not down to the flames.

Next, review YC's Competitive Positioning Chart. It should shed more light on the YC *Lived* Values Grid, and *vice versa.* In the case of my own YC? I think I could fall in love with this company, even though it's all cluttered up and engaged in too much wasted motion. Top management probably hires only MBAs from Harvard or Stanford or Wharton, thinking they can always grow their own top executives from these seeds, forever fearful of bringing in new blood from the outside that might shake things up with fresh approaches.

The internal climate or atmosphere seems too cold, even haughty, and a bit too formal. The thought of staging an annual company picnic would distress most of YC's top executives. The CEO (let's call him Foster Winslow) is brilliant, a warm-hearted man, but aloof. He's held the job for 15 years and just celebrated his 57th birthday. YC's people don't see him walking around the halls very often. The mornings he spends in town, he goes straight to his downtown Boston office, striding briskly from his car in his reserved place to the adjacent elevator in the underground parking garage. He arrives before dawn, before another soul has tread the beautifully appointed executive floor (except for Virginia, his faithful assistant for 14 years). Staff presentations in his presence, whether in groups or one-on-one, feel almost like formal courtroom meetings; most people feel intimidated. Presenters prepare doggedly for meetings with him because, even though he treats everyone courteously and respectfully, and has hardly ever fired anyone, he's quick to criticize shortcomings in very precise terms, and assumes most key people throughout the company take his pronouncements as the gospel truth. Similar to most CEOs Foster sets the tone for a lot of what goes on here.

Permit me to pause here and contrast YC with another company about the same size. It generates $325 million annual sales, has become a household name, and enjoys the guidance of a terrific CEO, who has held the job for more than 10 years, whose behavior and style differs markedly from our imaginary YC. The company is WD-40, and the CEO is an Australian, Garry Ridge, whose accent and informality alone prompt a smile from any stranger who meets him for the first time. WD-40 products are sold all around the world and sit on shelves in nine out of 10 U.S. households. It is among the most highly recognized brand names in the industry.

Garry's style doesn't make him an intrinsically better person than Foster and WD-40 isn't intrinsically better than YC. They're just different. But I'd rather work for Garry any day of the week, even though the sign on Garry's door, usually open, reads, "Danger! You are about to enter an intellectual collision zone." When he reaches the end of his rope with an executive he's worked with at length (he never gives up on anybody easily), he utters these last words: "I guess we'll have to share you with a competitor." Performance reviews, including his own from his outstanding board, adhere to one overriding principle, "Don't mark my paper, help me get an A." No one makes "mistakes" in this company; they experience "learning moments," which employees are required to share with colleagues, so everyone can learn from situations "when things didn't go right." Listeners greet their associates' disclosures with applause.

Garry would rather have his fingernails removed with pliers than work eight hours at YC, and Foster would feel the same after a few hours at WD-40. There are good reasons why Garry fits his firm and Foster fits his. Don't mistakenly assume that if Foster Winslow would just loosen up a bit, everything would run more beautifully at YC. While the CEO may set the pattern for the entire company, with his behavior cues cascading down through the layers of the company, changing him may or may not change YC.

From my decades of exposure to boards and top managements in virtually all industries, I've come to this conclusion: CEOs usually win their positions and have succeeded to the pinnacles of their companies not just because they display world-class talent, which most do, but because in demeanor, character, behavior, and outlook, they *confirm,* not *set,* the "lifestyle" of the company. Remember Charlie Hunter? For all his commitment to innovation and courage in change management, Charlie Hunter, young as he was, grew up in Obelisk, and shared in his bloodstream what that company was all about, even though he wasn't fully aware of it. The Board knew he had "something," and that the company needed that "something" in its leader to restore Obelisk to its former greatness. Even if he had been recruited from the outside by a top-flight executive search firm, he would have been selected by the board, because he possessed that elusive "something." Even if the board had helped engineer Obelisk's decline (through poor stewardship), they possessed the presence of mind and conscience to seek a remedy.

So, would it help the spirit of YC if Foster sought coaching from some consultant who could help him see how much he would *enjoy* the *contact* with his people and increase their competence that he now precludes with his aloofness and intimidating style? Would a team-building initiative with him and his direct reports help break some ice and bring fresh air to the company from the top down? Could that not help keep the ball rolling in the right direction? You bet. However, I still insist that YC's Style-of-Life "is what it is," and Foster Winslow lives more under its spell than the other way around.

Returning to YC's *Lived* values, assume that a perceptive review and candid discussion by a cross section of executives in the company determines these top three Primary Positive Lived Values: (1) Creativity, (2) Brilliance, and (3) Trustworthiness. Never mind, for the moment, that the other values in the upper left-hand quadrant represent additional great resources, because the top three alone can lead to greatness. A wonderful company can arise from just those three, because they're authentic. They convey who YC already *is*.

What, then, gets in the way? Look to the upper right-hand box for the answer, taking a stab at YC's Style-of-Life that accounts for the tension between the top boxes. The bottom boxes merely play supporting roles.

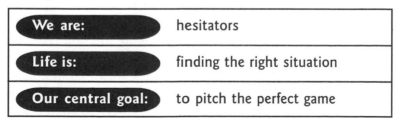

| **We are:** | hesitators |
| **Life is:** | finding the right situation |
| **Our central goal:** | to pitch the perfect game |

Aha! This Style-of-Life telegraphs a looming threat to YC.

Now, pick up a pen and paper, or sit down at your computer to apply this exercise to your real company.

## Step 3: Drafting YC's Vision Here-and-Now

To draft YC's Here-and-Now Vision, we'll capture in writing the answers to two familiar questions:

➤ Who are we?

➤ Where are we headed?

To answer accurately, we'll rely on any of the tools that might give us the insights we need. I recommend that you do this alone, and then do it with your associates and your board. Don't worry about streamlining your answers at this point; jot down as much detail as you like.

Here's an example:

> YC is a 62-year-old engineered products company that was founded in Peabody, Massachusetts. Founder Evan Collins came from a wealthy family, but dropped out of college to work as a field engineer for Cincinnati Milling Machine, a door his father opened for him. It turns out that Evan, in poor health throughout his childhood, showed remarkable genius, and soon grew restless to put his talent to work running his own company. With his father's financial support, he launched his business, and in 1945, one week after the war, he had already signed up three customers for his product. The business grew steadily, but not spectacularly, and always showed a profit.

> Foster Winslow, whom he met earlier, joined this modest business straight out of college, and before long, moved up to head of sales, a position he filled exceptionally well. A precise sort of person, not a stereotypical glad-handing salesman at all, he got on well with the introverted Evan. Evan praised him often, calling him "the absolute master of the soft sell." Neither of Evan's two daughters displayed the slightest interest in the family business, and though the men they married did, Evan found them dull-witted and never let them get near it. Fifteen years ago, Evan, age 67, turned the keys over to Foster, and said, "Take good care of my baby."

> Still privately held, YC enjoys a reputation as one of the best in its industry. Its growth has taken it into several countries, including Madagascar, from which it has established an

astounding foothold in a budding mechanical equipment service business in East Africa. Unfortunately, they have been unable to duplicate in the U.S. the imagination and daring it has shown for developing products and reaching markets in Africa. Foster and his top team can't tell you precisely why. "Perhaps it's a genetic defect," Foster says with a nervous chuckle.

When Evan walked away from the business, already wealthy from a large inheritance, he negotiated an agreement with Foster to let him buy YC, for an undisclosed amount, payable in installments every six months throughout 10 years. Given YC's consistent profitability, Foster could easily pay off the debt, though he found it increasingly difficult to meet his obligations throughout the last five years. Foster now owns the company outright, but has told his top management team that at some point, he may take the company public or create an ESOP (employee stock ownership plan.)

Today, however, YC boasts a more glorious past than a promising future. Product development (with the exception of Madagascar) has fallen off considerably, and YC's two finest young people in R&D have joined the firm's competitors. When YC does come up with new products, it takes too much time and effort. Like it or not, Foster still outsells anyone, and much of their business still comes from customers and contacts that he has maintained for years. Trouble is, many of those contacts have retired or died, while some companies they sold to have merged with larger ones. The new owners know little about YC's past, and only its less than illustrious past at that. The current VP of sales, who serves in name only, cannot replace Foster, and Foster has not developed anyone else to take his place.

When Foster and his team try to figure out their future, one executive points out, "We spin our wheels a lot by preparing brilliant reports (we shine at analysis) on possible new markets, acquisition targets, alternate financial models, procurement, building new plants, and even corporate relocation. We have a big budget for using premier outside consulting firms. Our competitors would love to have a fraction of our data! But what are we really doing with it?"

Though Foster himself demands most of these studies, he's not alone. Everyone at the top loves to assign research projects to their subordinates, and they, too, wonder why all the busywork fails to get results. One marketing manager jokingly says, "Our head of market research made a proposal to do a proposal." Once a report hits his desk, Foster tears it apart, nitpicking the tiniest details. That approach travels all the way down the line, making managers increasingly critical. "We beat each other up," observes one executive. Another displays a not-so-funny bumper sticker on his Mercedes: "Where are we going? And why are we in this hand basket?"

Concerned about all these signs of deterioration, Foster and his team began a Style-of-Life investigation with my help. To cut to the chase, we eventually came to this conclusion: "We're a Stage Three company (obsolescence and decline), not too far in, however. But if we don't make changes, we'll be headed for extinction. We're not the only ones doing acquisition studies. You can be sure we're in the cross-hairs of others that want to add us to their stable. They see the possibilities. Someone could come along with an offer we can't refuse, though no one wants that to happen.

We need capital. We're not profitable enough anymore to finance investment internally. We need to take on debt or go public to raise the money to invest in new products and acquisitions of our own. We've got the horses, and we're adventuresome at heart. Look at Madagascar! A smashing success! That's our jewel, and we can repeat it elsewhere in the developing world.

Now it's your turn. Craft a similar Here-and-Now Vision for your YC.

## Step 4: YC's Revised Style-of-Life

Given the current state of affairs at YC, the team needs to aim for a new Style-of-Life, an appropriate, realistic, and more positive one that captures the company's best self. How might they replace the present looming threat (hesitators, finding the right situation, and to pitch the perfect game) with a strong guardian presence? After a lot of deep thinking and debate, they came up with this:

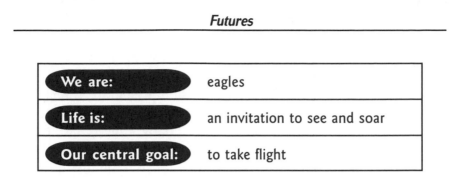

| **We are:** | eagles |
| **Life is:** | an invitation to see and soar |
| **Our central goal:** | to take flight |

Now write yours.

## Step 5: YC's Vision There-and-Then

To draft YC's There-and-Then Vision, you'll face two additional questions, using any or all of the tools we've discussed earlier.

➤ Who do we want to be?

➤ How do we get there?

This should take much less time than drafting YC's Here-and-Now. Here's what Foster and his team wrote:

> We want to be the eagles of our industry. We are (with all due modesty) the most creative and brilliant designers of one-of-a-kind equipment servicing tools for steel fabrication plants. We have shown again and again in years past that we see applications customers don't know are possible. Let our competitors imitate us; we'll dash onto the next! Research we have stashed away points to uses for equipment that our industry still hasn't caught on to.
>
> We will spread our wings and stop chasing our tail by overcoming our hesitancy. We will shed our naysaying, our waiting for the perfect time and situation to act. What we know in our heart of hearts we can do right now. Soar! We will overcome our fear and help Foster take off his own manacle. He's our chief eagle. He'll come alive.

Now write yours.

## Step 6: YC's New Mission

Many companies try to state their mission prematurely. Imagine writing YC's mission without completing all the necessary homework; it wouldn't work. It'll simply create more hollow rhetoric. Remember: you're ruthlessly seeking reality. Only when you know, for a fact, who YC is, can you legitimately ask more of it. Would you ask a NASCAR driver to enter the Tour de France? Or would you more properly suggest she try her hand at Le Mans?

Throughout the years, I have developed a set of guidelines and ground rules that help my clients state their new mission. First, let's keep clear in mind what it is: YC's *brief, compelling statement of purpose, uniqueness, and method.* Most mission statements overlook method.

YC's mission has to answer three questions:

1. What's does our customer need?

2. What product or service do we provide?

3. How do we do what we do? (In other words, what's our method? This can be more than merely action; it may be some unique or mysterious quality.)

The mission statement will not be effective if one of these three answers does not encapsulate YC's *uniqueness.*

Also, observe these guidelines:

First, bear in mind that YC's mission statement is an internal document. You wouldn't mind, certainly, if a supplier or customer sees it, but you write for your own people, the ones who will carry it out and identify with it personally. When they hear it, read it, or just think of it, you want them to say to themselves, "Yep, that's us, and we're darn proud of it!" Some missions *seem* pedestrian to outsiders who expect more hype and high-falutin words that read more like advertising copy. Seemingly dull language can send a strong message to insiders.

Second, a strong mission offers a first sentence that is brief, inspiring (to insiders), and memorable. People won't work to memorize it; they won't be able to forget it.

Third, be sure to limit YC's mission statement to 75 words or less.

Here's what Foster and his team wrote:

> We are eagles.
>
> Our small durable tools meet the need of steel fabricators around the world for ease of use in serving and repairing their machinery.
>
> Our knowing scan of the metal fabricating horizon allows us to respond with ingenious tool design and redesign for fabricators facing unanticipated challenges in their use of new machinery.
>
> "Trustworthy" is the label we cherish with our customers, all countries and communities in which we operate, and among ourselves.

Let's look at what makes this a strong mission statement:

▶ It articulates the customer's need for flexibility and ease of use.

▶ YC meets that need with speed and scan of the industry horizon with unmatched acuity.

▶ YC's ingenuity in product development is the industry standard.

▶ It aims straight at YC's people who proudly say, "Yep, that's us!"

▶ It has a first sentence that is brief, inspiring, and memorable.

▶ It is 75 words in length.

Now write yours.

## In this chapter you have learned:

➡ That each structure (form) *always* undergoes change to serve your organization's unshakable purpose (function).

➡ That the parts of "something" emerge in anticipation of the whole.

➡ That true vision begins with here-and-now awareness.

➡ That renewal starts with the discovery of buried values.

➡ That small decisions confirm an agenda, for better or worse.

➡ How to articulate your company's Style-of-Life, Vision, and Mission in a fresh, compelling way.

### Your Inner CEO Punch List

❒ Speculate how the future has entered the present in your company. Does it hold promise or danger, a guardian presence or looming threat?

❒ Think of some small decisions you have made that confirm an agenda beyond your awareness. How will you keep yourself on alert to those nails in the future?

❒ When you jotted down the *Lived* positive values of your company and placed them in the upper left-hand "power box" on the chart, did anything surprise you? Can you build greatness around them? How can you call attention to this "good news" among your associates?

# 8

# Models

*Science without religion is lame, religion without science is blind.*

—Albert Einstein

I have never met an executive with a purer Style-of-Life than Dom Dannessa. More than almost any of my clients, he has moved beyond his looming threat. A prototypical "pilgrim," he began his pilgrimage from looming threat to guardian presence long before I arrived on the scene. Blessed with a remarkable degree of receptivity, he's acquired a keen sense of himself at the half-century mark.

Dom, the executive vice president of manufacturing for USG, a 63-plant, market-dominant colossus, sees himself as a deliverer, his life as navigable, and his central goal to build and sail a seaworthy ship. Some of USG's facilities stretch a city-block long, with production lines carrying huge payloads. Overseeing this empire, Dom commands total trust among his associates. As one of his superiors told me, "If Dom says it can be done, we believe him."

His path has not been free from obstacles, however. His wife, Josette, faced and survived a life-threatening breast cancer crisis. Yet this event, which might hurtle many families into a state of despair, only served as a catalyst for the couple and their two daughters to forge an even deeper and more durable bond. Their spiritual faith has also buoyed them, with their local Catholic parish providing an anchor in their lives.

To get in a groove with life the way Dom has, you accept the boundaries you encounter on your own pilgrimage. As you cross each and every one of them you move closer to your Destiny. The milestones mark the points where you can rely on a sound purpose to move from threat to opportunity. You will never fulfill your Destiny without a sound purpose.

## Keeping the Faith

Throughout this book, I've often used the word *Destiny*, referring to it not mainly as a pre-ordained future, but as the natural result of living a life when you confront each situation consistent with who you are, steadily becoming the person you're born to be.

In Chapter 4, Gordon Parker, the managing partner we watched as he built his boundary awareness, stands out as an example. A natural learner, he continuously finds, enters and yields to Destiny's flow. In that same chapter on looming threats and test boundaries, I personalized the term Destiny by stating my own experiences in my mid-30s when I got the memo on "it."

When I urge you to become the person you're born to be, I don't mean that you move forward like a locomotive on a track. No, you choose Destiny just as surely as you choose a pair of shoes. You may not even believe in Destiny, but you can't overlook that you were born with certain potentialities, which you may freely accept or reject, cultivate or neglect. In that sense, at least, you make a choice about what happens next in your life.

When considering Destiny, you may or may not go at it in terms of religion. A Catholic might, and a Jew, Muslim, Presbyterian, or an Episcopalian might as well. But, then, so might an agnostic, or even an atheist. because even they place their faith in *something*. Faith in Destiny comes in many forms, as the late Dag Hammarskjöld, former U.N. Secretary General, so aptly put: "I don't know Who—or What—put the question, I don't know when it was put. I don't even remember answering. But at some moment I did answer *Yes* to Someone—or Something—and from that hour I was certain that existence is meaningful and that, therefore, my life in self-surrender, had a goal."

All of us are persons of faith, whether we designate it unnamable or science instead of God, Yahweh, Allah, Buddha, Krishna, Great Spirit, or the like. By faith, I mean a firm belief in something you cannot necessarily prove with cold, hard facts. In my own case, for the better part of two decades in my adult life, I participated in no formal religious practice in a house of worship. Now I do. But my faith has run like a stream, sometimes visible, sometimes hidden, throughout my life.

In early October 2006, I served as a panelist on a "Global Business Responsibility" program in Prague, part of a conference hosted by Forum 2000, an organization formed by Vaclav Havel, former president of the Czech Republic, Nobel Laureate Elie Weisel, and philanthropist Yohei Sasakawa, chairman of The Nippon Foundation. Honored to participate on one of the panels at this conference of world-class thinkers and scholars to discuss global business responsibility, I actually enjoyed even more a program titled "Interfaith Dialogue: The Risks of Globalization—Do Religions Offer a Solution or Are They Part of the Problem?"

This particular panel included 12 thinkers and leaders, among them Vartan Gregorian (President of Carnegie Corporation), Michel Dubost (Bishop, Eveche D'Evry-Corbeil, France), Michael Melchoir (former Chief Rabbi of Norway, now Member of the Knesset in Israel), Soho Machida (Professor, the Graduate School of Integrated Arts and Sciences, Hiroshima University), and His Holiness, the Dalai Lama. Two events during this two-hour session impressed me most.

One, when it came time for the Dalai Lama to speak, he referred to the rhetorical subtitle of the program, "Do religions offer a solution or are they part of the problem?" If you've ever seen the Dalai Lama in action, you know he displays a wonderful, even mischievous, sense of humor. Given his limited command of English, he often utters monosyllabic statements delivered with a chuckle. Imagine the audience's delight and surprise, when, after a graceful pause, the great religious leader proclaimed, with a twinkle in his eye, "Both!"

Who could say it better?

Two, near the end of the session, Moderator Joyce Davis (an African-American with Radio Free Europe) put a refreshing challenge to the panel: "I'm a Baptist! I need to feel my religion. I'd like to know what each of you does in times of stress or crisis to center yourself. What do you do to cope?" This challenge seemed to startle some of the panelists, but eventually all offered an answer. Two in particular, right near the end, touched a nerve in me. The first came from Vartan Gregorian, speaker of eight languages, who said the best advice he ever got for dealing with crisis was delivered by his illiterate

Armenian grandmother, who told him, "Be silent." The second came from Soho Machida, who said his response might not seem appropriate to the question and audience, but he would say it anyway. With that, he broke into a one-note chant that lasted perhaps for 30 seconds:

O O O O O O O O O O O O O O O O O O O O O O
O O O O O O O O O O O O A A A A A A A A A A
A A A A A A A A A A A A A A A A A A A A A A
A A A A A A A A A A A A A A A A A A A A A A
A A A A A A A A A A A A A A A A A A A A A A
A A A A A A A A A A A A A A A A A A A A A A
A A A A A A A A A A A A A A A A A A A-AH!

The walls of the large auditorium seemed to vibrate, as did my chair, and my heart, too. The program ended, and 700 people exited the hall in silence. If you care to, you can view the entire proceedings and hear the chant by clicking the following link:

*www.forum2000.cz/web_tv/video_2006.php*

"Both!" "Silence." A wordless note. Inspired by such simplicity, we all, in those moments, somehow came together in a faith-filled cradling, joined together no matter how we, as individuals, might define the mystery.

For many people, faith (in whatever form it takes), stems from their consideration of life's mysteries, beginning with the miracle of their own birth. It seems worthwhile to remind ourselves that in the final analysis, when we say we *believe* (no matter how firm that belief), we're admitting we can't prove our belief; we simply don't know all the answers. This recognition shouldn't discomfort us, because it merely articulates our human limitation, an incapability for which we bear no responsibility. No matter how we got here, we are what we are. As the *Tao Te Ching* admonishes, "Not knowing is true knowledge. Presuming to know is a disease." In our youth we think we know it all, then, as we mature with experience, we learn that we don't know as much as we once thought we did. That growth sows the seeds of faith.

Please don't mistake my discussion of faith as a challenge to your personal and unique set of beliefs. However, because I myself have learned so much from looking into a wide range of faiths, I suggest you try it yourself, but with one caution. At the dawn of the rebellious sixties, the late Alan Watts, Episcopal priest and Zen scholar, pointed out the dangers of such a romance with unfamiliar faiths:

> Foreign religions can be immensely attractive and highly overrated by those who know little of their own, and especially by those who have not worked through and grown out of their own. This is why the displaced or unconscious Christian can so easily use either beat or square Zen to justify himself. The one wants a philosophy to justify him in doing what he pleases. The other wants a more plausible authoritative salvation than the church or the psychiatrists seem to provide.

For anyone interested in exploring how a "foreign" faith might enhance your own, or simply widen your perspective, I strongly recommend Stephen Prothero's *Religious Literacy*. It is truly a book for our times.

In any case, our birth, an event that occurred without our permission, launched a life most often governed by the illusion that we can control it. As I've said so often in these pages, we'd all gain more peace and wisdom if we could only bring ourselves to shed that illusion and install, in its place, a faith that:

- Allows you to exercise free choice to build up your life, to wander through it like a sleepwalker, or to destroy it in a thousand different ways.

- Requires you to help build up the lives of those with whom you come into contact.

- Helps you understand that you're responsible for your actions; Destiny will account for results.

- Declares that an Unnamable exists and made you part of Creation.

- Declares you can create, but not control, your world.

Remember Jacob?

Despite his fear, he wrestled with the Unnamable throughout the night and *prevailed*. The Unnamable clearly found Jacob's perseverance not only acceptable, but commendable. "God" named his nation after him. Faith. Struggle. Choice. Welcome to your life. Welcome to the world of creativity.

As head of YC, how you can best apply creativity to enhance your world? As I've stated repeatedy, you can, first and foremost, improve your mastery of all the boundaries in your world. This will create authentic contact between you and all those with whom you come into contact, and it will help improve everyone's performance on and off the job.

Think about the word *faithful*. It means "loyal," yes, but it also means "filled with faith." Faithful people, especially faithful CEOs, provide the best *models* for how to live and work in the world with others. They don't tell us what to do, they *show* us how to live and work. They are masterful. They're so good they don't know it.

Aeschylus, the fifth-century B.C. dramatist, put it concisely:

> I am like all other men.
> I am like some other men.
> I am like no other man.

*You*, of course, possess certain unique traits and skills, and if you can discover and develop them and cross the boundary to give them to the world, you'll brighten the life of anyone you touch. Along the way you'll meet some others, kindred spirits (family, friends, associates) with whom you'll form strong bonds, and who will help you grow even more. And ultimately, you will, like everyone else, meet your Destiny.

Enough philosophy. Let's put it all to work with a few activities. First of all, keep your Style-of-Life in mind. After all, this captures your uniqueness in 10 words or less. If your Style-of-Life started out as a looming threat, I'm assuming you've done the excavation and recalibrated yourself so that you're operating with a guardian presence. If you haven't done that, do it now.

Begin by listing up to 10 ways you are like all other people, then up to 10 ways you're like some other people, then up to five ways that you're like no other person.

Ruminate a bit. Put your feet up. Remember Eric Hoffer's flashes from Chapter 1? Recall three or four "flashes" that have popped into your mind during the past three years, but failed to prompt you to act. Write them down. Did they not require that you employ your unique strengths? Why did you fail to do so?

| | Uniqueness Inventory | | |
|---|---|---|---|
| | **Like Everyone Else** | **Like Someone Else** | **Like No One Else** |
| 1. | | | |
| 2. | | | |
| 3. | | | |
| 4. | | | |
| 5. | | | |
| 6. | | | |
| 7. | | | |
| 8. | | | |
| 9. | | | |
| 10. | | | |

Look at the Uniqueness Inventory on page 184. I've partially completed it for Elaine Finn. You can deduce a lot about this 28-year-old woman from her entries:

| Uniqueness Inventory | | |
|---|---|---|
| | **Like Everyone Else** | **Like Someone Else** | **Like No One Else** |
| 1 | Human | Irish American | Mother, Lois, a social worker |
| 2 | Birth | MBA University of Minnesota | Father, Walter, an Episcopal priest |
| 3 | Death | 28-years-old | 1989 NCAA champion 100 meter freestyle |
| 4 | Taxes | Unmarried | I "come from behind" like nobody I've known |
| 5 | | Tax Accountant in "Big Four" firm | |
| 6 | | Employed | |
| 7 | | Ambitious | |
| 8 | | Workaholic | |
| 9 | | Physically Fit | |
| 10 | | Episcopalian | |

Elaine's "flash" gave her a mental picture of saving a small child from drowning, something far removed from her daily life as a tax accountant. Remembering that flash as she completes her Uniqueness Inventory, she realizes she *could have* put her skill as a swimmer (she won the NCAA Championship in the 100 meter freestyle as a senior at the University of Wisconsin) to work at the local YWCA, teaching inner-city kids a skill that might save a life one day. Why hadn't she done it? She was too busy with her career. Had she overcome her fear of not getting ahead in her work, might she have gained something even more valuable by applying her unique skill?

Suppose she acts on her insight and does start a swimming program for young girls at the Y. How much satisfaction might she get from doing something for others, from one of her students winning a swimming scholarship to Northwestern, from a life saved in a boating accident on Lake Michigan? Suppose Elaine becomes the sort of model that inspires 1,000 members of her classes and 1,000,000 residents of Chicago when she wins the city's Humanitarian of the Year Award. Was her uniqueness inventory worth the effort? Did this one little horseshoe nail not win a war?

Focus on any you have ignored or downplayed in the past. What makes you afraid to act on them? Should you act on them now? Why not? Face your fear, consult your heart, own your uniqueness. If you do all that, you may, similar to Elaine, gain something more valuable than you can imagine.

Determine *today* that you are not going to sleepwalk through life. Ban "woulda, coulda, shoulda" from your vocabulary, replacing these tired old excuses with "I will." Beat your own unique drum. March to your own unique beat. Contribute to your company's *culture of caring*.

Whoever you are, whether a senior executive with a Fortune 1000, who, up until now has been compromising yourself by riding on tradition, or an independent consultant who's been blaming the client company for your blahs, get back in gear by answering these four questions:

1. What does my company want to accomplish? Cite five goals.

2. In what area will my own superior performance produce the most impact? List no more than two.

3. Now, from the two options pick one and take it on.

4. On what other people does success depend? List four to six names.

Who will join the team? When will you act? Assemble the team; do it now. The details will begin to take care of themselves. The ever bold Stonewall Jackson, brilliant Confederate general, said it best: "Never take counsel of your fears."

## Real Boundaries from the Top

The activity you've just completed puts you on your way to becoming a unique and natural model. It makes you *transparent,* by which I mean that you shed your camouflage and pretensions, and live life with clear eyes and a full heart. Your actions reflect your intentions. In terms of boundaries, you cross from indirectness behind a façade to full frontal directness.

When I think about this point, Ed Phillipson, CEO of Benison Communications, comes to mind. I've gotten so close to him, I think of him almost as a brother. He's a Class-A player, and lives by personal values I respect. I would trust him with my life. He runs an enviably profitable magazine publishing conglomerate with periodicals you probably see scattered about your doctor's waiting room. He's the quintessential nice guy who finished first. He's a great model.

Still, he wasn't just born a great model. It took some soul-searching. In the early stages of his career, he liked to give and get only good news, a proclivity that derived from the fact that he desperately wanted to be liked. He found it hard to make strong declarations, the sort of pointed statements consisting of few words that a confident person delivers without any trace of swagger or bristle. As a result, his enterprises suffered from too little clarity about boundaries coming from the top. The less confident he felt about a subject, the more he talked about it. He managed by consensus, which may work when skies are blue, but when it's raining, consensus makes a poor umbrella. Unique and natural *models* know themselves, know their humanity, and know they can never not lead by example. Searching for consensus does not set a good example.

Here's the punch line: over a relatively short period of time, Ed changed. Conducting an exercise much like the one Elaine Finn performed, Ed recognized that he diluted his uniqueness and confused his organization. His unique gift? He's an "alchemist," able to blend complexity and disparate elements better than anyone I've ever met. People say he displays great instincts, and that's true, but even more than that, he has peerless insight into all the factors required for success, factors that others don't see in a complex, perilous undertaking, such as financing, marketing, and timing the introduction of a new magazine, which he's overseen brilliantly on numerous occasions.

Sounds great doesn't it? Well, sure, but Ed still felt he operated below his full potential. He misused his gift, not intentionally, but often enough to worry him. The alchemist in him offered both a blessing and a curse. His Creative Self made use of his broad comprehension to grasp tradeoffs overlooked by others, tradeoffs that "required" discussion and debate in a "consensus format" controlled by Ed. While Ed's team sorted out what needed to be done, and who would do it, he insisted on attending all those meetings. Before long, what he saw as collaboration deteriorated into micro-management, needless bottlenecks, and a team tethered to his approval on matters they could decide for themselves.

When the light went on for Ed, he did not defend his past practices but, instead, renamed himself *declarer*. The organization still enjoys a brilliant alchemist, but it has stopped the unwitting charade of "consensus." Ed states his insights up front, then lets a capable team take initiatives that lighten his load, add to their job satisfaction, and complement his gift.

Dr. Arnold Beisser, psychiatrist and practitioner of Gestalt Therapy, conceived what he called *The Paradoxical Theory of Change,* which I've edited just so slightly:

"Change occurs when one becomes what he is, not when he tries to become what he is not."

When Ed stopped trying to be what he's not, a people-pleaser giving what he thought others wanted ("consensus" that made everybody-but-nobody happy), he became what he is: a natural. He's *modeling* what he is, talking less, though still brilliantly, but also saying more, soundlessly. He grasped fully that only his actions can accurately and honestly convey his commitments. His people at Benison love these changes in him:

- He now knows that consensus produces the "lowest common denominator" and wastes a lot of time.

- He now makes and *receives* strong declarations.

187

▶ He now knows himself (and is known by his people) as someone to trust.

▶ He's moved *away* from indirectness and *toward* directness.

▶ He's transparent.

Back in Chapter 4 we discussed the *apparent* and *real* purposes of boundaries. A true and real purpose means a true and real boundary. People in organizations can sniff out the untrue and unreal. They know when a boss or a CEO tries to manipulate and control them. They know when the Emperor is naked, even when he parades about as if he's wearing the most resplendent garments. They also know honesty, integrity, truth, and reality when they see it.

As I worked with Ed Phillipson, we created the simple chart below. It revealed how his behavior led to erosion of trust and confusion among his own team, and undermined credibility among Benison's people, people who need to know the cold, hard truth.

| Benison's True and Real Boundaries | | |
|---|---|---|
| **False Model** | **True Model** | **Benefits** |
| Popularity of a decision creates commitment. | The correctness of a decision will make it popular. | Commitment |
| Consensus creates a sense of participation. | The right action will attract support. | Participation |
| People trust nice guys. | People respect authenticity. | Trust |
| You can talk people into belief. | People believe when you tell them the truth. | Credibility |

Now, investigate a more mundane case. David, a marketing director, has just declared a boundary to his staff, telling them that he'd choose the advertising agency their company would hire to promote Citrizone's new fruit drink line after he heard everybody's input one last time. Staff feelings ran strong on this topic with three people expressing quite different views on which agency would do the best job. Each marshaled cogent arguments for his or her preference, and each presented his or her preliminary recommendations skillfully. David listened to it all, then awarded the job to the Avery Agency.

This pleases Brad, who argued strongly for Avery. He doesn't gloat, however, because, for the most part this team feels comfortable and trusting with each other. He would like to think he would have acted just as graciously had the decision not gone his way. He assumed Kay and Ev felt the same way. The five other members of the team, who remained basically neutral on the choice, applauded the decision and looked forward to getting started on the campaign. No one could fault Avery's reputation for creativity and effectiveness.

All of that occurred last Friday afternoon. Now it's Monday, just before lunch. First thing this morning, David had circulated a memo to his team, saying that over the weekend, he changed his mind and decided to go with Walters & Collins instead of Avery. This abrupt shift, after such an orderly decision-making process, is described in his memo, saying that Ev had contacted him over the weekend and had ardently pressed his case for Walters & Collins. David relented. Shocked by his unilateral betrayal, Brad seethes with anger, and the rest of the team freezes when anyone mentions David's name.

What would Sherlock Holmes say about this crime? How would he solve the "Case of the Violated Boundary?" He'd ask a few penetrating questions:

- What caused David to jeopardize the team's good chemistry?

- What does David's action say about his decision-making?

- Why did David seemingly abandon his code of ethics?

- Did David consider how the shift would affect the team's relationship with Ev?

- Why has the energy level of the team dropped?

- Did David consider what might happen?

The answer is quite simple: David forgot *himself,* relinquished his responsibility as a model, and went against his natural gift for leadership because he let the importance of the decision overrule his basic instinct for honesty, trust, consistency, and credibility.

You can see from this mundane example how easily modeling can be compromised by passion and stress. I do not, for one moment, suggest that David can't work himself out of this predicament, though he'll pay a price no matter what he does. As a first step, he needs to embrace humility and come clean with the whole team that he blew it. At the same time, the team and Ev need to mend a fence (cross a boundary) by exploring the meaning of his behavior. The team, and especially Brad, needs to extend forgiveness to David and Ev and then discuss what, if anything, they might do about the damage to trust and credibility. Finally, should Avery or Walters & Collins get the account?

When you make missteps like David did, you can repair, but not retrace them. My wife often says that the most important words in any CEO's vocabulary should be "please," "thank you," and "I'm sorry." Never underestimate the power of an honest, heartfelt apology, even when you've committed the corporate crime of the century: a betrayal of trust.

## The Pilgrim

Back in Chapter 1 I used "the pilgrim" as an example of a guardian presence Style-of-Life, the same sort of guardian that pulls Dom Dannessa toward his Destiny. The very first pilgrim, (I'll call him Jim McGuire) became my client in the early 1970s. He was a founder and CEO of a remarkably successful real estate development firm that built a prestigious apartment complex in midtown Manhattan that houses prominent people you know from films, TV, and public life; resort properties in Colorado ski country; major commercial bank office buildings; the tallest reinforced concrete structure in the world; plush residential communities in La Jolla, California and Shawnee Mission, Kansas; and a host of other architectural award-winning structures.

Today he's 82 years young, wealthy as ever, yet even more charitable, madly in love with his wife of 57 years, warm and good-natured, a proud parent of four achievers, grandfather of 17, great-grandfather of two, all of them the greatest joys of his life. I've never admired a friend more.

Not a Catholic myself, I appreciated his strong faith, exemplified by an incident during the construction of the world's tallest (at the time) reinforced concrete high-rise. When the building reached its zenith at 70 stories, Jim hosted the typical topping out ceremony, complete with the frightening ride with his family to the summit on the construction elevator, champagne toasts, press party, and a final symbolic last pouring of concrete.

In Jim's own words, "We said a prayer of thanksgiving to St. Francis and my Mom. She had died recently, but had been praying the Rosary for two years for the safety of the workers. Her prayers were answered; unlike most such projects, this one was completed without any loss of life and no tragic accidents. We carefully placed her Rosary inside the form where the concrete was going to be poured." Everyone present at that "holy moment" knew they stood in the presence of an admirable model.

When I work intensely with an executive, we not only craft a Style-of-Life, but we work up and distill a one-page profile that serves as a guide to the executive's future and personal development. In 1976, we crafted Jim's Style-of-Life profile, a document that reveals the fact that even the pilgrim travels an endless road.

## Jim Maguire's Style-of-Life Profile

**Basic Strengths**

Strong family ties.

Cooperative, team player, charitable.

Good sense of humor, convivial.

Loves flair, the big event.

Persistent in the midst of difficult chores.

Honest, disciplined, shuns excesses.

**Growth-Blocking Attitudes**

I must do things right; I'm being judged.

If I'm not good, I'll be punished.

Good people go further, get the best rewards.

I have to do a lot of things I don't like to do.

I have to cope with a lot of unethical people.

I sometimes envy rebels, but rebellion's not for me.

My way is the moral way.

**Style-of-Life**

I am: a pilgrim.

Life is: rewards and punishments.

My Central Goal: never fall from grace.

**My Centering Statements**

When I've been wronged? I let it go.

I am more accepting of people.

I forgive myself, too.

I compete without blaming others for my failures.

I loosen up; I play.

I show my real SELF to the world.

Heaven is on earth.

———

Using Jim's Style-of-Life Profile as a guide, try your hand at crafting your own. Begin by referring to your original or revised Style-of-Life. Although brief, it serves as a seed from which will sprout a more detailed profile. Ever since Chapter 1, you've put your life under a microscope, and just a few pages ago, you wrote down how you're like everybody else, like some others, and like no other person.

So let's walk through the elements of your profile, just as they appear in sketching a developmental road map, subject to change, of course, that you can use to lead you through the rest of your life. Open with "Basic Strengths." Review all that you've recorded and thought about yourself since you began the process of discovering your inner CEO. It should be relatively easy for you to cherry-pick and organize a list from that material. Make sure every item you select reflects positive attributes. Feel free to include strengths that match those of others, but also enter a quality or skill unique to you alone. Take some time with this exercise because it does take a while to boil it all down to a true assessment.

For example, at one point Elaine Finn listed "hard worker" as a strength, but the more she thought about it, she realized that her gift for swimmer training and long hours of practice, while a strength, had also led to one of her weaknesses (working to the exclusion of other important aspects of her life, such as personal relationships and personal growth in other areas). Finally, she settled on "works steadily to accomplish a goal." Note the subtle difference between work for work's sake and work to reach a destination.

Next, you'll compile your "Growth-Blocking Attitudes." This poses more of a challenge. Again, review all the material you've collected as you've considered those traits or beliefs that can fuel a looming threat: your shortcomings, hang-ups, fears, and weaknesses.

For Elaine Finn, "workaholic" sums it up, but as she thinks more deeply about it, she concludes that the word is an easy cliché. What, really, lies at the root of her tendency to focus on work (or training for a swim meet) to the exclusion of all else? Eventually she writes, "I can focus too hard on one goal.

Again, take your time drafting your own Growth-Blocking Attitudes. You can play with these over time and revise them as you get better at figuring them out, but never ignore them. They guide you as you draft your Centering Statements (which we'll cover shortly). The idea is not to drown in negative thoughts, but actually to have a little fun with yourself over the "creative" ways you've introduced distortions into your life. ("Yes, I really do this. Can you believe that?!") Acknowledge them clearly and they have a much better chance of disappearing on their own. As Peter Drucker put it so well, "The effective executive is one who has learned how to make his strengths productive and his weaknesses irrelevant."

You've already completed your Style-of-Life, so just enter that onto the page now and move on to "My Centering Statements." If I were advising Elaine Finn, I'd encourage her to strive for what I call "aha moments." Similar to many high-performing people, Elaine's strength (dedicated effort) can become a weakness (obsession). Contemplating her strengths and weaknesses, without harshness to herself, she might conclude that "Centering" involves balance. So she writes, "I balance professional and personal growth." Jim could help her, I think. He found his own "aha moment" when he saw that he needed to strike a balance with a life that was too judgmental; and a life based on doing the right thing. As he confided during this exercise, "it's not always right to be right."

When Jim and I did this work together, he and seven other top executives met with me for a half-day on eight consecutive Saturdays. All eight went through the same process of working up their one-page profiles. As you would expect, they got to know each other quite well, bonding the way many people do in such circumstances. At the end of one of these sessions, a light bulb went on for me. I said, "Fellas, pull your chairs into a circle." After they did that, I turned to Jim and said, "Jim, I'd like you to stand up, walk around this circle, face each one of us and tell us, one-by-one, one thing you don't like about us. Start with me."

I could tell from his flushed face that Jim would rather walk on hot coals, but he agreed with a grimace. Towering over me, he looked down at me and said, "I'm not going to describe this in specifics, but you disappointed me, and I think you know it." I replied, "Yes, I do, you mean the hospital." He nodded. (He'd asked me to join a hospital board in Chicago; I agreed to do it, and then backed out when I saw how much work it involved.) Now, I said, "Thank you for telling me. Do the same with everyone." He did, and they responded much they way I did.

When he completed the circle and sat down, I asked him how he felt about what he had just done. "I didn't like it," he said. "How do you think these guys feel?" I asked. He said, he didn't know, but guessed they were probably Okay. "Ask them yourself," I suggested. Well, you can imagine the overwhelmingly favorable feedback he got. Jim, the severe judge and critic, had masked that tendency by keeping those judgments bottled up in himself. He lived by the adage that if you can't say something good about somebody, don't say anything.

That "goodness" kept him from indulging in gossip, but it didn't keep from judging "inside." Quiet judges build walls between themselves and others, and what he had just done was open a gate. By talking straight with the guys, he became eminently more likable, more relaxed, and more trustworthy.

Stop here; ponder the extremes in your life, including the strengths that, taken to the edge, can become weaknesses, and the weaknesses, moderated properly, that can become strengths. Then compose your Centering Statements. One final caution: Centering doesn't mean compromise. Compromise, similar to consensus, provides a false foundation on which to erect a meaningful life. It's not about the averaging out of your existence or finding its lowest common denominator. Centering establishes appropriate behavior for each situation you encounter. You may whisper and pray in the darkness at 2 a.m., and you may yell yourself hoarse at Yankee Stadium. Forget "one size fits all." Honest and trustworthy behavior comes in every size imaginable.

## Arriving at Your Deeper SELF

Remember Zeno's Paradox from Chapter 2? Basically, it says you walk halfway to the wall, halfway again, and halfway again and again and again. And again. You never reach the wall, but you get very, very close. While the journey to self-discovery never ends, as with Zeno's Paradox, you can get closer and closer to your deeper SELF.

Let's return to our initial discussion of Style-of-Life, and the idea that an organized set of convictions beyond our awareness pulls us forward. Before you began reading this book, I expect you had a fairly orderly outlook on life, and a consistent governance system in place for it, although that outlook and governance resided beyond your full awareness. You "understood" yourself in a defined way (self-image), "scanned" your horizon through a prescribed lens (world view), and "navigated" the sea of life in accordance with a central goal (encompassing, hidden, magnetic) that you relied on to land you on a peaceful shore.

If you've engaged in the exercises throughout the book, you should have "come closer to the wall," growing more and more aware of it. If you have arrived at a guardian presence Style-of-Life, congratulations! If, on the other hand, you discovered a looming threat in your Style-of-Life, you may now (if you haven't done it already) revise that Style-of-Life to become a guardian presence.

You'll remember that it took me two steps to get closer to my own wall. Essentially, the journey went like this.

Starting Point:                  I am an observer

Step One Advancement:     I am an angler

Step Two Homeward Bound: I am a laser

At the Starting Point, I became aware of the self-image that governed me. With Step One, I took corrective action and became less passive and more proactive; more in tune with myself, more aware and adept. With Step Two, I came closer to the wall, a true SELF, increasingly unaware and adept. Now more natural, I see that possibilities may exist for my making occasional contributions to other people's lives without knowing it. My Creative Self has taken me from self to SELF. You may make this journey more quickly and easily than I did, but if not, my own example proves that you can get there if you work at it.

My first conception of myself emerged in Philadelphia when I was enjoying great financial success. While I don't disdain that self, I see it as stunted and under-developed. Step by step, I navigated my self until it developed more fully into a true SELF. You may remember that I gave you a foreshadowing of this process when I sketched it out as the "A-B-Cs of Change" at the conclusion of Chapter 2.

How many adjectives can you use to describe your true self? Start with:

SELF: grateful, outgoing, masterful, grounded, flexible, receptive, healthy, other-centered, spiritual, patient, attentive, brave.

Now add a dozen of your own:

SELF: _____  _____  _____

_____  _____  _____

_____  _____  _____

_____  _____  _____

Pause, as well, for a minute to remember Jim McGuire's and Elaine Finn's and your own Centering Statements from a few pages back. They, too, stepped closer to the wall.

## The Adventurer

My close friend Pepper de Callier strode as close to the wall, to SELF, as anyone I've ever known. His Style-of-Life:

| I am: | a participant |
| --- | --- |
| Life is: | a full arena |
| My central goal: | to play well with others |

Pepper grew up in central Indiana's Pike Township, in the most modest circumstances. A high-school dropout, he began working as a barber, manning the middle chair of a small shop, flanked on both sides by men who later served time in federal penitentiaries. Shunned by his former mates, he dubbed himself a loser. One day, however, his high school's principal, Edwin White, paid him a visit and scolded him for throwing his life away.

Mr. White pulled no punches. Then he delivered a proposition. If Pepper would agree to take an all-day test and pass it, Mr. White would sponsor his application to a decent college or university. Overwhelmed by his former principal's caring intervention, Pepper agreed to take the test. He passed it, and applied to three top universities: Northwestern, Indiana, and Arizona. All three accepted him, but wishing to put distance between himself and his recent past, he headed west to Tucson. When he arrived there, Admissions Director, David Windsor, took him aside and said, "I just want you to know I don't approve of this sort of thing. You're here under a cloud." Pepper worked his way through school, mopping floors at a fraternity house, doing other odd jobs, and eventually graduated with a major in business administration.

He began his career selling insurance, then founded and served as president of a regional employee benefit consulting firm in Tucson. After he sold that business, he became publisher and editor of *Monterey Life Magazine*, an award-winning, but troubled, monthly publication detailing life on California's central coast. Despite lacking any background in publishing, Pepper turned this enterprise around, then entered into serious negotiations to become publisher of a prestigious New York fine arts magazine. When that job fell through, Pepper found himself out of work for six months. Life went downhill from there. A difficult divorce coupled with a betrayal by the owner of a company who hired him as president, but then refused to honor his pledged investment, plunged Pepper into a dark place.

Broke and terribly discouraged, he finally saw a glimmer of light when an opportunity presented itself for him to enter the executive search profession. It was a dream come true, and he never looked back as he stepped toward what he saw as his Destiny. Long story short, he became a partner in the Los Angeles office of Heidrick & Struggles, one of the premier firms in the business, and seemed set for life. He remarried and moved to San Diego. Soon thereafter, however, his new wife, Priscilla, underwent surgery for breast cancer, and Heidrick & Struggles abruptly closed the San Diego office and asked Pepper to return to Los Angeles. He refused.

In the fall of 2003, Pepper and Priscilla faced a major decision: Where do we go from here? Priscilla's late father, an army officer who had taught at West Point, had served in several European posts, and Priscilla spent much of her youth living abroad and learning new languages. She longed to go back.

With no job on the horizon for either, they scooped up their savings. Too young to retire, they took stock of their finances and made a bold, exciting investment in their future. Choosing to view these recent disruptions in their lives as natural transition points, they sold their two cars and their beautiful San Diego house that overlooks the Pacific. Then they put their furniture in storage, and promptly took off for a rented country house 75 kilometers outside of Paris. They planned to spend three months there, three months in Tuscany outside Florence, then possibly settle for a while in Cairo, Egypt, where Priscilla's mother lived and Pepper could fashion a new career. Doing what? Who knows? They'd cross that bridge when it caught fire.

While in Tuscany, Pepper and Priscilla hosted a party for their new local friends and invited her mother and a couple they'd met earlier, through her mother, as house guests. The wife of her mother's friend, it turned out, was Dana Hunatova, Ambassador to Egypt from the Czech Republic. One night at dinner, when Dana asked Pepper about his plans, he replied that he was content to enjoy this great adventure with Priscilla for now. As for later, perhaps he would consult or teach.

Surprisingly, the Ambassador wondered if he would consider coming to Prague to meet some business and government people there. "We need people like you." She said that since ex-President Vaclav Havel, had left office (he served in that post for 13 years following the fall of Communism), the country had continued its ascent, which was begun under him, and could use a good consultant. "We've come out of Communism and are growing fast."

Though flattered, Pepper didn't take the offer seriously until on the night before departing, Ambassador Hunatova asked again, rather forcefully. Pepper and Priscilla agreed to go to Prague, where he would attend a conference sponsored by the Organization of Security and Cooperation in Europe. The conference centered on developing small and medium-sized businesses in the region. Prague itself in 10 years could become the capital of corporate headquarters in central Europe.

While Pepper attended the three-day conference, Priscilla explored the city, which had transformed itself, from a rather dreary city into a vibrant and lively center of business and culture. At dinner one evening, she suggested they make Prague their home. "My answer had to be yes," recalls Pepper, who believed in his wife's uncanny ability to seize life's opportunities.

Through a professor friend at California State University in San Marcos, he met a professor at Georgetown who knew a man in Prague named Jan Bubenik. Bubenik, the youngest member of Parliament in the new government formed in 1990, had traveled with President Havel to the United States, explaining to all who would listen, their dream of resurgence for the Czech Republic.

After that, Bubenik had served as a European associate of America's most prestigious consulting firm, McKinsey & Company, then had branched out and formed his own executive search firm, Bubenik Partners, now the premier search firm in central Europe. Today, Pepper is that company's Chairman. He coaches top executives, conducts key searches, and enjoys a position as senior advisor to Vaclav Havel's Forum, one of the most distinguished annual conferences for global responsibility in the world. What a journey! From the middle chair in a small Indiana barbershop to a chair at the top of the world.

If you ask Pepper how it all happened, he'll answer with one word: "Serendipity." Call it what you will, luck or Destiny or good fortune, but few great careers develop in a linear fashion. Life ebbs and flows. Obstacles pop up. Detours abound. Several setbacks delay one's success. But the surprising journey goes on, one step at a time.

Pepper has accepted a beckoning Destiny. Will you? He has grown into an admirable model. Follow in his footsteps, and you will, too.

### In this chapter you have learned:

➡ That you are like all other people, like some other people, and like no other person.

➡ That traversing real boundaries will greatly benefit your organization.

➡ How to write your Centering Statements.

➡ The difference between self and SELF.

➡ That you never reach the wall; the journey never ends.

### Your Inner CEO Punch List

❏ Have you thought lately that you might too frequently avoid risk? Be overly risk-averse? When might you go out on a limb, and try something that frightens you a little, or a lot? Try taking some major leaps into new territory.

❏ Think about the times when you talked too much. Remember the maxim: "I would have said less if I'd taken more time to think." Think twice, speak once.

❏ Think about your reaction to the idea that you're responsible for your actions, but not results. Does this notion strike you as foolhardy? Does it deserve your consideration?

❏ When you think you've discovered all you can about yourself, take one more step toward the wall.

# 9

# Mentors

*Unconditional love, that's what mentoring is about.*

—Garry Ridge

One of the most admired CEOs in college textbook publishing, the late Jim Leisy, loved mentoring young executives and often gave surprising advice. "Kings never accept collect calls," he once said to a friend of mine. What? Back then, when a long-distance call cost real money, Jim used that fact to teach a lesson: an effective executive attracts admirers and can waste valuable time talking with people who wanted to associate with the king, whether or not the conversation relates to the king's, and the kingdom's, mission. "Make sure, Mike, that people have a good enough reason to talk to you, so that they'll spend their own money on the call."

Throughout the past three decades, I have worked closely with, and studied dozens of, effective CEOs like Jim Leisy, and I've learned a lot of their secrets about succeeding in the top job. I've done my best to share some of these secrets with you, whether you serve as the CEO of a Fortune 100 company, the president of your local school board, the managing partner of a law firm, the head of a small start-up, or simply yearn for a top job at any sort of organization.

Now that we're nearing the end of our little journey together, and as you continue your personal pilgrimage on your own, I'd like to conclude with one secret that empowers all the others. To quote Dr. Spock from *Star Trek*: "Learn long and prosper." Putting it another way, "Every teacher learns, and every learner teaches."

Mentoring. Do you believe in it? Does it strike you as a bit too touchy-feely or bed-rock essential? Is it just about teaching and learning? How does it differ from personal training? If you believe in mentoring, how do you find a good one? How can you be a good one yourself? Good questions. Let's look for some answers.

First, I'll offer my own definition of mentoring: *the shared learning between mentors and the people they mentor that results in the autonomy of the latter.* By autonomy, I mean self-sustaining competence, what the fledgling eagle acquires when its mother lovingly pushes it out of the nest. Autonomy created by shared learning takes place in many different ways, as we'll see in the pages ahead.

## The Endless Spiral

Christopher Weil, age 70, is the founder of the extraordinarily successful San Diego-based investment firm that bears his name. When you walk through the door, you can see with one glance all the people who make the firm tick. Weil employs 13 people at present, seven of them full-time. Look around, and you'll see no vice presidents, but 10 or 12 cheerful, smiling faces welcoming you into their home.

All seven full-timers answer phone calls, depending on who's free at the moment, and all can field a call from either a complete novice or the most sophisticated investor. Nobody screens a call by asking "Who's calling?" In an office slightly more than 2,200 square feet, which includes a conference room, kitchenette, and a nursery to accommodate a new mother's needs, everyone works in a cubicle, and can't help but overhear any conversation, phone or face-to-face, taking place in such close quarters. A recipe for chaos? Not at all. You cannot find a more congenial work place in town. The company's unofficial motto? "We all learn from each other's buzz."

Actually, Chris Weil himself occupies a tiny corner office with a door, but only because it would have cost the firm more to dismantle it when they moved in three years ago. Only two other two spaces boast a door: the conference room (small, but tasteful) and the nursery, used by Jennifer Sturak, director of investments, and Winston, her infant son.

Had you known Chris Weil in his teens, or even mid-20s, you never would have imagined that he would become such a class act in the investment world. After dropping out of high school, he joined the Navy, served for a time as a Navy recruiter, obtained his G.E.D., and ultimately graduated from UCLA, as a philosophy major, without ever having taken a single course in business or economics. He grew up in a family that nurtured a pro-work but anti-business ethic. "This arose," he says," from my father's commitment to the labor movement, and my mother's conviction that business was unworthy of the attention of first-rate minds."

As a young father, however, struggling in a difficult employment climate, Chris eventually landed a job with Investors Diversified Services, passed the securities exam, and began work as a mutual funds salesman. Always a fast learner, he did so well he started his own investment firm in 1971, grew it steadily, and finally sold it in 1985, remaining aboard with the new owners as chairman of that unit. Restless for new horizons, however, in 1988 he formed Christopher Weil & Company (CWC), an investment firm involved in portfolio management, private equity, and financial advisory services. CWC ranks in the nation's top 3 percent of all S.E.C. registered investment advisors for assets under management. In the last decade, the firm has quintupled the volume of those assets, working mainly with 250 wealthy families.

When I ask Chris about mentoring, he sounds like a contrarian. "There are people very conscious about mentoring. They do it deliberately. I've never done that. Every leader, by virtue of his position, has influence. Not all leaders are good leaders. Good leadership is in the demonstration. I pay attention to see if people are learning. I'm not here to teach, except by example. If I do my job right, that's all the 'mentoring' I feel I need to do. Mentoring as a project has always seemed a little artificial to me. Others have done well with it, so this is not some nullifying cosmic statement. It just seems that sometimes the mentor wants too much from the relationship for himself. I've never been comfortable with it. For me, it puts dye in the water."

Now chairman of the firm, Chris has placed the CEO mantle onto his son-in-law, John Wells, and become, along with his wife, active in San Diego philanthropic activities. John doesn't match any of the images most people conjure up when they picture the guy who married the boss's daughter. A graduate of the Johnston Center at the University of Redlands in California, John took advantage of the school's program wherein students create their own major, take mostly tutorials with selected professors, rather than traditional courses, and perform on a pass/fail basis. Similar to Chris, John was allergic to the conventional form of business education. Majoring in Chinese-American history and politics, he won the election for president of the student body at the end of his freshman year. The sort of man who knows how to present a point of view, he dazzled, then married fellow student, Kit-Victoria Weil.

After graduation, Kit went to work in her father's business while John pursued a career in international affairs with a Chinese company. He ended up going Japanese instead, and hired on with joint venture Nippon-Yusan-Kaisha where he arranged American corporation visits for Asian executives looking to acquaint themselves with U.S. business methods. This involved an excruciating mastery of detail, for which a computer proved quite useful.

Surprised by his natural affinity for this kind of learning, John began to moonlight at CWC to help the firm automate its complex business transactions. In 1994, he joined CWC full-time, sequentially mastered every job in the business, and today holds the top job. For his part, father-in-law Chris says the firm has excelled with the right mix of hardware, software, and intellectual capital. "We have an enormously sophisticated platform for transactions that's run day-to-day by Terence Kelling. It's equal to the major houses like Goldman, Sachs, and Morgan Stanley. But it's not just the platform that has led to our wealth management delivery process. The real difference is made by our people who have an unusual attitude about service."

Chris continues: "It's not just the people, it's people in a system, more sophisticated than a culture. What makes them valuable is not how good they are and how well they do their jobs, but the extent to which they contribute to a system based on collaboration between people who trust fully that what you give to it will somehow come back to you." In other words, learning at CWC is a two-way thoroughfare, where teachers learn and learners teach. It works because the people at CWC, highly competent, caring, and blessed with an abundance of mutual respect, never tire of the learning process.

When I asked John if he and others in the company considered Chris as a mentor, he offered some fascinating observations. John differs with his father-in-law. "It's clear. Here, Chris is the mentor. His bold steps are usually right on, and we learn from him. I'm not the risk-taker he is, and I get comfort from his strength. To give you a specific example, Chris is mentor to Rob Gaan (a Chinese-American, who, more than anyone, except Chris, is in charge of client relations and sales). Rob is now totally comfortable in his job and handles 99 percent of complex client issues."

What makes him a good mentor? John describes Chris as a consummate people person and a careful listener. He says that anytime the team hits a snag on some initiative, Chris comes up with three options for people to explore on their own. Everyday, Chris teaches those around him to use old tools in new ways, always stressing a creative way of looking at client needs. Because he does that so well, he provides a model on which others can base their behavior. However you say it ("walk the walk," "lead by example," "show, don't tell"), it all comes down to providing a template without forcing a cookie cutter onto people's beliefs and notions.

Then something magical happens. Everyone who benefits from the mentor's model turns into a model as well, creating an endlessly expanding spiral of learning with all the power of a tornado. As Chris says of John, "We've learned together. I knew more about the business, but he knew and was insistent about what we needed to grow and improve. We talk things over. He argues with me when he feels strongly about something and accepting when I have a prevailing argument. We both know there's no such thing as not having more to learn."

Chief Financial Officer Laura Gordon, and Director of Investments Jennifer Sturak, are prime examples of CWC having a diverse work force. No glass ceiling here.

Laura has worked with Chris from the beginning. Responsible for all of the firm's accounting, she knits together all their elaborate deals. Day-to-day she works with bankers, lawyers, accountants, and CEOs. Calm, pleasant, and unpretentious, she handles negotiations with aplomb. "Chris is the deal guy," she observes. "I do the dirty work. I'm analytical. I like things in a box."

When she went through a rough divorce a couple of years ago, she didn't miss a day of work, though some days she did little more than stare into her computer. She did not hide her feelings, because, as she plainly told me, "There's no need to hide who you are in this place."

Similar to everyone else, she speaks of CWC's nurturing environment, which encourages freedom of expression and mutual respect between associates. This attitude also extends to the clients. "A key lesson I've learned from Chris," she says, "is that there's a value to every relationship, and you don't know where it will go. Who's going to cross your path again? It's not about burning bridges; you just don't know."

The fact that the company includes its clients in the endless spiral of learning, learning from them as much as they learn from each other, and teaching them as much as they teach each other, accounts for a great deal of CWC's success.

Jennifer is the main influence on all the decisions made by the investment committee of the firm on behalf of the 250 wealthy client families. Her associates admire her for her diligence and discipline. She says point blank, "The reason I've been able to excel is the environment. I flourish here. Our good work for our clients is not exceptional. We do it every time."

Mentoring at CWC functions like a two-way radio, with both sides of the communication constantly transmitting and receiving important lessons as shown in the chart on page 207.

Before we leave this company, I'd like to share some notes I took as I interviewed Chris, John, Laura, and Jennifer about mentoring:

## Notes on Continuous Learning at CWC

1. Concentrate on the heart of the matter.

2. Expand your breadth of knowledge by learning about other people's jobs.

3. Everyone is a brother or sister, even when a fight breaks out. This includes clients.

4. Provoke and challenge comfortable belief systems because danger often lurks in the comfort zone.

5. Never lose sight of the company's strategy (the big picture).

6. Worry about the details (little pictures that make up the big picture).

7. Automate, automate, automate whenever possible. Technology is the lynchpin to efficiency.

8. Practice ethical behavior, integrity, and absolute honesty.

9. Educating your clientele, should they want to be educated, is in the best interest of the client and us. We get the chance to explain our value compared to regular industry practices and clients receive valuable information.

10. Participate in community life (charity, politics, neighbors and the environment).

| The 2-Way Radio | | |
|---|---|---|
| **Transmitter** | | **Receiver** |
| General: someone models behavior | ↔ | Someone studies model, practices modeling. |
| General: Someone delivers honest feedback | ↔ | Someone welcomes criticism, suggestions, evaluations. |
| General: Team develops clear, concise, compelling mission | ↔ | Everyone listens carefully, internalizes lessons. |
| General: All bestow and receive love | ↔ | All receive and bestow love. |
| General: Everyone makes time for contact | ↔ | Everyone takes time to build relationship. |
| Specific: Everyone approves of a diverse work force | ↔ | CWC network generates candidates who meet the standards for hiring. |
| Specific: Jennifer exercises her firm discipline and insight to generate investment options | ↔ | Investment Committee listens, critiques, and decides. |
| Specific: John takes Danny Cung under his wing to teach him how to master the complex trading system | ↔ | Danny trains, studies, passes the Equity Trader Exam, and prepares to succeed John in that role. |
| Specific: Jennifer gives birth to Winston | ↔ | Instead of enduring a long maternity leave, CWC creates a nursery on the premises. |
| Specific: Chris represents strong moral, intellectual and risk-friendly presence, and makes stock available to all associates | ↔ | Everyone trusts Chris's word, and appreciates his wisdom. |

When CWC hires a new person, they look for these traits in a candidate. "We don't hire based on credentials," says Chris. "We don't hire based on technical proficiency. We are looking for brains, old fashioned ambition, curiosity, character, and a service orientation." In a word, they look for "a good student." And good students, like good mentors, constantly engage in constructive dialogues.

## Conversations With Water

Philosopher Martin Buber ("All real living is meeting"), gave a lot of thought to dialogue. He wrote that a satisfying conversation with someone depends on honest sharing of words and ideas. That does not mean that you never hold anything back. Carpenters "measure twice, cut once." Good communicators "think twice, speak once." I once stood behind a voluble, complaining woman in a supermarket checkout line. After the exasperated checker failed to get in one word of response or explanation, he shouted "Lady, have you ever had an unexpressed thought?"

Why am I harping on dialogue and the careful use of words? Because all teaching and all learning involves dialogue, even if that "conversation" only appears in your head as you read a book. Cynthia Ozick, one of our finest writers, observes that "Language makes culture, and we make a rotten culture when we abuse words." Poor use of language makes rotten mentors as well.

Research by a brilliant Japanese scientist demonstrates the power of positive care-giving speech, clearly written language, compelling graphics, and beautiful music. Dr. Masaru Emoto summarizes his research in his short book *The Hidden Messages in Water* and in his video *Messages from Water*. I urge you to take a look at them. (See the "Your Inner CEO Bookshelf" section at the back of this book.)

An ardent environmentalist, Dr. Emoto is a student of water. Starting from the notion that no snowflake looks exactly like any other, Dr. Emoto wondered if frozen water crystals drawn from various water samples from around the world would also exhibit such individualistic properties. At first they seemed to do so. However, as he photographed frozen droplets from 50 different sources thawing in 50 different petri dishes, he discovered that the astonishing range of crystal formation (or lack thereof) depended on the environment from which a particular sample was drawn.

While 100 percent pure water produced well-formed, hexagonal, beautiful crystals, water drawn from natural sources reflected those sources. Samples from Rocky Mountain glaciers in North America produced ice crystals that looked as if they were encased in snow. Ice crystal formed from water drawn from the enormous Victoria Falls in Zimbabwe formed crystals whose wide columns looked like plunging water.

When Dr. Emoto and his colleagues placed a jar of water on top of photographs of beautiful scenery, and then photographed the crystals that formed from their exposure, they "reflected" aspects of the scenery. A photograph of the sun produced a large crystal much like the sun itself. The Korean folk song, "Arriang," tells the sad story of separated lovers, and, when "heard" by a jar of water placed in front of a stereo, the water crystals were shaped a broken heart. Yodeling from Austria produced a crystal that mimicked an open mouth. A beautiful crystal forming from Mozart's Symphony No. 40 seems to mirror the unreserved way Mozart lived his life. The color photos reproduced in Dr. Emoto's book and video will delight you.

Tap water that had undergone "purifying treatment" from Paris, Tokyo, London, Sydney, and Bangkok failed to produce crystals at all. Here's the surprising thing, though. While some waters captured beauty, others behaved rather badly. Water from New York City and Washington, D.C. formed crystals, albeit rather unlovely ones. Words typed on plain paper and wrapped around a jar of water produced varying results: beautiful if the words conveyed positive and kind feelings, or ugly if they communicated negative and mean-spirited ones.

Beautiful crystals emerged from "thank you" in all languages sampled, as well as "let's do it," "I'm sorry, "wisdom," "you're cute," "you're beautiful," "angel," and "cosmos." Ugly and mal-formed crystals came from words such as "you fool," "do it," "you make me sick," "I will kill you," "must," and "Satan." Water that was *ignored* fared even worse than that which was insulted or threatened.

Can you guess what experience led water to form the most beautiful crystal of all? A paper wrapping displaying the words, "love" and "gratitude." Think about it.

The words "love" and "gratitude" easily won out over "love" alone. Dr. Emoto muses: "What is the relationship between love and gratitude? For an answer to this question, we can use water as a model. A water molecule consists of two hydrogen atoms and one oxygen atom, represented by H2O. If love and gratitude, similar to oxygen and hydrogen, were linked together in a ratio of 1 to 2, gratitude would be twice as big as love.

"I suggest that having twice the amount of gratitude as love is the balance we should strive for. At a seminar after I had mentioned this in my presentation, two young women came up to me and said, 'We were very impressed. Weren't you saying that people have one mouth for speaking and two ears for listening?'

'That's right—that's absolutely right!' I exclaimed, and I knew I had become a little wiser. When we observe the natural world, we can see that the passive energy has greater strength."

If water registers the affect of negative and positive words, imagine what happens in the human heart? People listen carefully to a mentor like Garry Ridge, so skilled and caring in his speech. They turn a deaf ear to the ego-driven executive who rambles on and on about *himself* and *his* goals and *his* needs. Every morale survey I've seen backs up that fact.

## The Power of "With"

Do you want authentic power? Yes? Then share is it *with* others. You want people to follow you? Travel *with* them. You want people to learn? Learn *with* them. Good mentors replace "and/or" thinking with a *with* philosophy. It's not CEO *and* team; it's CEO *with* team; not leadership *or* management, but leadership *with* management; not us *and* our customers, but us *with* our customers. Life and work is not a monologue. It's a dialogue.

The best mentors (teachers *with* learners) use careful and caring speech not to reach consensus, but to express who they are and what they believe the company can be at its best. The conversation occurs at the boundary between you and people who, more than anything else want to belong and grow and gain and give. They long for love and respect for everyone with whom they work. Your careful and caring speech, both its tenor and content, builds a sturdy bridge over the often troubled waters that lie between rhetoric and essence.

Note that both contact and conversation begin with the same prefix "con," which in Latin means "with." Think about other words that begin with "con."

- Concentrate
- Conserve
- Contain
- Confide
- Console
- Context
- Conjoin
- Constitute
- Continue
- Connect
- Construct
- Contract
- Consent
- Consult
- Convince

Starting with you, YC provides a place of *contact* where conversations occur. In that place, continuous learning thrives, nurtured by careful and caring communication.

My friend Garry Ridge, age 50, the warm, unpretentious Australian CEO whom we met in Chapter 7, maintains just such a place. He calls it "Servant leadership with an edge." At WD-40, the transmitters and receivers of mentoring lie on the cutting edge of learning.

Let me give you an example of how Garry uses one word to connect with his people: *tribes.* To anyone who will listen, Gary insists "Tribal leaders sit around a fire and share their learning with younger tribe members. So that's the number one responsibility of the WD-40 Tribe, to make learning inclusive and evolutionary." Concentrating on the task of maintaining a robust learning culture, Garry uses the tribal metaphor to give his people a sense of identity and sense of belonging. The tribe creates folklore, the stories people share to teach what works and what doesn't work at WD-40. A company's folklore socializes and congregates (there's that old "with" prefix again) people behind the tribe's mission. Stories, like parables in the bible, *show* rather tell a moral.

The tribe includes warriors, hunters, and gatherers, healers and Shamans, all the individual contributors who do proud work to sustain the tribe. It conducts tribal ceremonies that honor traditions. I could go on for pages, but you get the idea: a rich culture springs from a single, simple, powerful word, a concrete word that creates a clear mental image. "There's no question," Garry says, "that our mission and goal in life is to create shareholder value. But as part of that process, we are using this learning laboratory to create great leaders that we send out in the world to be better leaders in the business world, in the community, and in their personal lives."

Garry's commitment to "servant leadership with an edge" shows up most when he shares his theory that mentoring is all about unconditional love. He says he's not a religious person, but he does think of himself as *spiritual*. Every tribe uses some form of spirituality to generate faith, the sort of faith we discussed in the previous chapter.

He describes mentoring as two people traveling down a road side-by-side. Although the mentor knows the road well, he lets his friend make his own discoveries. When the mentor knows there's a pothole ahead, he may warn his friend to step wisely, but he doesn't necessarily tell him exactly where the danger is. However, he won't let his friend hurt himself. While he cares deeply about his friend, he doesn't meddle in his life. He rejects control. He promotes autonomy. Even if the friend stumbles once or twice, he learns from the experience.

At WD-40, mentoring is a way of life. Garry says, "We've formalized a mentoring program. Anybody can volunteer to be a mentor when they think they have something to contribute to a learner in a particular area, but they do it as collateral activity, not in place of their day-job in any way."

Garry himself mentors everybody. He travels the world regularly, keeping in touch with WD-40's 240 people everywhere via frequent, warm, colorful broadcast e-mails that detail his own learnings from the trip, and praise for people who have contributed to the business in some imaginative or thoughtful way. To see how the spirit of good will and energy permeate this company, check out the Website (*www.wd40.com*) and Garry's own site (*www.thelearningmoment.net*).

Maria Mitchell, WD-40's vice president of corporate and investor relations, began working for the company as a secretary 11 years ago, before Garry became CEO. She owes much of her amazing advancement to her mentor. "Garry helps a lot of people, just as he's helped me. I'm blessed to know what it takes to learn, thanks to him. He helped me see the possibilities. Many others will say the same thing. He's remarkable."

Maria acts as corporate secretary, managing external relations, such as global legal affairs and customer loyalty programs, with a staff of four. In her early days, however, she lacked confidence in herself.

"I didn't have a college degree, but he wanted me to enroll in the Master of Science of Executive Leadership program at San Diego

University. He has a technical degree from Australia, and graduated from the SDU program himself in 2001. The school makes admission exceptions for some applicants, and I felt honored to be one of them, but was terrified when I saw the credentials of my fellow students. I got past that, though, and found I'm good at learning. I'm a developing leader and maybe always will be. Garry won't let anyone take being 'a leader' an ego trip. More than anything else, by way of mentoring me, he helped me articulate my growth plans and opportunities in plain English."

Maria says that when Garry speaks, he chooses his words carefully, and when he acts, he does so with great precision. Once, when she submitted a 500-word report for his review, he scanned it quickly, summarized it concisely, and suggested specific ways in which she could make it tighter, crisper, clearer, and more compelling. That lesson helped her improve all of her communication. Garry's skill with connection matches his skill with communication. Maria points out, "He reads people extremely well and fast, too. He has an eye for the stages they're in and where they'll be down the road and what more they need. He peels away egos." In other words, he replaces "I" with "we," so that any one person walks the path to success *with* everyone else.

To make all this practical, I asked Garry to jot down 10 questions that might help a mentor develop the sort of care-giving speech so prevalent at WD-40. It took seconds for him to come up with this list:

- Do you interrupt people, finish their sentences?
- Do you use *questions* to make judgments or express criticism?
- Do your voice mail and e-mail messages remain courteous?
- Do you speak with a smile in your voice?
- Do you insist on having the last word?
- Do you glare?
- Do you threaten?
- Do you hold grudges rather than forgive?

▶ Do you find it difficult to say "I'm sorry" when you've wronged someone?

▶ Do you consistently show others love and gratitude?

In keeping with the notion that leaders work, workers lead, teachers learn, and learners teach, Garry Ridge has formalized mentoring at WD-40. The following memo presents the company's 2006 program:

## Leaders Coaching Leaders

# A WD-40 Company Mentoring Program

**Leaders Coaching Leaders** is a mentoring program that will provide a resource for WD-40 teammates around the world who want to improve their leadership and business skills by learning from an internal teammate. This program will pair up the mentor/mentee (coach/learner) depending on skill development, geography, interest, and functional area. The coaching teams will develop and agree to their own perfect transaction for their experience, as relates to time commitment, schedule, skills to be learned, and any other specific expectations.

### Goals of the Leaders Coaching Leaders Program:

➡ Provide an opportunity for WD-40 teammates to improve their leadership skills and business knowledge.

➡ Provide an opportunity for WD-40 coaches to improve their mentoring and leadership skills.

➡ Allow teammates around the world to come into contact and share business and cultural knowledge.

➡ Broaden the knowledge base of WD-40 teammates across departments and functional areas.

➡ Develop strong inter-departmental and international communication between teams.

### Who Will Be the Coaches?

➡ All coaches will not necessarily be a "manager." We are looking for Leaders!

➡ Some coaches will volunteer by contacting Carol Chappie in the San Diego office.

➡ Some coaches will be asked to volunteer by a teammate who wants to learn from them.

➡ Some coaches will be requested to participate based on specific skills, geography, or knowledge base.

## How Do You Get Involved as a Learner?

➡ Contact Carol Chappie in the San Diego office #1131.

➡ Have a specific topic or skill that you would like to improve or learn.

➡ If you already have a coach or a request for a specific coach, let Carol know, or she can help pair up the teams with the coaches who have volunteered.

## When Does the Leaders Coaching Leaders Program Begin?

➡ Coaching teams will be matched up in April/May 2006.

➡ These coaching teams will continue through 2006, until the new teams for 2007 are created.

➡ Depending on your own Perfect Coaching Transaction, your coaching relationship may end earlier or later than the calendar year end.

————

Can you see a way to adopt WD-40's mentoring program for your company? Note how the WD-40 program describes the process, sets goals, identifies resources for coaching, tells people how they can get involved, and establish a timetable. It fulfills the old reporter's checklist: "who, what, when, where, why, and how?"

## Full Frontal Contact

I'd like to conclude this final section of the book with another good mentor, Jim Metcalf, the 48-year-old president and chief operating officer of USG, the $6 billion-plus market-dominant company I presented earlier. Jim grew up in Toronto, Ohio, population 8,000, about 30 miles west of Pittsburgh. The youngest of three children and the only son of a steelworker and World War II veteran, he graduated from Ohio State University in 1980 and immediately went to work with USG in Los Angeles as a trainee. His career followed a straight trajectory to the top operating job.

His Style-of-Life looks like this:

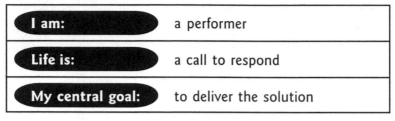

| I am: | a performer |
|---|---|
| Life is: | a call to respond |
| My central goal: | to deliver the solution |

From discussions with members of Jim's team and my own observations from many hours spent with him throughout the years, I've concluded his superior performance relies heavily on mentoring. When asked about mentoring, he doesn't hesitate: "Be fully present, a consummate net-worker, and a grounded positive leader."

## Fully Present

It simply doesn't matter who you are; when you come into contact with Jim Metcalf, you feel like the only other person in the room. He focuses on you like a laser, making you feel important, valued, and respected. Unlike so many self-centered executives, he leaves his ego at the door.

He shows up at meetings early and greets everyone with genuine enthusiasm, instantly conveying his accessibility. He makes any meeting with him informal and relaxed, and he strives to create a climate where people feel confident expressing themselves honestly and forthrightly.

Whether he stands behind a podium making a formal presentation to a large audience, sits at a conference table with a few staff members, or relaxes in an easy chair for a conversation with you, he engages others with a remarkable blend of directness, candor, and clarity.

People find him supportive in a hands-on way. Never passive in his dealings with colleagues, he makes "full frontal contact" without micro-managing the situation. He cares about people. His care-giving speech includes a number of stock phrases: "Is there anything we can do to help?" "Do you need to talk anything over?" "You're new in this job, but we expect big things from you. While you're getting your footing, I'll give you air cover throughout the company."

Unlike a lot of big-shot bosses, he doesn't summon people to his office. He'd rather go to them; yet he always keeps his door open for anyone who needs him for anything. The benefit to this practice flows two ways. When Jim visits you, you feel honored; when you visit him, you feel welcomed.

All of Jim's team members see him as a model for *balance,* a leader fully present both on and off the job. With a strong wife and three exemplary kids, his family functions as a fully integrated and loving unit. He admires his mother-in-law, and seeks her company. He gives himself to key community organizations, plays a lot of golf, and he loves sports, particularly Ohio State and Pittsburgh Steelers football.

He knows when to turn off the Blackberry and notebook. Three years ago when he went off to the Stanford Executive Program for seven weeks, he left Dom Dannessa, his EVP of manufacturing, in charge. Because he had mentored his people so well, his organization didn't miss a step, and, as a matter of fact, grew in his absence.

## Consummate Net-Worker

Rick Lowes, USG vice president and corporate controller, tells a simple story that illustrates how Jim Metcalf pulls people into his orbit. Jim's team had just completed a day's work at their offsite meeting at The Renaissance Esmeralda Resort and Spa in California's Palm Desert.

"A couple of our guys peel off and head back to their rooms to take care of some details before we reassemble later for a group dinner. But a few of us, along with Jim, are walking down one of the paths leading to the lobby, when Jim spots a placard outside a large meeting room that announces a reception for Yogi Berra.

"Immediately, Jim says, 'Hey, let's go in and see if we can meet Yogi.' Well, we open the door and sure enough, we see a room full of people, and a couple of them off to the side speaking to Yogi. Jim heads straight for that little enclave, and we follow.

"He stops a suitable distance from them, they notice us, and the two people with Yogi, apparently feeling their allotted time with him is up, smile and gracefully take their leave. Yogi turns; Jim steps up, extends his hand, introduces himself and us, and tells Yogi that we're with USG Corporation, here for a meeting, saw this reception, and crashed the party because we just couldn't pass up this opportunity to meet him. Yogi laughs easily and says it's a pleasure to meet us, too. He and Jim banter a bit with sports talk, we then all thank him, shake his hand, and leave."

This brief encounter with the great ballplayer may seem trivial, but it epitomizes Jim's skill as a consummate net-worker. Rick benefited from this little lesson, which Jim himself picked up from his own caring mentor, Jim Phillips, who's now retired from USG. Metcalf says of Phillips: "I worked with him in 1988 and we kept close contact throughout my career after he retired. He helped me navigate some of the personalities in the building materials industry and our company, teaching me to trust my gut. He believes in helping people inside and out of USG and gives himself, still, to charities that he feels good about and make a genuine contribution to the community."

Phillips maintains countless contacts throughout Chicago, people he networks into Jim's and USG's world. These people learn about USG, and vice versa, expanding the endless spiral of learning we discussed earlier.

Jim Metcalf extends his influence by sharing his mentor, Jim Phillips, with some of his subordinates who can benefit in specific ways from Phillips's perspective. Fareed Khan, executive vice president of sales and marketing, says, "I've learned a lot about Jim Metcalf's values by learning about Jim Phillips's values." Dom Dannessa has broadened his understanding of marketing and sales through association with Phillips, and was appointed to the Advisory Board of Catholic Charities of Chicago by virtue of Phillips's introduction.

Chris Griffin, president of CGC, USG's Canadian subsidiary, shares another example of Metcalf's networking ability. Ten years ago, when Chris had just become manager of a faltering, but vital product line, Metcalf offered an idea. "Here's a list of five people in the company that I want you to call and set up a time to get together with them to get their perspective on the product, where we've fallen short, and what we can do to improve the product and our service around it." Realizing that all the names on the list outranked him, Chris resisted the advice. Metcalf countered, "What do you have to lose?" Reluctantly, Chris complied.

"Well," said Chris, "I was stunned. All five agreed to meet with me, and that was valuable not only for what I learned from them, but because I got to know them, they got to know me, and the product truly got on the radar. I went back to Jim with a big smile and he gave me a new list!" Networking, Chris learned, teaches you even more than the school of hard knocks.

## Positive Grounded Leadership

Although far from perfect, and with a temper he sometimes needs to keep in check, Jim Metcalf exhibits an exceptional degree of positive leadership, largely because he remains so grounded in his life.

He does not issue orders: he asks penetrating questions. Instead of "I think you should...." He asks, "What do *you* think?" Rather than detailed tactics and goals, he relies on broad, clear parameters. Brendan Deely is president and COO of L&W, USG's subsidiary, which is by far the largest wallboard-related products distributor in the world. He says Jim leads by "judging our judgments." Says Brendan, "I thrive on that kind of direction." Dom Dannessa speaks volumes about Jim in a few words: "He's steadily helped me raise my game."

Jim gets high marks from his staff, too, for his balanced temperament, good will, and resourcefulness. If some project fails early, he knows how to rescue it without making anyone feel like a failure. His message conveys, "There are a lot of ways to do this, so what should we try next?" As Fareed Khan says, "I watch him with admiration, and remind myself I can do these things, not his way, but my way."

Despite this flexibility under pressure, Jim keeps a steadfast heart. He'll stay the course when things get shaky. He'll feast on pressure, his body language signaling, "We're all in this together." Chris Griffin argues that, "He's more than a cheerleader."

Fareed underscores Chris's view: "Jim's transparent and consistent. We're never on a zigzag course. Things just seem to build on themselves. Therefore he doesn't have to be so exact. He looks at all sides of the prism. His flexibility is awesome. I learn from his instincts when we talk about stressful challenges or shifts in the business. I'll test the situation with a declarative statement of what we need to do. Then he looks at me and says, 'Go ahead. Fix it.'" Bottom line: Jim Metcalf teaches the essential habits of high achievers."

## The 20 Habits of a Good Mentor

In 1985, long before I met Chris Weil, Garry Ridge, and Jim Metcalf, I published a book titled *The Making of the Achiever*. In it, I listed and described what I considered the 20 essential qualities in a top executive that produce world class performance. I grouped those 20 qualities under four broad categories: (1) Other-Centered, (2) Courageous, (3) Judicious, and (4) Resourceful.

Not long after the book came out, I led a workshop for the top management of a key division of Avery Dennison. In preparation for that offsite meeting, Jim Shaw, the head of the division, assigned the book for homework, asking Gene Woynoski, a member of Avery Dennison's corporate staff, to conduct a literature search to capture the "best practices" of top executives in the leading companies of the day.

Gene compiled the list, added another column indicating Avery Dennison's own "best practices," and then placed them side-by-side with my 20 qualities. (See page 221.) The two columns came out remarkably similar, and served as a discussion guide for our meeting. I've reproduced the result below with just a few modifications. You won't be surprised that I'd award "A's" to all the mentors you've met in this chapter. This chart can provide a handy checklist to measure your mentoring skills and those of others, either your own mentor or people who might become mentors in the future.

# Team Monitoring

Of all the qualities contributing to the making of a great mentor, none matters more than "collaboration," because, if you fail to master it, you'll fail abysmally as a mentor and leader. I stressed that quality in Chapter 5, but I'm stressing it again because it plays such a crucial role in mentoring. I also want to offer a simple tool I think you'll find quite effective when assessing and assuring team collaboration.

*Mentoring always means nurturing a team.* Seventeenth-century English poet John Donne said it best: "No man is an island." Whether serving as a mentor or receiving mentoring, ultimately you succeed or fail because your team succeeds or fails. Remember, you don't collaborate to reach consensus, but to select from the many *ideas* developed by energized team members that *one option* that will most likely provide a superior outcome.

## 20 Habits of a Good Mentor

| Habit | Activity: Is/Does | Weil/Ridge/Metcalf |
|---|---|---|
| Warmth | Accessible, welcoming, winsome, supportive | A |
| Listening | Listens and speaks clearly to advance the dialogue | A |
| Encouragement | Not bland, mild support, but "to make courageous" | A |
| Affirmation | Confident, believing, optimistic | A |
| Sharing | Forthcoming, steps back, makes room | A |
| Vulnerability | Treats failure as learning, sees critics as teachers, risk-friendly | A |
| Discretion | Trustworthy, tasteful, poised | A |
| Nurturance | Teaching, caring, loyal, truthful | A |
| Decisiveness | Makes *yes, no*, and *wait* decisions quickly | A |
| Uniqueness | Acts on unique strengths | A |
| Orgnizational Savvy | Ardent student of behavior and structure | A |
| Priority | First things first, second things never | A |
| Tenactiy | Sometimes, the only course is staying the course | A |
| Sense of Humor | Can poke fun at self and enjoy it, sees absurdities without cynicism | A |
| Luck | *Seems* to live a charmed life | A |
| Quality | Practices quality in all ways, including own performance | A |
| Perception | Senses what others don't sense | A |
| Gifts Refinement | Unaware and adept, so good she doesn't know it | A |
| Collaboration | Seeks full voices and superior choices, not consensus | A |
| Vision | Sees how "what is" can become something greater | A |
| *The Making of the Achiever"* | Other-Centered, Courageous, Judicious, Resourceful | CWC/WD-40/USG |

That one option may come quickly from a teammate, or it may emerge more slowly as various elements of various ideas combine in the midst of concentrated thinking and careful speech of colleagues who care deeply about each other and their organization. The team leader may start out as the chief collaborator, but as the team grows, all members grow by actively honing their skills as collaborators. Nothing energizes an organization more as teammates expand their skills as mentors and models for the rest of the organization

My own favorite team motto is *"Full Voices and Superior Choices."* Keeping it in mind helps assure your team's collaborative success. I've also found the Team Collaboration Scorecard quite useful. All team members can fill it out periodically as a monitoring device. Share the results. Talk about how you can improve your team's collaboration. Take the lead on this. If you make it a habit, I think you'll like the long-term results.

Look at Chris Weil and John Wells at CWC, Garry Ridge at WD-40, and Jim Metcalf at USG. They're masters at pulling and keeping a team together. You can do it, too. The average executive spends 17 hours a week in meetings and another five hours preparing for those meetings. Nearly everyone complains about it, but the real problem is not meetings, but what happens in them.

## Team Collaboration Scorecard

For each of the following six items, please circle the number that best captures the climate of the team meeting you've just completed. (1=lowest, 5=highest)

**Inclusiveness**

     1     2     3     4     5

Why did you choose that number? _____

_____

**Directness**

     1     2     3     4     5

Why did you choose that number? _____

_____

**Engagement**

    1      2      3      4      5

Why did you choose that number? _____

_____

**Experimentation**

    1      2      3      4      5

Why did you choose that number? _____

_____

**Accountability**

    1      2      3      4      5

Why did you choose that number? _____

_____

**Sensitivity**

    1      2      3      4      5

Why did you choose that number? _____

_____

———

## Your Mentor's Inventory

Now, in closing, think of all the people you've worked with or have observed at home, at work, or participating in community sports, church, or school activities. Which had the most positive effect on you? Jot down the names of 10 or so, then rate them on the 20 Habits of a Good Mentor. I bet they will all do well. How about yourself? How would others rate your mentoring skills?

Revisiting the qualities of people you keep in your heart because they kept you in theirs will help put you on the path to great mentoring, both as a teacher and learner. Phil Jacklin, father of my best friend in grade school, held a white-collar job in a local dairy, then became a salesman for the Glidden Paint Company. He never rose to the top in the business world, but he volunteered as our scoutmaster and youth baseball coach. I count him a significant mentor in my early life. He would get an "A" on most all the habits. The same holds true for Keith Ackman, a YMCA executive who hired me for his staff. A brash, young college freshman, I happily let him take me under his wing and teach me organizational and social skills that I use to this very day. My hard-nosed, tobacco-breathed junior-high teacher, Florence Murdoch, told me, a fumbling student, and our whole class, that I had, as she put it, "gray matter." That simple act changed my life.

### In this chapter you have learned that:

➡ teachers learn and learners teach; mentors model and models mentor.

➡ good mentoring induces *autonomy* in others.

➡ mentors can come from any background.

➡ words make a difference.

➡ "with" rightly replaces "and/or."

➡ mentoring relies on full frontal contact, networking, and positive grounded leadership.

### Your Inner CEO Punch List

❑ Review your hiring methods and standards. Do you rely too heavily on credentials or past proficiency? Consider recruiting for "brains, old fashioned ambition, curiosity, character, and a service orientation."

❑ Read Dr. Emoto's short book. If you do, you will probably exercise more care with words.

❑ Designate someone *with* whom you'd like to become engaged in a mentoring role. Explore that connection with the person you have in mind.

# Appendix:
# Your Inner CEO Bookshelf

If you would like to explore the ground-breaking ideas of Alfred Adler and others who have influenced my work, I suggest you add these books to your executive library. I have also included two earlier books of mine, which I hope you'll find useful, especially if the final chapter on mentoring intrigued you.

1. Ansbacher, Heinz L. & Rowena R. Ansbacher, eds. *Individual Psychology of Alfred Adler: A Systematic Presentation in Selections from His Writings*. New York: Harper Torchbooks, 1964.

    This is not something to read in just a few sittings. It's a scholarly, exhaustive work and the most authoritative and comprehensive treatment of Adler in one volume. It is well-written, however, so your eyes shouldn't glaze over if you read it in short spurts.

2. Collins, Jim. *Good to Great.* New York: Harper Business, 2001.

    Probably the best business book in the last decade written by a class-act author. The Level 5 Leadership Collin's describes and espouses runs down the same track as *Your Inner CEO.* Big Picture thinking based on solid exhaustive research.

3. Cox, Allan. *The Making of the Achiever.* New York: Dodd, Mead, 1985 and *Straight Talk for Monday Morning.* New York: Wiley, 1990.

    I recommend *The Making of the Achiever* if you'd like to know more about each of the 20 qualities that I've listed in the final chapter on mentoring. I'm recommending *Straight Talk for Monday Morning* for its introduction only. There, in the first 20 pages, you'll find detailed guidelines for master collaborators.

4.  Dyer, Wayne D. *Meditations for Manifesting: Morning and Evening Meditations to Literally Create Your Heart's Desire.* Carlsbad, Cal.: Hay House, Inc., 2004.

    You can get this CD from Amazon, too. It, along with the following one, will help you practice the art of meditation. I use this method every morning.

5.  Emoto, Masuru. *The Hidden Messages in Water.* New York: Atria, 2004, *Messages from Water.* (DVD)

    I hope Dr. Emoto's ideas kept you awake at night. His book is short and contains beautiful photographs. The video will enlighten you further after you've read the book. I ordered them both from: *www.amazon.com*

6.  Greenleaf, Robert K. *The Servant as Leader.* Indianapolis, Ind: The Robert K. Greenleaf Center, 1991.

    Don't buy the book with the same title, but this marvelous 37-page orange pamphlet that launched the "Servant Leadership" movement. Order from the Robert K. Greenleaf Center: *www.greenleaf.org*

7.  Katie, Byron, with Stephen Mitchell. *A Thousand Names for Joy: Living in Harmony With the Way Things Are.* New York: Harmony, 2007.

    Byron Katie is a remarkably wonderful woman. With this book you get a "two-fer." Katie (that's what they call her) is married to Stephen Mitchell, her coauthor. Mitchell is the author and translator of many books, including *Genesis*, which led to his appearance on Bill Moyers's *Genesis* for PBS. I have read a passage from his translation of the *Tao Te Ching* virtually every morning for the past 11 years. Similar to Dr. Emoto, Katie will jar you into alternative considerations. Visit their Websites to learn more.

    Mitchell's Website: *www.stephenmitchellbooks.com*

    Katie's Website: *www.thework.com/index.asp*

8. Tapscott, Don, and Anthony D. Williams. *Wikinomics: How Mass Collaboration Changes Everything.* New York: Portfolio, 2007.

Don Tapscott is the best-selling author of *The Digital Economy,* a perceptive, clear book that enlightened the non-geek world about the powerful technological changes taking place in our economy that continue to change our lives forever. Now, in *Wikinomics,* he's back, with his colleague, Anthony Williams, showing us in a compelling way how mass collaboration through the open-source movement and peer production processes are lifting us to never-before imagined efficiencies and knowledge application on a global scale. *Wikinomics* demonstrates that wherever people practice the kind of collaboration espoused in *Your Inner CEO,* and wherever they practice it on a broad scale, geometric growth benefits accrue to the participants. Tapscott truly understands boundaries. You'll want to be part of this!

# Bibliography

Baker, Wayne. *Achieving Success Through Social Capital.* San Francisco: Jossey-Bass, 2000.

Barks, Coleman, trans. *The Soul of Rumi.* San Francisco: Harper San Francisco, 2001.

Bennett, Nathan and Stephen Miles. *Riding Shotgun: the role of the COO.* Palo Alto: Stanford Business Books, 2006.

Bly, Robert, trans. *Selected Poems of Rainer Maria Rilke.* New York: Harper & Row, 1981.

Buber, Martin, and Maurice L. Friedman, ed. *The Knowledge of Man.* Atlantic Highlands, N.J.: Humanity Books, 1998.

Buber, Martin, and Ronald Gregor, trans. *I and Thou.* New York: Scribner, 2000.

Buckingham, Marcus, and Curt Coffman. *First, Break All the Rules.* New York: Simon & Schuster, 1999.

Dalai Lama, and Victor Chan. *The Wisdom of Forgiveness.* New York: Riverhead Books, 2004.

Gendler, J. Ruth. *The Book of Qualities.* New York: Harper & Row, 1988.

Georgescu, Peter with David Dorsey. *The Source of Success.* San Francisco: Jossey-Bass, 2005.

Gleick, James. *Chaos: Making a New Science.* New York: Viking Penguin, 1987.

Gregorian, Vartan. *Islam: A Mosaic, Not a Monolith.* Washington, D.C.: Brookings Institution Press, 2003.

Hammarskjold, Dag. *Markings. New York: Knopf, 1964.*

Hawkins, David R. *Power vs. Force: The Hidden Determinants of Human Behavior.* Carlsbad, Cal.: Hay House, Inc., 2002.

Hoffer, Eric. *Reflections on The Human Condition.* New York: Harper & Row, 1974.

Horney, Karen. *Neurosis and Human Growth.* New York: W.W. Norton, 1991.

Kung, Hans. *Freud and the Problem of God.* New Haven: Yale University Press, 1979.

La Mott, Anne. *Traveling Mercies: Some Thoughts on Faith.* New York: Pantheon Books, 1999.

Markova, Dawna. *No Enemies Within.* Newburyport, Mass.: Conari Press, 1994.

Mitchell, Stephen, trans. *The Poetry of Rainer Maria Rilke.* New York: Random House, 1982.

———. *Tao Te Ching.* New York: Harper & Row, 1988.

Murphy, Emmett C. *Talent IQ.* Avon, Mass.: Platinum Press, 2007.

Olins, Wally. *Corporate Identity: Making Business Strategy Visible Through Design.* Cambridge, Mass.: Harvard Business School Press, 1989.

———. *On Brand.* London: Thames & Hudson, 2004.

Osbon, Diane K., ed. *A Joseph Campbell Companion.* New York: Harper Collins, 1991.

Poitier, Sidney. *The Measure of a Man: A Spiritual Autobiography.* New York: Harper Collins, 2000.

Prothero, Stephen. *Religious Literacy.* San Francisco: Harper San Francisco, 2007.

Rilke, Rainer Maria, and Joan Burnham, trans. *Letters to a Young Poet.* Novato, Calif.: New World Library, 2000.

Sonnenfeld, Jeffrey A. "What Makes Great Boards Great." Harvard Business Review, September-October 2002, 106–113.

Stafford, William. *The Way It Is: New & Selected Poems*. St. Paul, Minn.: Graywolf Press, 1997.

Tapscott, Don and Anthony D. Williams. *Wikinomics: How Mass Collaboration Changes Everything*. New York: Portfolio, 2007.

Wackerle, Frederick W. *The Right CEO*. San Francisco, Calif.: Jossey-Bass, 2001.

Williams, Miller. *The Ways We Touch*. Champaign, Ill.: University of Illinois Press, 1997.

# Index

## A

A-B-Cs of Boundaries, 93, 96

ABCs of Change, 57, 196

Adler, Alfred, 12, 31, 34, 37, 43, 61, 67, 82, 99, 159

adventurer, 197–200

Alliance Care, 94–95

Altman, Roger, 23–24

analogies, animal, 68, 145, 162, 164

Analyzing Boundries, 31

Angus Corporation, 138–140

Angus, Harold, 138–140

Angus, Morton, 13

animal analogies, *see* analogies, animal

art, four qualities of, 77–78

A-T-A Question, 82, 87, 91

authenticity, 97

## B

BAM Grid (Boundaries Awareness Mastery), 13, 84, 87–88, 107, 130

Basis for Strategy, 160

Benison Communication, 186–188

Benison's True and Real Boundries, 188

Berra, Yogi, 143, 217–218

Big Three Questions, 16, 19, 31, 34, 68–69, 72

board, 14, 20, 107–134
    CEO's collaboration with, 118, 122–126
    CEO's reasons to join, 113
    integrated, 113
    meetings, 14, 119–120
    peer reviews, 114
    self-assessment, 113

Boundary Reality Check, 103, 156

boundary, 12–13, 20–22, 24, 26–27,
        33–34, 74, 81–84, 88–96,
        100–105, 186–190
        experience, 109
        flags, 99
        mastering, 100–101
        purpose of, 101
bright side, 22–24, 27, 31–32, 94, 104
Brummer, George, 24-27, 30
Buber, Martin, 92
Buchanan, John, 144–147

**C**

Campbell, Joseph, 22, 48, 51
Canavan, Pat, 119–120
Carlson, Anita, 23–24, 26, 30
Carstairs Computing, 46
catalyst, *see* CEO, as catalyst
Centering Statements, 14
central goal, 16, 18, 26, 31–32,
        34, 37, 43, 45, 50, 59, 61,
        63–64, 70, 72–73, 99, 140,
        159, 169, 173, 197, 216
CEO Boundary Quiz, 125–132
CEO
        and boards, 107–134
        and organizations, 12
        as catalyst, 112–116
        inner, 12
        lost, 88
        "real," 97
        successful, 11
Christopher Weil & Company,
        202–208

Churchill, Winston, 155
Citrizone, 189–190
Coca-Cola, 149
community, 18
consensus, 125, 187
control, 64, 112, 120–125
Corporate Diagnostic, 61, 72–74
corporate magnetism, 136–140
courage, 17, 22, 51, 93
craftsmanship, 77–78
creative self, 41–43, 196

**D**

Dalai Lama, 67, 179
Dannessa, Dom, 177
dark side, 22–24, 27, 31–32, 94, 104
Davis, Joyce, 179–180
de Callier, Pepper, 197–200
Destiny, 11, 16, 43–44, 46–48, 51,
        64, 72, 75, 83, 88, 200
disconnect, 20
Dreikurs, Rudolph, 31

**E**

Ehrhart, Karl, 38–40
8 Rules of Engagement, 110–112
Emoto, Masaru, 208–210
Engdall, Ted, 15, 20, 30, 59
Esau, 49–50
essence, 13, 76

## F

facades 13, 59, 76
faith, 53, 178–182
Farley, Neal, 114–116
fears, 12, 50, 93
Filkin, Len, 94–95
Finn, Elaine, 183–185
Fiorina, Carly, 29–30
fly-on-the-wall coaching, 108–112
form, 14, 155–156, 159
Fourth Presbyterian Church, 144–147, 161–162
full frontal contact, 215–216
function, 14, 155–156, 159

## G

Gaylord InterScience, 109
Geldmacher, Jay, 22
Georgescu, Peter, 27–30
goals, 12, 15, 18–19, 157
Gregorian, Vartan, 179–180
Griffin, Chris, 218–219
Grounding Quiz, 40–41
grounding, 11–12, 21–22, 38, 41, 46,48, 93, 107–108, 219
Grove, Andrew, 74
guardian presence, 12–13, 18–21, 24, 34, 44–45, 67, 74, 93

## H

Halsey-Frickert, 114–115
Harley-Davidson, 149

*Hidden Messages in Water, The*, 208–210
historical perspective, *see* perspective, historical
Hoffer, Eric, 20, 90, 182
Horney, Karen, 82–83
Hunter, Charlie, 59–60, 62, 70–71, 157, 168–169

## I

I Am Questionnaire, 51, 53–56
identity, corporate, 64–70
Intel, 74

## J

Jacklin, Phil, 223–224
Jacob, 48–50, 181

## K

keel-of-boat values, 14, 145
Klimek, Lisa, 47

## L

Labyrinth, 87, 90
Laidlaw Cement, 120–122
Lamott, Anne, 47
land between, 91–92
Lassiter Corporation, 81
Leisy, Jim, 201
life cycle, 75
Lloyd, Frank, 155
looming threat, 12, 18–22, 24, 29, 34, 44–45, 67, 74, 93

# M

Machida, Soho, 180
Madison, Mark, 51–53
Maguire, Jim, 190–195
management, "open book", 112
mastery, 84–86
McCartney, Paul, 131
McCauley, Curt, 81, 92
Mellencamp, John Cougar, 78
mentoring, 13, 201–224
    habits of a good, 220–221
Metcalf, Jim, 216–220
model, 13, 186–187
Mosco Nutrition, 42
Motorola, 119
moving,
    against, 13, 34, 82–84, 90
    away, 13, 34, 82–84
    toward, 13, 34, 82–84,
      88–90

# N

Napoleon, 22
National Association of
    Corporate Directors
    (NACD), 109

# O

Obelisk, Inc, 59, 70–71, 157, 168–169
obstacles, 27
Ockham's Razor, 155–156
Ogilvy & Mather, 76

Ogilvy, David, 76–77
Olins, Wally, 148, 150
    view of corporate success,
      148–149
"open book" management, *see*
    management, "open book"
opportunities, 22
organizations, 20
    *see also* CEO and
      organizations
Overby, Phil, 46–47

# P

Parker, Gordon, 87, 90, 99, 178
Parsons, Nicole, 86
Pat's Paradigm, 119–120
Penrose, Wally, 47–48
personality
    ideal, 13
    real, 13
perspective, historical, 77–78
Phillips, Jim, 218
Phillipson, Ed, 186–188
pilgrim, 177, 190–195
Porsche, 148–149
power, *see* control
    presentations of, 116–118
purity, 77–78
purpose, *see* function

# Q

Quest Music (QM), 60, 63–64, 156

# R

rationalization, 102

reality, 22

Reserve Resources, 159–161

revelation, 77–78

Ridge, Garry, 168, 210–215

# S

Sahm, Doug, 97

self
    creative, 41–43, 196
    ideal, 60, 62–63
    real, 60, 62–63, 133

SELF, 13, 195–197

self-image, 31–32, 64, 74

self-knowledge, 17

Shaw, Robert, 77

soul, 22

Southwest Airlines, 149

Starbucks, 149

strengths, 12, 195

structure, *see* form

Style-of-Life, 12–13, 30–34, 37–38, 42, 50, 53, 57, 69–72, 99, 101, 131, 140, 155, 161, 164–169, 177, 195

Sullivan, Louis, 155–156, 159

Summers, Gary, 159–161

# T

*Tao Te Ching*, 85

Team Collaboration Scorecard, 222–223

2-Way Radio, The, 207

Theories of Personality, 82

threats, 22, 29

Tomlinson, LaDanian, 85

top team, 107

top team, 14, 113, 115, 118, 126
    decision-making process of, 189–190
    point of view of, 118

Twenty 20 Habits of a Good Mentor, 221

# U

Uniqueness Inventory, 183–185
    values, 161–164
    vision here-and-now of, 170–172
    vision there and then of, 173

# V

values, 68, 78, 97, 151, 161–164
    corporate, 151
    feet, 33–34, 62, 153
    mouth, 34, 62, 153
    negative, 163
    of YC, 161–164
    positive, 67, 161, 163

vision here-and-now, 14, 143, 149–150, 170–172,

vision there-and-then, 14, 143, 149–150, 173

vulnerability, 44–45

# W

wake-up call, 22, 24, 27
Wallace, Bill, 109
Wardlaw, Arch, 107, 116
water crystals, 208, 210
WD-40, 168, 215
    mentoring program at,
        214–215
Weil, Christopher, 207–208
Wells, John, 203–208
Whiteside, Steve, 42
Winslow, Foster, 167–169, 175
Witherspoon, Nate, 120–122
Wolsley, Av, 121–122
worldview, 31–32, 64, 100

# Y

YC Identity Kit, 147
YC Qualities Chart, 150
YC's Comparative Positioning
    Chart, 165, 167
YC's Lived Values Grid, 163, 166
your company (YC), 137, 141–143,
        150–153, 155, 157–159
    mission, 174–175
    Style-of-Life of, 164–169
        revised, 172–173

# Z

Zastrov, Norman, 98–99
Zeno's Paradox, 48

# About the Author

ALLAN COX is a CEO coach and founder of Allan Cox & Associates, Inc. He has authored seven previous books, including the best-sellers *Confessions of a Corporate Headhunter* (the first book ever written about the executive search profession), *The Cox Report on the American Corporation*, *The Making of the Achiever*, and *Straight Talk for Monday Morning*. He has advised CEOs and top management teams of many corporations and not-for-profit organizations, including USG, Motorola, Consolidated Communications, Columbus McKinnon, Kraft, Pillsbury, the Minnesota Vikings, Child Welfare League of America, and The Christian Century magazine. He served for five years as chairman of the board of Chicago's Center for Ethics and Corporate Policy. He and his wife, Cher, live and maintain offices in Chicago and San Diego.

## Other Books by Allan Cox

*Confessions of a Corporate Headhunter*

*Work, Love and Friendship*

*The Cox Report on the American Corporation*

*The Making of the Achiever*

*The Achiever's Profile*

*Straight Talk for Monday Morning*

*Redefining Corporate Soul* (With Julie Liesse)

# VISIT *WWW.YOURINNERCEO.COM*

Visit *www.yourinnerceo.com* and enhance your Style-of-Life on-and-off the job.

Download *free,* the *Your Inner CEO Workbook* that supplements *Your Inner CEO* and shows you step-by-step how to excavate your existing Style-of-Life, and follows through on other exercises in the original book.

Read and respond to Allan Cox video and written blogs and dialogue with fellow visitors to the site.

Acquaint yourself with the benefits of coaching for you, your associates, your superiors.

Download and distribute *free,* Chapter Five, **"Boards,"** from *Your Inner CEO,* that can serve as a working model for the governance of your organization, and the catalyst role played in it by your CEO.

Contact Allan Cox to arrange *Style-of-Life* workshops and presentations for your organization.

Find links to additional products and services that may be useful to you and your organization.